ROMAN WARFARE

Roman Warfare surveys the history of Rome's fighting forces from their inception in the seventh century BCE to the fall of the Western Empire in the fifth century CE. In nontechnical, lively language, Jonathan P. Roth examines the evolution of Roman warfare over its thousand-year history. He highlights the changing arms and equipment of the soldiers, unit organization and command structure, and the war and battles of each era. The military narrative is used as a context for Rome's changing tactics and strategy and to discuss combat techniques, logistics, and other elements of Roman war. Political, social, and economic factors are also considered.

Full of detail, up to date on current scholarly debates, and richly illustrated with halftones and color plates, *Roman Warfare* is intended for students of the ancient world and military history.

Jonathan P. Roth is a professor of history at San Jose State University. A scholar of Roman military history, he is the author of *The Logistics of the Roman Army at War.*

CAMBRIDGE INTRODUCTION TO ROMAN CIVILIZATION

Cambridge Introduction to Roman Civilization is a program of books designed for use by students who have no prior knowledge of or familiarity with Roman antiquity. Books in this series focus on key topics, such as slavery, warfare, and women. They are intended to serve as a first point of reference for students who will then be equipped to seek more specialized scholarly and critical studies. Texts in these volumes are written in clear, jargon-free language and integrate primary texts into a synthetic narrative that reflects the most up-to-date research. All volumes in the series will be closely linked to readings and topics and presented in the Cambridge Latin Course.

ROMAN WARFARE

JONATHAN P. ROTH

San Jose State University

CAMBRIDGE UNIVERSITY PRESS
Cambridge, New York, Melbourne, Madrid, Cape Town, Singapore,
São Paulo, Delhi, Dubai, Tokyo

Cambridge University Press
32 Avenue of the Americas, New York, NY 10013-2473, USA

www.cambridge.org
Information on this title: www.cambridge.org/9780521537261

First published 2009

Printed in the United States of America

A catalog record for this publication is available from the British Library.

Library of Congress Cataloging in Publication data
Roth, Jonathan P., 1955–
Roman warfare / Jonathan P. Roth.
p.   cm. – (Cambridge introduction to Roman civilization)
Includes bibliographical references and index.
ISBN 978-0-521-83028-7 (hardback) – ISBN 978-0-521-53726-1 (pbk.)
1. Military art and science – Rome – History.
2. Rome – History, Military.   I. Title.   II. Series.
U35.R68 2009
355.020937–dc22   2008025380

ISBN 978-0-521-83028-7 Hardback
ISBN 978-0-521-53726-1 Paperback

CONTENTS

ILLUSTRATIONS

ACKNOWLEDGMENTS

Many thanks are due to Cambridge University Press for the opportunity to work on this project, and especially to Beatrice Rehl, my long-suffering editor, Barbara Folsom for her copyediting, and Holly Johnson for production editing. The careful reading of various drafts of this work by colleagues such as Jasper Oorthuys, Myles McDonnell, Gaius Stern, Jean-Jacques Aubert, and Robert Knapp saved me from many egregious errors. Many thanks to Nick Marshall and the Batavi for their kind help in providing a picture of late Roman reenactment. My brothers, David and Andrew, both took time from busy schedules to read drafts and offer suggestions. As this book has no footnotes, I wish to acknowledge here the many works, both academic and popular, written by my fellow students of Roman military history. In addition, I extend my thanks to the many anonymous authors of articles in Wikipedia, which provided an enormous and readily available handbook on any number of subjects. My colleagues and friends at San Jose State University have been very supportive through this entire process. My largest debt, however, is to my wife, Susan Heidenreich, who helped me in a myriad of ways, including wording, organization, and illustration. Without her constant encouragement and support this book quite literally would never have been written.

INTRODUCTION: SOURCES AND METHODS

The story of Rome is a story of warfare. It is through war that a small and insignificant town in central Italy rose into one of greatest empires that ever existed. It was war that maintained the Roman Empire's power and its institutions over hundreds of years. Although there were many factors involved in its decline, the collapse of the western part of the empire ultimately occurred through war. Although ancient war was very different from that of modern times, there are elements of Roman warfare that are just as relevant today as they were two thousand years ago.

By "warfare" we mean not only the fighting of wars, but also those institutions, such as the army, that made fighting possible. While there were certainly changes, warfare remained remarkably stable over the course of antiquity. On the other hand, the definition of "Roman" changed dramatically over the more than thousand years covered by this book. The word begins by describing the inhabitants of a small town in central Italy and ends by referring to virtually every person who lived in southern and western Europe, western Asia, and northern Africa. It is important to note that the Roman population was ethnically mixed from its very beginning. Although mainly Latin speakers, there were also Oscans, Etruscans, Greeks, and quite possibly Phoenicians in early Rome. Throughout its history, Rome's openness in granting citizenship to other peoples was an important factor in its success. Although proud of their traditions, the Romans also freely borrowed foreign customs, especially where fighting was concerned.

Rome's geographic position was a key factor in its rise, something already noted by the historian Livy in the first century BCE. The Tiber, one of the few navigable rivers in central Italy, formed an early east–west highway. Rome arose next to a ford where a north–south trade route could cross the river. Western Italy had fertile volcanic soil, which, along with abundant rainfall, meant that the western coast of Italy had one of the largest population densities in the ancient world. Thus Rome, once it developed a way to exploit this manpower for military purposes, could field substantial armies and navies. Italy also had access to significant mineral deposits, especially the rich iron deposits on the nearby island of Elba. This led to an early industry in the forging of weapons and armor. Geographic factors, however, did not predetermine Rome's empire. This book introduces the complex social, cultural, and political elements in Roman militarism. We will only be able to scratch the surface, though, and historians continue to explore and debate the reasons for Roman military success.

Whatever its causes, one can hardly exaggerate Roman military might. By the third century before the Common Era (BCE) the Romans controlled or dominated the lands around the western half of the Mediterranean Sea and, by 100 BCE, its eastern half as well. At its height, the Roman Empire directly ruled western and southern Europe, northern Africa and the Middle East, an area of 2.3 million square miles (5.9 million square kilometers), larger than the size of the continental United States. By the traditional date of the "Fall of the Roman Empire," 476 CE, the western part of the empire had collapsed into independent German kingdoms. The eastern half, however, survived for another thousand years. We refer to this surviving state as the Byzantine Empire, but its inhabitants called themselves Romans, and their state, the Roman Empire.

We learn about warfare from much the same sources as those that inform us of other aspects of ancient Rome. These include the Latin writings of historians such as Sallust (ca. 86–35 BCE), Caesar (100–44 BCE), Livy (59 BCE–17 CE), Tacitus (ca. 55–ca. 120 CE), and Ammianus Marcellinus (ca. 330–395 CE). This is due to the fact that one of the main themes of Roman historical writing was war, and each of these authors describes the Roman army and its battles, as well as the political causes and results of these wars. Our sources are not only in Latin. As the poet Horace famously put it, Rome, having captured Greece, was captured by it. By the second century BCE, Greek had become a second language to educated Romans, and Rome and its institutions an important theme for Greek writers. Two of the best descriptions of Roman military institutions are written in Greek by Polybius (ca. 200–118 BCE) and Flavius Josephus (37–ca. 100 CE). Other Greek sources for Roman warfare are the writings of Dionysius of Halicarnassus (ca. 60–ca. 5 BCE), Plutarch (ca. 50–ca. 120 CE), Dio Cassius (ca. 155–ca. 230 CE), Appian (ca. 95–165 CE), and Zosimus (ca. 460–ca. 530).

History was a literary genre in antiquity, and when writing about war, or any topic, ancient historians followed certain conventions and themes, called *topoi*. In their writings Roman historians, for example, would usually include valuable information, such as the names of units and commanders, and the size of military forces. On the other hand, matters of equal or more interest to modern historians, such as the way in which individuals fought or how armies were supplied, are rarely mentioned. It is true that ancient historians sometimes distorted, and even invented, events in order to improve the impact of their story. Therefore students of Roman warfare should always read the sources carefully and critically. Nevertheless, they should remember that "literary" is not necessarily the same as "fictional." Even highly rhetorical writing can give us important historical information.

Unfortunately, though not surprisingly, only a very few military handbooks and technical manuals were of enough interest to medieval copyists to have survived the centuries. What we have includes a collection of military tricks or stratagems by Frontinus (ca. 40–103 CE), a book on tactics and a sort of guidebook for fighting against the Alans (a steppe people) by Arrian (ca. 86–160 CE), a manual on building a camp by Pseudo-Hyginus (dating from the second or third century CE), and a very important but enigmatic Late Roman book on the army by Flavius Vegetius, written in the late fourth or early fifth century.

Since warfare and the army were such significant parts of Roman society, it is not surprising to find many military references in various different genres of literature, both poetry and prose. The writings of Plautus (ca. 254–184 BCE), Virgil (70–19 BCE), Lucan (39–65 CE), Silius Italicus (ca. 26–ca. 101 CE) and Juvenal (late first to early second century CE) give us valuable information on the Roman military.

The Latin or Greek books we read, whether in the original or in translation, virtually all come to us through what is called "manuscript transmission." This means that each book was painstakingly copied and recopied over the centuries, until it was finally edited and printed starting in the fifteenth century. Of course, many mistakes, omissions, and other corruptions naturally occur in texts when they are copied so many times. During the Renaissance, the science of philology was developed to correct ancient texts. This process continues today and is vital to our understanding of the ancient past, including warfare.

In addition to the manuscript tradition, we learn much about Roman warfare through so-called documentary sources, such as inscriptions, papyri, ostraka, and wooden tablets. Both the study of inscriptions, called epigraphy, and that of papyri, called papyrology, are highly informative. Roman soldiers, especially officers, had the habit of putting up inscribed tombstones with a great deal of detail about their careers, including the units in which they served, the ranks they attained, and occasionally the wars in which they fought. Scholars have learned much about the army in this way. In addition, there are hundreds of other Latin and Greek inscriptions erected by individuals, units, cities, and states that describe victories, building activities, laws, treaties, and so forth. All these help us to understand the Roman army and ancient warfare.

Papyri, made from the pith (the stem center) of the papyrus plant, was used much like modern paper. Most surviving ones are mostly written in Greek, although there are also some Latin ones. Papyri survive mainly in Egypt, but also in Israel, Jordan, and Syria. We have found unit rosters, pay records, letters, and other documents that detail the day-to-day life of soldiers. Ostraka (writing on broken pieces of pottery) and writing on wooden slips were used as we do note paper today, and are also valuable. For example, hundreds of military ostraka have been found at Bu Njem, a fort in North Africa, and more and more wooden slips are being discovered at the auxiliary camp at Vindolanda in northern England. There are also a few dozen metal *diplomata*, or discharge documents, that give us much information about auxiliary units.

Archaeology also is of great help in understanding Roman warfare. Dozens of military camps and forts have been excavated, providing information about daily life, equipment, and weapons. In rare cases, we even discover the remains of battles, mainly sieges such as Numantia and Masada. Recently, the battlefield at Teutoburger Forest (9 CE) has been discovered and scientifically studied. Together with the descriptions given by Tacitus and Cassius Dio, and some inscriptions, archaeology helps us paint a picture of the course of this important battle. An increasingly important way of understanding the Roman army is through the reconstruction of their equipment. Reenactors have discovered, for example, the proper method for using the *furca* as a pack and the workings of the Roman cavalry saddle.

Of course, we have no videos or photographs of ancient battles, but war was an important theme in ancient art. There are pictures of soldiers and their equipment in stone reliefs, frescoes, painted pottery, and illustrated manuscripts, as well as statues and figurines with military themes. Although we are grateful for what we have, we must remember that ancient paintings and sculpture were highly stylized. There is much debate about the accuracy of even very realistic-looking images, such as those seen on Trajan's famous column in Rome. As a result, there is much uncertainty about the reconstruction of ancient equipment and the course of battles, particularly over the Romans' use of missile weapons and cavalry.

Another difficulty facing the military historian is the fact that the number and quality of our sources differ greatly for various time periods.

With few exceptions our earliest reliable sources, both written and pictorial, date to after the second century BCE. There is a "golden age" of evidence for the army, in the first centuries BCE and CE, subsequent to which sources again become scarce, until they virtually end in the fifth century. There are regional differences as well. We have hundreds of military documents from Egypt, for example, and now some from Britain, but virtually none from elsewhere.

Overall, what is important is that we combine our sources and analyze them critically to gain an overall picture of Roman warfare. Although this is a difficult task for historians, those interested in the subject have benefited from the work of generations of dedicated and talented military historians. The task of refining and correcting this picture will continue and there is much for future military historians to discover and understand about Roman warfare.

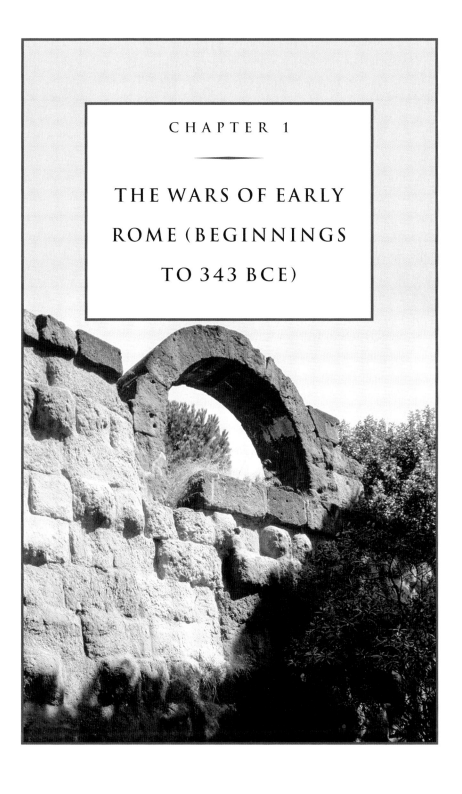

CHAPTER 1

THE WARS OF EARLY ROME (BEGINNINGS TO 343 BCE)

There are numerous stories about Rome's beginnings, and dividing fact from fiction is a difficult chore. This is as true of warfare as it is of other aspects of society. We frankly have few reliable details of Roman warfare in this early period, and there is an intense debate among historians about what little we do know. Modern archaeology is revealing more of early Rome, but there is a limit to what excavated finds can tell us. Nevertheless, we can say something about how early Romans fought. The original Romans inhabited villages along the Tiber River, perched on hills surrounding a marsh. Livy gives the date of the founding of Rome as the equivalent of 753 BCE. This may be too early: most historians think several Latin villages merged into a town sometime around 650. Recent discoveries, however, may push Rome's beginning back into the eighth century. Its inhabitants were mainly Latins, sharing their language, customs, and a myth of common origin with their neighbors in Latium (now the province of Lazio in central Italy). All the adult men fought in wartime. Indeed, the Latin word for "people," *populus*, originally meant "army."

At this time, most Roman weapons were still made of bronze, with only a few iron ones. A wealthy aristocrat might have had an iron sword, as well as a conical iron helmet. An unusual feature of some early Roman helmets was a tall tiara-like plate running from one temple to the other, making the warrior look taller. Better-off warriors also wore leather armor, perhaps with a square metal disk, or pectoral, to protect the chest, and a round or oval shield. The wealthiest drove two-horsed chariots. In contrast, most Roman warriors, the commoners, would have gone into battle with little or no armor and perhaps just a spear as a weapon. Rome's ruler was called the *rex*, which meant "king," though at the time this "kingdom" had no more than ten thousand inhabitants. "Chief" or "warlord" might possibly be a better translation, as Rome's earliest "wars" probably were little more than cattle raids. Livy relates exciting, but fictional, stories of the exploits of heroic rulers like Romulus and

Ancus Marcius. Although these are legends, not history, the office of king likely did originate as a war chief and, the most important function of the *rex* was leading the Romans into battle. The *rex* had what the Romans called *imperium*, the power to command (*imperare*).

Royal Rome raised its army from the city's three tribes (*tribus*, from the Latin for "thirds"). According to Livy, each tribe contributed a thousand men, neatly subdivided into ten centuries (*centuriae*) of one hundred men and commanded by a military tribune (*tribunus militum*). Rome's aristocrats, called patricians (*patricii*) were supposed to have contributed three hundred cavalry under a cavalry tribune (*tribunus celerum*). Livy's numbers are notional – there is no reason to think that the tribes contributed equally, but his total of three thousand is probably approximately correct for this period. Rome's early cavalry may not have been solely aristocratic. The use of chariots had certainly been abandoned by this time, and horses were probably not very important in war; the "cavalry" may have ridden into battle and dismounted to fight on foot. In all likelihood, patricians fought other patricians in one-on-one battles, while common soldiers skirmished among themselves.

Livy's reference to centuries in the royal army is anachronistic: the clan, or *gens*, was the tribe's military subdivision. The names of certain clans (*gentes*) like the Iulii (or Julii), Aemilii, Cornelii, and Fabii abound all through early Roman military history. The leading patricians led their clan followers into battle. As late as the early fifth century, we hear of the Fabian clan fighting as a group. At the Battle of the Cremera River, traditionally dated to 477 BCE, virtually the entire *gens Fabia* was said to have been wiped out. The Senate (*senatus*) grew up as a council of the most powerful clan leaders, who served both as subcommanders and advisers to the king.

Trumpets would announce the beginning of a military campaign, which generally started with the onset of spring in March (*Martius*, the month of Mars, god of war). After a victory, the king led a celebratory parade through the city for which the Romans borrowed an Etruscan word: the triumph. Indeed, it is likely that the Romans derived much of their early military culture from their more advanced neighbors to the north, the Etruscans, and from the Greeks to the south.

War was an integral part of Roman life and religion, as indeed it must have been for most cultures in the period. Special priests called *fetiales* carried out rituals to ensure that Rome's gods would grant the city victory. Some have suggested that this shows that early Rome was peacefully inclined toward its neighbors. It is true that there was not much expansion during this period: Fidenae, with whom Rome fought for more than a hundred years, lay only five miles (8 km) upstream. It may be that Rome's militarism, like that of Sparta, developed long after its founding, but this is unclear.

Livy writes that King Servius Tullius (traditionally 578–535 BCE) first divided citizens into wealth classes for military purposes. Some scholars think this reform actually occurred in the fifth century, after the establishment of the Republic, but a date in the mid-sixth century seems more likely. Whenever it happened, this "Servian Reform" was simply the adoption by Rome of Greek-style hoplite warfare. Under this military system, every adult male in a city-state seventeen years or older was required to buy weapons and armor if he had sufficient property to do so. A census was held every five years to determine who would fight. Those with enough wealth to serve as infantry were called *assidui*, literally "those present (at the muster of the army)." The wealthiest were *equites* or horsemen (also called equestrians). Those who were too poor to buy weapons were the "proletarians," who could offer only children (*proles*) to the state. The hoplite system allowed a city-state to raise a large military force relative to its population. The army was essentially self-arming, without the need for a bureaucracy to buy and distribute weapons. In addition, those who derived the greatest benefit from the city-state, its wealthier citizens, were personally responsible for its defense.

Since the army was now drafted, or levied, from among the eligible male citizens, the Latin word for levy, *legio*, became the term for the army as a whole. This is where we get our word "legion." A later Roman tradition suggests that Servius' hoplite-style army had six thousand heavy infantry drawn from the four urban and sixteen rural tribes. Like the Greeks, the Romans originally divided the army into units of ninety-six men (twelve across and eight deep). The Romans called this a century (*centuria*) or "hundred-man unit." There were supposed to have been sixty centuries in the royal army of the sixth century BCE. While we have no way of knowing for certain, in general terms this rings true, as Rome's army would have been the same size as that of a medium-sized Greek city-state. The richest Romans supposedly contributed six centuries of cavalry, who may now have started to fight on horseback. Cavalry, however, played little role in hoplite warfare except for chasing down fleeing enemies after the battle ended.

At first, the legionary carried the same weapons as a Greek hoplite, with the names simply changed into Latin. Each soldier wore a metal helmet (*cassis*) and carried a round, wooden shield covered with bronze, called a *clipeus*. He fought with an eight-foot spear (*hasta*) and a long, iron slashing sword (*ensis*). Wealthier Romans could afford a breastplate (*lorica*). Some of these may have been the form-fitting "muscle cuirasses" we see in statuary, but more commonly they were simply plates of hammered bronze. Common soldiers made do with a leather jerkin, and possibly the older square pectoral or "heart protector," also of bronze, attached with leather straps. Greek hoplites wore two greaves, but it seems to have been a Roman custom to wear only one, on the left shin. In battle, hoplite soldiers were organized into ranks and files, forming a rectangular unit, called a phalanx in Greek. An enemy thus faced a solid wall of shields and spears. Hoplite-style helmets protected soldiers from arrows and other missiles, but greatly restricted a soldier's vision.

There is a vigorous scholarly debate about how a hoplite battle was actually fought. According to one theory, the hoplites pushed against the enemy line, the soldiers behind adding their momentum to those in front. Another view is that the front rank dueled with the soldiers immediately in front of them, the soldiers behind stepping forward to replace fallen men. Whichever the case, it took a great deal of courage, what the Romans called *virtus*, and physical endurance (*vis*), especially for those in the front line of battle (*acies*). Evidence from Greek sources

1. Two Italian hoplite soldiers are shown on plaques found in Palaestrina, the ancient Praeneste, a Latin city that fought both with and against the Romans in wars of the fifth and fourth centuries BCE. Photo: Réunion des Musées Nationaux/ Art Resource, NY.

suggests that even victorious armies suffered some 5 percent casualties. Battles were necessarily short, as soldiers could not fight for long wearing such heavy armor. When one side broke and ran, greater losses were incurred, around 15 percent of the defeated force, due to the soldiers exposing their unprotected backs in flight. Traditionally, hoplite-style battles did not result in annihilation of the losers.

The new "Servian" army was very successful. There are indications of a growing Roman militarism. The Alban Hills and the lower Tiber valley were conquered sometime in the sixth century, and around this time Rome built its first city walls, a reflection of its increased power. They were constructed partly of the local volcanic rock (called tufa) and partly of earth. After an Etruscan family, named the Tarquins (Tarquinii) established a dynasty at Rome in the late sixth century, the city expanded considerably. Rome's last king, Tarquin the Proud (Superbus) seems to have brought all of Latium under his control, an area of about 350 square miles (900 square kilometers). Around 500 BCE the Tarquins were overthrown and the monarchy replaced by an aristocratic and oligarchic republic. This was a not uncommon occurrence among ancient Mediterranean city-states with hoplite armies, though whether there was a causal relationship remains a topic of debate.

Under the new Roman Republican constitutional arrangement, two patricians served for a year as consuls, sharing military and civilian leadership of the state. The consuls did not divide power, as we might expect; rather, both held equal power simultaneously. This arrangement was designed to prevent a new king from emerging. In the case of extreme danger, usually of a military nature, a single ruler was elected, but only for a six-month term. Originally called the army commander (*magister populi*) he was better known as the *dictator*. Consuls were elected by an assembly of Roman citizens, organized in centuries and called the Centuriate Assembly (*comitia centuriata*). The link between the assembled Roman people and the army continued all through the Republic. Although the electoral century grew to have thousands or even tens of thousands of voters, the smaller military century of one hundred soldiers was still drawn from its ranks, and identified with it.

Patrician clans still dominated the Republic politically as well as militarily. Only patricians could hold positions of command in the army. Although the assembly was the body that declared war and passed laws, the Senate conducted warfare. The Senate was still technically only an advisory body, but it assigned the command of each military campaign, usually to one of the two consuls. The area in which the war was to be fought was called his province (*provincia*) and he had *imperium*, that is, the right to command within it. The soldiers took an oath (*sacramentum*) to obey all of the commander's orders and to turn all plunder over to him. Around 500 BCE, a disaffected Sabine leader, Attus Clausus (called Appius Claudius in Latin), defected to Rome and was inducted into the Senate. This willingness to absorb foreign peoples, and share power with their leaders, continued to be an important factor in Rome's political and military success.

Around the time of the founding of the Republic, Romans seem to have lost control of Latium, possibly due to the political upheaval that accompanied the overthrow of the monarchy. Thus they seem to have had to conquer Latium a second time. In a legendary battle, dated sometime around the 490s BCE, the Romans are supposed to have defeated the Latins at Lake Regillus with the help of the gods Castor and Pollux. Even if the battle was genuine, the victory was not decisive. The Romans could not establish direct control over the Latins, but instead formed the Latin League in a treaty called the Treaty of Cassius (*Foedus Cassianum*). The Latin League helped Rome to fight off the attacks of hill tribes to the east, the Sabines, Aequi, and Volsci, which were still powerful enough to threaten Rome's existence. The Romans and the Latins combined to defeat the Sabines around 450 BCE.

Securing the loyalty of the clan leaders to the new Republic turned out not to be a simple matter. Some Roman aristocrats seem to have joined Rome's enemies out of ambition or injured pride. Legends speak of a Volscian attack led by a renegade senator named Gaius Marcius Coriolanus (the subject of a play by Shakespeare), who almost succeeded in taking Rome. Nevertheless, by the 430s, the Aequi and Volsci had been decisively beaten, and Rome gained control over the mountainous

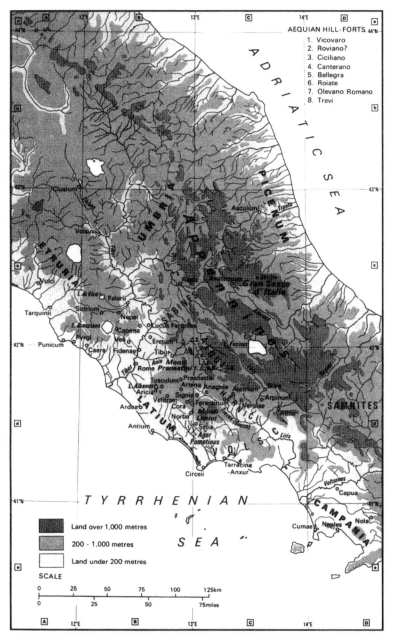

AEQUIAN HILL-FORTS
1. Vicovaro
2. Roviano?
3. Ciciliano
4. Canterano
5. Bellegra
6. Roiate
7. Olevano Romano
8. Trevi

ADRIATIC SEA

PICENUM

UMBRIA

APPENNINES

SABINES

ETRURIA

Clusium

Volsinii

Vulci

L. di Vico

Faleri

Tarquinii

Sutrium

Nepet

L. Bracciano

Capena

Veii

Lucus Feroniae

Pyrgi

Punicum

Caere

Fidenae

Eretum

Tibur

L. Fucinus

Gran Sasso d'Italia

Asculum

Truentus

Aterno

Gizio

Gavis

Saras

Anio

Rome

Praeneste 7.

Momo

Sabini

Tusculum

Artena

Anagnia

Alatrium

Arpinum

Albanus

Aricia

Signia

Velitrae

Ferentinum

Verulae

SAMNITES

Ardea

Cora

Norba

Lepini

Liris

Antium

Setia

Ager Pomptinus

VOLSCI

Tarracina

Anxur

Circeii

Volturnus

Capua

CAMPANIA

TYRRHENIAN SEA

Cumae

Naples

Nola

Land over 1,000 metres

200 - 1,000 metres

Land under 200 metres

SCALE

0   25   50   75   100   125km

0   25   50   75miles

2. A map of central Italy during the time of the Roman monarchy and the early Republic. Photo: © Cambridge University Press.

region east of the city. The story of Coriolanus' treachery suggests violent political struggles within the early Roman state. There are other stories as well, of the so-called Conflict of the Orders, pitting patricians against the *plebs*, or plebeians. In Rome, all free citizens not born patricians were called plebeians. This category included both wealthy and poor Romans. Since propertied plebeians made up the bulk of the army, they could use the threat not to fight as a tool to obtain concessions. On the other hand, since the patricians were the army's officers, they used their command positions to maintain their hold on power. As a result, the plebeians' goal was to gain access to high ranks in the military and political office, which in Rome was the same thing. The office of *quaestor*, originally established to make sure plunder was distributed fairly, was opened to plebeians after 421. Around the same time the elected position of military tribune was created, to replace the hereditary patrician clan leaders in the command of tribal contingents. In the fifth century, these military tribunes were sometimes given consular power – that is, de facto command of the army as well as of the state – a sign of the political struggle between the orders.

Although the Romans had established control over Latium by the end of the fifth century BCE, they faced a powerful enemy to the north, the city of Veii. This Etruscan city was ten miles (16 km) from Rome. When the Romans took Veii, around 400 BCE, it almost doubled the size of Rome's territory. Shortly after conquering Veii, however, Rome was itself defeated by the Gauls (also known by their Greek name, Celts). The Gallic expansion into northern Italy in the previous century had already led to the decline of the Etruscans. In 390 (or, according to another reckoning, 387) BCE, an expedition of Gauls plundering through Etruria wiped out a Roman army on the banks of the Allia River, a tributary of the Tiber some eleven miles from Rome. According to tradition, the Gauls then took and sacked the city of Rome itself. Some scholars, noting the lack of archaeological evidence of destruction, suggest that the "Sack of Rome" was not a huge defeat. There is reason to think, however, that it was a serious setback: in the 380s the Romans were again fighting the nearby Latins and hill peoples

3. A remnant of the Servian Wall on the Aventine Hill, built with blocks of tufa, a volcanic rock, in the 370s BCE. Note the arched opening for a torsion artillery piece, added later. Photo: Scala/Art Resource, NY.

such the Volsci and the Aequi. Rome, however, bounced back, and in 389, Antium (now Anzio) on the west coast of Italy was crushed. That city was required to furnish ships and sailors to Rome, the beginning of the Roman fleet. Soon, the Volsci and the Aequi were again defeated, and Tusculum to the south was annexed. In the 370s, the Romans began building substantial new walls on the foundations of the sixth-century fortifications. Though still called the Servian Walls, they were much larger than before, over 4 m (13.1 ft) thick and at least 8.5 m (27.9 ft) high. Skillfully made by hired Greek artisans, the walls were more a sign of Rome's increasing wealth and power than of fear of a renewed Gallic attack. Portions of these fourth-century Servian walls can still be seen next to Rome's main railway station and elsewhere.

In 367 BCE a law opened the consulship and command of the Roman army to plebeians. This ended the Conflict of the Orders and

The Siege of Veii (ca. 400 BCE)

Veii was not only the closest Etruscan city to Rome but also the wealthiest. Livy's narrative of the siege of Veii is quite detailed, but much, if not most, of this account is probably anachronistic fiction. Nevertheless, there may well be some real particulars in the account. The elaborate circumvallation that Livy describes was beyond Rome's capability at the time. The Romans probably utilized a blockade camp, which did not surround the enemy city but was used to interfere with relief attempts. On the other hand, the assertion that the Romans built their first winter camp (*hibernacula*) at Veii is probably true. Around 400 BCE, the Romans began paying a small amount – called a *stipendium* – to soldiers, though they still had to provide their own equipment. Rome could now keep its army in the field over a winter. Roman tradition connected this to the siege of Veii, and this is not unlikely.

Livy claims that the siege lasted for ten continuous summers and winters, a length of time meant to mirror the duration of the Trojan War. This is doubtless too long. The siege was certainly lengthy by the standards of the time, and may well have lasted for several years. The Romans apparently suffered a serious setback at one point, losing their camp to enemy attack, and it would have taken a year or more to recover. Livy says Veii fell when Marcus Furius Camillus, the Roman commander, ordered a mine (*cuniculus*) dug into the citadel. Historians have questioned the story of the mine, but the soft tufa rock in Latium is ideal for digging tunnels. Whatever details are true or false, there is no question that the Romans ultimately took the city.

resulted in the creation of a new ruling class: the senatorial nobility. This new order was made up of the old patrician nobles and the heads of the wealthiest plebeian clans. With minor exceptions, this senatorial order would provide the military command and political leadership for the Romans for the next six hundred years. In the same year that the consulship was opened to plebeians (367), a new office was created, the praetorship. Although the praetor, like the consul, had civilian duties, he also had *imperium*, so he also could lead armies if necessary. Soon, sometime in the 360s, the army was doubled in size. There were now two legions, one under the command of each consul. The number of military tribunes, and centurions, also doubled. The term "legion" (*legio*) now changed its meaning from the army as a whole to that of an individual military unit.

Several other important military reforms were enacted sometime in the fourth century. The Romans attributed most of these changes to a senator and military leader named Marcus Furius Camillus, and we call them the Camillan Reforms. Some historians prefer a date in the middle of the century, arguing that the changes were in response to Gallic warfare, as the Gauls fought in a more open fashion than hoplites. Other historians, however, think the reforms came at the end of the fourth century in response to a series of difficult wars against the Oscan-speaking peoples of the Apennines, including the Samnites. In any case, it is worth remembering that the fourth century BCE was a period of profound military change among the Greeks as well.

By this time, the number of Roman citizens and potential soldiers had grown substantially, partly through natural growth, partly through granting citizenship to conquered peoples. In addition, under a law virtually unique in the ancient world, freed slaves became Roman citizens. This may well have been done to increase military manpower. Whatever the motivation, the Romans did significantly expand their army, adding a second and third wealth class: the former were not required to provide a breastplate or pectoral, and the latter lacked greaves. Each of the wealth classes was now divided into *juniores* (men from seventeen to forty-six years of age) who were on active service, and those forty-seven and over, the *seniores*, who served as a reserve force and defended the city.

The legion, made up of 4,200 infantry, was divided into three lines. The first-class soldiers, called *principes*, did not stand in front, as one might suppose from their name, but formed the middle line of battle.

Marcus Furius Camillus (445–365 BCE)

Livy related many legends about Marcus Furius Camillus, one of Rome's great heroes, and it is difficult to tell how much, if any, truth there is in any particular detail. Said to be a vigorous leader of the patricians during the Conflict of the Orders, he nevertheless was supposed to have been open to reform if it benefited Rome militarily. Livy says he served as a military tribune with consular powers in 401 and 398, campaigning against Capena and Falisci, both allies of Veii. With the siege of Veii dragging on, the story is that Camillus was made dictator in 396, and succeeded in taking the city, Rome's greatest military triumph to date. As more experienced commanders were available, Camillus' appointment seems to be evidence of his military reputation. In 394, again as military tribune, he is said to have defeated the Falerii and, in thanks, dedicated a golden bowl at the shrine of Apollo at Delphi in Greece. Livy says Camillus was again made dictator after the Sack of Rome in 390, but if this is true, the story of his defeating the Gauls and retrieving a thousand pounds of gold ransom almost certainly is not. Another story claims that Camillus arrived with an army just as the Romans were paying the gold tribute. Camillus is supposed to have said, "Rome buys its peace with iron, not gold." He stopped the payment and drove out the Gauls. For this, the Romans are supposed to have named him Second Founder of the City (after Romulus). This story, although colorful, is doubtless fiction.

After the Gauls left, our sources say that Camillus was military tribune three times, fighting successfully against the Volsci, the Latins, and the Etruscans, and capturing Bola and Tusculum. The military changes attributed to him, the so-called Camillan reforms, might date to this period. In 367, the Gauls again raided Latium. Camillus is supposed to have become dictator once again, although he was seventy-eight years old, to have defeated the enemy, and celebrated a triumph. According to tradition, the old general died at the age of eighty.

In the front line were the more lightly armed soldiers of the second class, the *hastati*, and the oldest, most experienced, third class (*triarii*) stood in the rear. Each line was now divided into ten subunits called maniples (*manipuli*), of 120 men each in the first and second lines, and 60 in the third. Each maniple consisted of two centuries, of 60 men in the *hastati* and *principes*, and 30 *triarii*. Note that by now "century" had ceased to mean literally one hundred men. The smallest subunit of the legion was the squad or *contubernium* (literally, a "tenting-together") of six soldiers. It is not clear if the *triarii* had fewer, or smaller, *contubernia*.

The numbers in these subunits could change: the Senate might vote to establish larger legions for especially demanding tasks. This was not done by adding more maniples but by increasing the size of each maniple, and of the centuries and *contubernia*, that composed it. Conversely, casualties and illness would gradually reduce the legion's size. After a campaign was over, the legions were dissolved, and so the "First Legion" of one year technically bore no institutional relation to the "First Legion" of the next, though in reality they were often the selfsame unit. Soldiers normally did at least six years of service continuously with a particular legion; thus, there was continuity and unit cohesion. In this period, legions had not one but five standards (*signa*), but the maniple was the only subunit of the legion to have a standard. It is clear, therefore, that the maniple was the basic tactical unit, as standards were used for signaling and as rallying points. In addition to the infantry, each legion included about three hundred *equites* or cavalry organized into ten squadrons, each called a *turma*, and led by a decurion. To control the quality of mounts, the government now provided horses to the cavalry, who were called "horsemen with a public horse" (*equites equo publico*).

It was in this period that the tribunes, who had previously commanded tribal contingents, became legionary officers. An assembly of the Roman people as a whole now selected the tribunes, not their individual tribes. There were now six tribunes in each legion, and every two months a pair of them commanded the legion, alternating every day until replaced by another pair. The centurion (*centurio*) originated as an experienced soldier who took his place in the century first and on whom the rest of the unit formed. By the mid-fourth century BCE, the centurion had become the century's tactical commander. Every maniple had two centurions, one for its right-hand century, the *centurio prior*, and one for the left, the *centurio posterior*. Each centurion appointed an *optio* from the ranks, who served as a second-in-command, and who could expect eventually to become a centurion himself. Just as the centuries were ranked according to their wealth class and their position in line, so were their centurions. Eventually, the centurion of the first century of the *triarii* was recognized as the legion's senior centurion and functioned as its tactical commander. As the senior centurion stayed in his post while the nominal commanders – the six tribunes – rotated in and out of their posts, this practice provided important command continuity. In this way, the Romans developed a every effective two-tiered system of officers, a first tier made up of educated and sophisticated nobles, and a second tier of skilled and experienced soldiers drawn from the ranks.

There were also changes in armor and weaponry. The Romans adopted a new type of shield, the convex, oval-shaped *scutum* replacing the round "hoplite" *clipeus*. This new shield was borrowed either from the Samnites or the Gauls. Some thirty inches (75 cm) in width and four and a half feet (1.4 m) in height, the *scutum* was curved to better protect the individual soldier, and an iron rim protected against sword blows. An iron boss was fixed in the shield's center. *Scuta* may have been adopted gradually, but were eventually used by all the wealth classes. Another innovation was the introduction of chain mail, possibly borrowed from the Gauls. Small iron rings were linked together to form a metal shirt. Chain mail was lighter and more flexible than scale or plate armor, and almost as effective in deflecting blows. High-ranking officers, however, continued to wear the traditional breastplates. The helmet also underwent a change. The older hoplite-style helmet protected the entire head but obstructed the soldier's vision. The Romans adopted a new conical helmet with two metal flaps to protect the cheeks. Feathers, probably from swans, were placed on the helmet's crest, both as an identifier and to make the soldier appear taller. When discussing equipment, it is important to keep in mind that each soldier provided his own arms and

4. A bronze sculpture of the fourth century BCE, showing two Etruscan hoplites carrying a wounded comrade. It served as the lid for a burial urn, quite possibly that of the injured soldier. Photo: Scala/Art Resource, NY.

armor. Clearly there were some rules and conventions, but the details of both weapons and defensive gear would have varied from person to person.

In 358 BCE the Romans won a decisive victory over some Latins who had allied themselves with the Hernici, in violation of the Treaty of Cassius. Rome took this opportunity to impose a new relationship on their allies. Although the name of the Treaty of Cassius was kept, the Latins were no longer equal partners; rather they were dependents, forced to provide soldiers who would fight under Roman command. This system of unequal "alliances," which would gradually be applied to states throughout Italy, was another important factor in Roman military success. By 343, Rome was the major power in central Italy, but it would soon face one of its greatest challenges: the Samnite Wars.

Links: Livy 2.10.1–13 (Horatius at the bridge), 3.26.7–29.7 (Cincinnatus), 5.1.1–28.8 (Siege of Veii), 8.8–10 (early Roman legion).

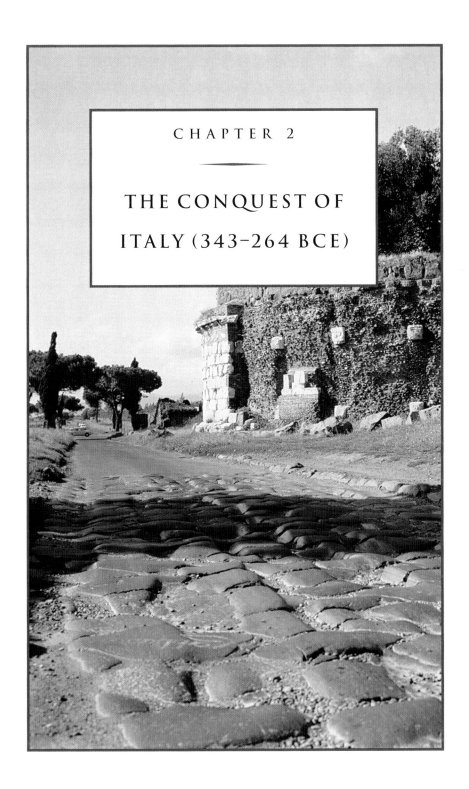

CHAPTER 2

THE CONQUEST OF
ITALY (343–264 BCE)

The period between the beginning of the Samnite Wars (343 BCE) and the outbreak of the First Punic War (264 BCE) was a key one in Roman history. Rome went from being a local power to one dominating all of Italy – the second most populous region in the Western world after Egypt. In the year 343 BCE, however, it was not at all clear that Rome would accomplish such success. While the Romans were winning control of central Italy, the Oscans were becoming dominant in the southern region of the peninsula. The most dangerous of these Oscans were the loosely organized but warlike Samnites who blocked Roman expansion to the west and south. They were divided into four tribes, the Caraceni, the Caudini, the Hirpini, and the Pentri, joined together in a confederation. Although most scholars think the First Samnite War (dated to 343–341) was a historic event, there are those who have doubted it. It says much about our lack of knowledge that in discussing a period as late as the mid-fourth century BCE, the age of Alexander the Great, historians are not sure about something so basic to Rome's development. There is no question, however, that the Samnites were major regional rivals of the Romans and in any case, the First Samnite War was not decisive. The Romans are supposed to have allied themselves with the Capuans, but fighting was cut short by a mutiny in the legions, leading to a renewal of the Samnites' treaty with Rome. The story of disobedience in the ranks suggests that ill feelings generated by the Conflict of the Orders were still affecting military operations.

There was another threat to Rome at this time, which may explain the willingness to make peace with the Samnites. In 341 the Latins demanded that Rome restore their former status as equal partners in the Treaty of Cassius. The Latins allied themselves with the Campanians, but the Romans, in an early example of their "divide and conquer" strategy, broke the alliance by offering favorable terms to the latter. The Romans then defeated the isolated Latins in two campaigns. After reconquering Antium (Anzio), they took the bronze beaks, called *rostra*, of the Antiate ships and placed them on a monument in Rome. This monument, called the Rostrum, became the spot from which Roman politicians addressed the assembly.

After the Romans won the "Great Latin War" in 338, some Latin communities, such as Antium and Tusculum, were given full Roman citizenship and their land made part of the territory of Rome (*ager Romanus*). Adult males with sufficient property were required to do military service in the legions. The rest of the Latin cities were granted the private rights of Roman citizenship but not the right to vote or serve in the legions, another indication of how citizenship and military service were linked in the Roman mind. Latin allies (*socii*) were still required to provide soldiers to the Romans, under Roman command, whenever Rome decided to go to war. Thus, the "Roman" army was made up increasingly of allies. Rome, however, allowed each Italian city to run its own internal affairs. At the beginning of each year, the consuls informed each allied state how many soldiers it had to furnish. This number depended on the size and wealth of the state. Individual contingents called "cohorts" ran to around five hundred infantry and were under the command of an allied officer called a prefect. Ten of these infantry cohorts were combined into an Allied Wing (*ala sociorum*), not to be confused with the later cavalry unit of the same name. The "wings," the equivalent of the legion, were so called, of course, because they were placed on the flanks, the Romans taking the center of the line. A Roman rank, prefect of the allies, was created to command this unit. There were probably six prefects, rotating command in the same way as the military tribunes. As a general rule, the number of allies equaled that of Romans in any given force. The Italian soldiers were paid by their own cities, and although they also provided their own equipment, this came more and more to resemble that of the Romans. We do not know how the Italians viewed these drafts. We occasionally hear of discontent, and ultimately there was an Italian revolt over the issue (in 90–89 BCE), but during the years of expansion the prospect of booty (and adventure) led many young Italians to volunteer for military service. An elite group of Italian allies called the "extraordinaries," who were under the direct command of the consul, probably represented such volunteers. The Romans also began a program of military colonization, placing Roman citizens in settlements at strategic points. This practice firmly established their control over Italy and the surrounding seas. Indeed, the first colonies were maritime ones, located at Ostia and Antium along the coast.

The Romans now turned their attention to Samnium. An alliance with the Greek city of Tarentum, which was at war with the Samnites, and a military colony established at Fregellae, cut Samnium off from Campania. The Second Samnite War (326–304) is the point at which we can begin to write Roman military history with more confidence. This conflict was divided into two phases, from 327 to 321 and 316 to 304, divided by a five-year cease-fire. The war began promisingly. The Romans pushed to the Adriatic for the first time and won over the Marsi and Paeligni, who lived in eastern Italy, as allies. Then, in 321, disaster struck at a place called the Caudine Forks. Livy writes that a Roman army of about twenty thousand marched into a narrow ravine where they were trapped by Samnite forces. To prevent a massacre, the Roman commander is supposed to have surrendered, and the entire army marched "under the yoke," that is, under an archway made of tied spears. Scholars have hotly debated Livy's account, especially about where a location can be found that fits his description, but there is no question that the Romans suffered a humiliating loss, recalled for centuries with a combination of shame and anger. In the time of Augustus Caesar the anniversary of the Battle of Caudine Forks was still remembered as a "black day" (dies ater).

This was also probably the time when the Romans doubled their army from two to four legions and began numbering them: the First, Second, Third, and Fourth legions. Each consul commanded two legions and an equivalent number of allies. This meant that a Roman army in the field now numbered some 35–40 thousand men. Victory against the Samnites not only required more soldiers but more lightly armed ones who would be useful in mountain fighting. It is likely that at this point the fourth and fifth classes were added to the army. The fourth

5. Two Samnite infantrymen and a cavalryman from a tomb dating to ca. 350–325 BCE. They carry trophies of a victory, perhaps over the Romans. Photo: Erich Lessing/Art Resource, NY.

class, known as *velites*, functioned as light infantry. At first they carried a spear (*hasta*) and a small round shield (*parma*). At some point they began using a throwing javelin (*pilum*) with a range of about 100 feet (30 m). The point of the javelin, shaped like a pyramid, was designed to punch through an enemy's shield, disabling it. The fifth class, the *accensi*, was armed as slingers. These slings were basically leather straps that hurled bullets (*glandes*) made of lead. Sling bullets traveled at high speeds and could do serious damage if they hit an unarmored spot. Soldiers molded their own lead bullets, which sometimes had a tag line such as the number of the legion, the commander's name, or even an expression such as "Take that!" or "Catch!" (Or something more vulgar, like "For Pompey's butt.")

The dating of the various changes in the army and the assembly's organization are complex problems. By this time, however, there were five property classes contributing to the army and a total of 193 centuries making up the Centuriate Assembly (*comitia centuriata*) and serving as recruiting categories for the army. These were broken down into eighteen centuries of cavalry, eighty in the first class (plus two of "engineers"), twenty in each of the next three classes, thirty in the fifth class, plus two of trumpeters, and a single century for all the proletarians.

In 316, the second phase of the Second Samnite War began. The Romans restarted the war, repudiating the treaty made after Caudine Forks, but suffered initial setbacks, losing the Battle of Lautulae and seeing Capua, an important Campanian town, join the enemy. The Latins, however, stayed loyal and the tide gradually turned. The Romans captured the Samnite stronghold at Luceria and took the cities of Taracina and Capua. These strategic points were connected to Rome by the building of the Appian Way (Via Appia) a 132-mile (211 km) road constructed by the censor Appius Claudius Caecus in 312. Eventually this road ran all the way from Rome to Brindisium at the southern tip of Italy. Roman roads were not merely tracks but sophisticated pieces of engineering. First a ditch was dug and filled with sand, stones, and gravel. Only then was the roadbed laid. This provided drainage that drew off water and prevented the road from flooding and becoming too muddy for wagons. This made the movement of armies, and more important supplies, significantly easier. The Roman custom of building fortified camps each day might also have been connected to the fighting in Samnium, because of the danger of ambushes. Although this practice slowed down a Roman army's rate of movement, camp building added a great deal of security and helped to improve discipline. Roman armies could, and did, move rapidly when necessary.

The Samnites stubbornly fought on. Beginning in 312 they formed a "grand alliance" of Etruscans, Marsi, Paeligni, Aequi, and Hernici against the Romans. In 310, however, the new consul, a brilliant general named Fabius Rullianus, led a march through the forests of the Ciminian mountains, outflanking the surprised Etruscans and defeating them decisively at a battle near Lake Vadimo. One after another, the Romans defeated the Etruscan city-states, until the whole region had fallen under their control. After this, Rome moved into Umbria, making treaties with the Picentes, and then into central Italy, exterminating or absorbing

6. The Via Appia about six Roman miles from the walls of Rome, where it is paved with flagstones. The road was begun in 312 BCE and subsequently lined with villas and monumental tombs. Photo: Scala/Art Resource, NY.

their ancient enemies, the Hernici and Aequi. The Marsi and Paeligni were forced to become Roman allies. Like the Latins, the Oscan allies kept their independence but were required to provide a specified number of troops to Rome under Roman command. As in their earlier conflicts, the Romans utilized strategic alliances during the Second Samnite War very effectively, using them to break up possible enemy coalitions, provide staging points, and supplement Roman forces, especially in light infantry and cavalry. As they moved farther from their own territory, the Romans also used food supplies requisitioned from allied states to support the fighting in northern and southern Italy. By the end of the conflict, Rome had become the most powerful state in Italy. Most of the central part of the peninsula was ruled directly from Rome, and it had established indirect, but firm, control over Campania to the south and Etruria to the north.

The Romans increased the number of military colonies. One at Sora guarded the Samnites' northern border and another, at Narnia, protected the strategic route to Umbria. Colonies dominated the central Appenine mountain range, and the Romans had begun a second major military road over them, the Via Valeria, connecting the capital to Italy's eastern coast. Other colonies were set up at strategic points inland to break up the territory of their enemies, especially the Samnites. The colonists, who were Roman citizens, guarded important passes and watched over Rome's enemies. They were subject to military service and frequently called upon to fight. The colonies were often used to settle landless Romans, thus increasing the number of *assidui* and the potential strength of the legions.

In 312, a new maritime colony was established on the island of Pontiae (today called Ponza) off the west coast of Italy. The next year a two-man Naval Board was established. Each naval *duumvir* commanded a fleet of ten ships, probably triremes, the main type of warship of the day. The trireme sank other ships with a bronze ram or beak (*rostrum*) attached to the bow just under the waterline. Maneuvering to ram took great skill, determination, and courage on the part of the rowers. Therefore, the sailors who rowed Roman warships were always free, never slaves. Rome continued to expand its maritime colonies; by 218 there were twelve of them. Such colonists were exempt from legionary service, but rather served in the Roman fleet. There is a widespread belief that the Romans did not have a fleet until the First

Punic War – an idea stemming from a famous story in Livy – but this was clearly not the case. Republican Rome understood the importance of naval power, but generally relied on allies and maritime colonies to provide it.

By 300 BCE, the Romans had surrounded Samnium on the west, north, and east. The Samnites attempted to compensate by pushing south against the Lucanians in southern Italy. In 298, the Lucanians asked for Roman help, which led to the Third Samnite War (298–290). An army under L. Cornelius Scipio Barbatus marched south and drove the Samnites out of Lucania. This is the first mention of a Cornelius Scipio in Roman military history – the men of this patrician family would lead Roman armies for the next 150 years. In 296, the Samnites counterattacked, commanded by a skilled general named Gellius Egnatius, and struck deep into Roman territory, picking up forces from the Etruscans, Umbrians, and Senones, a Gallic tribe living north of Etruria. The next year Egnatius crushed an army under the command of Scipio Barbartus. The Romans raised a new force, calling up old men and freeing slaves to fight in the legions. The veteran Fabius Rullianus and a plebeian consul, P. Decius Mus, shared command. The Samnite alliance and the Romans met at the Battle of Sentinum in 295. The Romans crushed the Samnites, killing Gellius Egnatius.

The Romans then invaded Samnium itself and in 293 defeated a Samnite force that included the elite Linen Legion at the Battle of Aquilonia. Three years later, the consul Manius Curius Dentatus marched throughout Samnium destroying crops and burning buildings. Samnite power was permanently broken, and from this point on, the Samnites formed an important part of Rome's allied forces, although seething hostility toward Rome occasionally resulted in revolt. The defeated Umbrians and Senones were also forced into alliance. In 284 the Senones revolted. They besieged the city of Arretium and defeated a Roman force sent to relieve the city. Curius Dentatus defeated the Senones by repeating the strategy he had used against the Samnites. He first defeated the Gallic tribe in battle and then mercilessly laid waste their farms and towns. So thorough was the destruction that the Senones'

The Battle of Sentinum (295 BCE)

The Battle of Sentinum was the climactic event in the Third Samnite War. The Romans faced a coalition of powerful enemies: the Samnites, Etruscans, Umbrians, and Gallic Senones. This anti-Roman alliance was under the command of the talented Samnite general Gellius Egnatius. The Romans sent both consuls, the patrician Fabius Rullianus and the plebeian Decius Mus, to face him. The combined consular armies had four Roman legions and a larger force of Latin allies, plus a thousand Campanian cavalry – some 30 to 35 thousand men in total. The Samnite force was about the same size. The Romans deployed a diversionary force to Etruria, forcing the Etruscans to abandon their allies in order to defend their homes. In the battle, the Samnites were on the right, facing Fabius Rullianus, while the Gauls faced Decius Mus on the left. The fighting between the Samnites and the Romans was a long stalemate, but when Decius tried breaking the Gauls with cavalry, he was confronted by the Gallic chariots, long abandoned by most contemporary armies. Unfamiliar with them, his cavalry fell into disorder. His infantry also faltered under a renewed Gallic assault. With the Roman left near to defeat, Decius Mus decided to dedicate himself to the gods (the *devotio*). This ritual involved the commander performing certain ceremonies and then charging, alone, into the enemy ranks, offering his own death as a sacrifice to the gods. The consul's dramatic act rallied the Romans. At this point, Fabius brought up his reserves, which forced the Samnites into retreat, then ordered the Campanian horse to hit the Gauls in the rear. This led to a rout. According to Livy, 25,000 of the enemy were killed and 8,000 captured, at a cost of 8,700 Roman dead.

region remained a wasteland for fifty years. Another tribe of Gauls, the Boii, fought the Romans around the same time but was crushed in 283.

At this point, only the Greek city-states in the south of Italy remained independent of Rome, but not for long. Over the next few years, most of the Greeks voluntarily submitted themselves as Roman allies, partly because the Romans could, and would, protect them from warlike hill people such as the Lucanians and Bruttians. There was an exception, however. Tarentum, the most powerful of the Italian Greek cities, proudly refused to yield. The Tarentines had long used mercenary soldiers and generals, and they now appealed to Pyrrhus (319–272), the king of Epirus, a state in northwestern Greece. Pyrrhus was a bold military leader and adventurer. He took Alexander the Great (his cousin) as a role model and aspired to create a great empire to the West, as Alexander had done in the East. In 280, Pyrrhus sailed to Italy with an army of 25,000 infantry, 3,000 cavalry, and 20 elephants. The latter were a new element in Western warfare and had never been seen in Italy before. It was also the first time the Romans faced the Macedonian phalanx, which had dominated warfare in the Western world for three generations. The new legions were sorely tested. Nevertheless, at Heraclea in 280, although the Roman force of 20,000 was out-numbered, the consul P. Valerius Laevinus did not hesitate to attack Pyrrhus. The Roman cavalry, however, was thrown into disarray by the elephants, and Rome was defeated, although the Epirotes suffered heavy casualties.

By the next year, Pyrrhus had built his forces up to about 40,000 or 50,000 men with the help of Oscan and Samnite tribes, who were seeking to free themselves from Roman rule. At Asculum (279), he met a Roman army of about the same size, and again won, although at a high cost. (After this battle, Pyrrhus commented that another such victory and he would be defeated. This is the origin of our expression "a Pyrrhic victory.") Attempts to come to terms with the Romans were rebuffed. During the Republican period, the Romans seldom negotiated with their enemies from a position of weakness, preferring to tough it out. At this crucial point, the city-state of Syracuse in Sicily appealed to Pyrrhus for aid. Impatient and frustrated by the lack of progress in Italy, Pyrrhus went to Sicily.

While Pyrrhus was away, the Romans hammered the king's Oscan and Samnite allies, effectively isolating him, so that when Pyrrhus

Quintus Fabius Maximus Rullianus (ca. 364–ca. 290 BCE)

Many of the stories Livy relates about Fabius Maximus Rullianus are fictional, and others may be in fact about his grandson, the more famous Fabius Maximus who fought Hannibal. We can guess, however, that as a young man, Rullianus served as a quaestor, curule aedile, and/or praetor: he certainly was in the army. Livy says that he won a victory over the Samnites in 325, but because he disobeyed orders, the dictator Lucius Papirius Cursor ordered him punished. According to Livy, Rullianus was elected consul in 322, defeating the Samnites and the Apulians, and then consul four more times (in 310, 308, 297, 295) and dictator in 315, taking the town of Saticula. However, he was then defeated by the Samnites at the battle of Lautulae.

According to the Greek historian Diodorus Siculus, Rullianus was dictator again in 313 and captured Fregellae, Calatia, and Nola. Between 310 and 308, he is said to have campaigned in Etruria and Samnium. Rullianus was censor in 304 and is supposed to have instituted the *transvectio equitum*, a parade of Rome's cavalry, intended to inspect the horses provided by the state to the equestrians. During the Third Samnite War, he campaigned in Samnium in 297 and possibly again in 296. Rullianus was consul once more in 295, along with the plebeian Decius Mus. In this year the two consular armies were joined and defeated the Samnites, Etruscans, and Gauls at the battle of Sentinum. There is a military scene on a frieze found in a fourth-century BCE tomb on the Esquiline hill that identifies a figure as a Q. Fabios [*sic*]. This may be a portrait of Rullianus.

returned to southern Italy in 276 he had to face the Romans alone. The next year he fought them again at the battle of Malventum (later called Beneventum). Avoiding an ambush, Curius Dentatus forced the king into open battle. Again, Pyrrhus won a technical victory but took such heavy losses, including eight of his remaining elephants, that soon

7. The sarcophagus of Scipio Barbatus, a consul of 298 BCE. The inscription says in part that he "was a brave and wise man, whose handsome looks (*forma*) were equal to his courage in battle (*virtus*)." Photo: Scala/Art Resource, NY.

afterward he gave up his dream of conquering Italy and went back to Greece. What had turned the tide of war was the fact that the Romans, with their system of allies, were able to replace their losses whereas, Pyrrhus, reliant on professional troops, could not. Tarentum, along with the city of Croton, was forced into alliance with Rome in 270. With some minor exceptions, all the territory south of the Rubicon River that separated Italy from Cisalpine Gaul was now directly or indirectly under Roman rule.

Links: Livy 8.9.4–10.8 (Decius Mus devotes himself), 9.1.1–6.9 (Caudine Forks); Justin *Epitome* 18.1.1–7.2 (the Pyrrhic War).

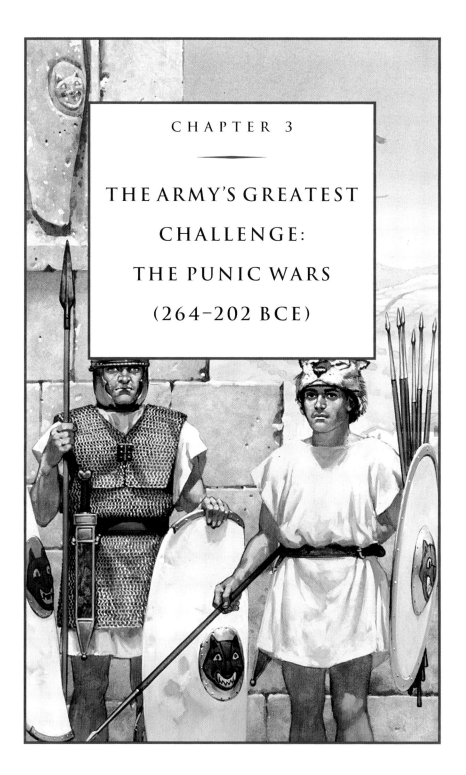

CHAPTER 3

THE ARMY'S GREATEST
CHALLENGE:
THE PUNIC WARS
(264–202 BCE)

Rome's conquest of Italy brought it face-to-face with the Carthaginian Empire, centered in the region of North Africa, modern Tunisia. It was soon drawn into a struggle between Carthaginians and Greeks who had long been fighting over the wealthy and populous island of Sicily. In the course of this conflict, a group of Italian mercenaries called the Mamertines had seized control of the important Sicilian city of Messena in a dispute over pay. When the Carthaginians threatened to attack them, the mercenaries appealed to Rome for help.

Livy portrays a debate in the Senate between those who contended that intervention in Sicily would be raw aggression and an unjust war, and others who argued that it was in Rome's strategic interest to intervene. Whatever the reality of this debate, in the end the Romans went to war. A Roman army had no trouble in securing Messena. They then invaded the territory of Hiero II, the king of Syracuse, but the fighting ended when Hiero agreed to join the Roman side. Hiero supplied the Romans with food during their invasion, as they apparently did not yet have the infrastructure for overseas logistics. The Romans marched across the island to Agrigentum (now Agrigento), the main Carthaginian base. Although themselves surrounded by Punic forces, the Roman force captured and sacked the city in 262 BCE.

Supremacy at sea was necessary to obtain victory. The Romans realized that their relatively small fleet was no match for the Carthaginians' 120 quinqueremes, or "fivers." Since more than three banks of rowers was not practical, it is likely that the term meant something like "five rower-powered" (think of five horse-powered), rather than that there were five banks of rowers. Significantly longer and more powerful than triremes, these ships probably sported three banks of oars in a 2–2–1 pattern. The Romans, drawing on Italy's immense resources, including its many maritime states and colonies, quickly built up a fleet of 140 quinqueremes, plus a smaller number of triremes.

8. Bronze coin issued by the Mamertines, Italian mercenaries who had seized the town of Messena and made it a base for piracy and banditry. Threatened by the Syracusans and Carthaginians, the Mamertines appealed for help to the Romans, whose intervention led to the First Punic War. Photo: © The Trustees of the British Museum.

9. The prow of a warship and its ram shown on an *as*, a Roman bronze coin minted at the end of the third century BCE. Below the vertical line one can see the ship's forward "castle," where archers could be stationed. Photo: Bildarchiv Preussischer Kulturbesitz/Art Resource, NY.

In 260, the two fleets met at Mylae, off Sicily's north coast. The Carthaginians fought in the traditional manner, each ship rowing toward an enemy at top speed and using its ram to smash a hole in it, then backing up to watch it sink. The Romans, however, were equipped with the newly developed *corvus*, or raven, a device for boarding ships. The *corvus* was a bridge attached to a pole at one end, so it could swing, and a hook at the other, to grab the enemy ship. The Carthaginians were confident, even overconfident, and their ships raced to engage the Romans, but many fell victim to the *corvus*. Turning a sea battle into a virtual land battle, Roman troops swarmed over the enemy's ships, overwhelming their crews. Unable to deal with the new tactic, the Carthaginian ships retreated. After the battle, Gaius Duilius celebrated Rome's first naval triumph.

The Romans followed up their victory by seizing most of the rest of Sicily, bottling up the Carthaginians in three strongholds: Panormus (Palermo), Drepana (Trapani), and Lilybaeum (Marsala). Rome then planned an invasion of Africa. The Carthaginians tried to stop the Romans at the naval battle of Ecnomus (256), but despite fierce fighting, the Punic fleet was defeated. A Roman force of fifteen thousand under Marcus Atilius Regulus then landed and after winning a victory at the Battle of Adys pushed to within a day's march of Carthage. With the help of a Spartan mercenary named Xanthippus, however, the Carthaginians trained a citizen army, which, in an astounding turnabout, defeated the Romans at the Battle of Tunis (255). Roman legend maintained that Regulus was captured and, after vowing to return, was sent back to Rome with a peace proposal. He is supposed to have promptly advised the Senate to reject any talk of peace and then, true to his word, returned to the enemy's capital, leading the infuriated Carthaginians to torture him to death. This story of Regulus was held up by later Romans as a classic example of *virtus*, courage, and *officium*, duty to the state. In fact, Regulus seems to have been killed by the Carthaginians immediately after the Battle of Tunis.

The Romans now put their energy into conquering the remaining Punic strongholds in Sicily. Panormus fell in 254, but despite its first use of battering rams, Rome failed to take Lilybaeum in 249. The Roman use of siege works had gradually increased over the course of the third century. Siege walls, called circumvallations, were being routinely built by the time Sicily was invaded. The Romans' logistical capabilities had also improved: convoys transporting provisions to armies had grown in size, and by 249 the Romans were using 800 transports, guarded by 120 warships, to bring supplies to the army besieging Lilybaeum.

The war dragged on. In 249, the Carthaginians under Adherbal soundly defeated the Roman fleet commanded by P. Claudius Pulcher at the Battle of Drepana. The Romans lost ninety-three ships and thousands of men. Soon, the Carthaginians entrusted their army in Sicily to a brilliant young commander named Hamilcar Barca, father of the famous Hannibal. Hamilcar carried out a guerrilla war from two mountain bases but only had sufficient troops to delay Roman victory, not prevent it. The reluctance, or inability, of the Carthaginians to reinforce their overseas forces led to Hamilcar's defeat. The reason for it remains a mystery, made more enigmatic by the fact the Carthaginians had possessed the most sophisticated logistics in the region a century earlier. It is possible that political rivalries at Carthage undermined Hamilcar.

The Roman losses in the First Punic War were enormous: the census of 247 suggests a decline of some 17 percent in the citizen population. Losses among the aristocracy may have been even higher. Nevertheless, the Romans refused to give up or even consider negotiations. As long as they maintained the will to fight, they held a decisive advantage – more money and a larger population than the Carthaginians: they could afford to replace losses and their enemy could not. By the late 240s, the Carthaginians, who were running out of funds, dispersed their fleet in an attempt to save money. Thus a Roman fleet easily defeated Carthage at the Battle of the Aegates Islands in March 241. At this point the Carthaginians surrendered. Rome forced Carthage to pay a huge war indemnity: 1,000 talents (30 tons) of silver immediately and 220 talents a year for ten years. In addition, Carthage had to hand over its possessions in Sicily. Soon after the war, breaking the terms of the treaty they had just made, Rome also seized Sardinia and Corsica. In 235, the consuls closed the gates of the Temple of Janus, a ritual act performed only when there was complete peace in areas ruled by Rome. The next time this happened would be over two centuries later, in the reign of Augustus Caesar.

Peace, however, lasted for only seven years. The Illyrians, who lived in what is today Croatia in the northwestern Balkans, had long been harassing the Romans with piratical attacks in the Adriatic. In 229, when a Roman ambassador to Illyria was murdered, the Romans went to war. A Roman army and a fleet swiftly took control of Illyria. The Romans did not make the local cities and tribes into allies but introduced a new category, "*amicus*," or "friend [of Rome]," which involved a vague, but very real, submission to Roman power.

Soon Rome faced another threat. In 225, a confederation of Gallic tribes numbering some 70,000 invaded Italy. By this time, Romans were able to raise an enormous force of 130,000, divided into several armies, and to annihilate the Gauls at the Battle of Telamon (224). Despite this decisive victory, the alarm raised by the Gallic invasion led the Romans to embark on a conquest of northern Italy, then known as Cisalpine Gaul. By 200 almost all of the Gallic tribes in the region had surrendered. The Romans secured Cisalpine Gaul with two colonies, Placentia and Cremona, and a military road, the Via Flaminia. Another road, the Via Aurelia, was extended along the western coast from Rome to the Arno River. Cisalpine Gaul would gradually become more Romanized and integrated into the rest of Italy, although formal annexation was more than two centuries away.

Meanwhile, Carthage was faced with the task of paying Rome its enormous indemnity. In 236 Hamilcar Barca led an expedition to Spain and over the next eight years conquered a large portion of the country. This allowed the Carthaginians to exploit Spain's lucrative silver mines. Since the Romans were now used to considering security issues well outside the boundaries of Italy, they negotiated a treaty with Carthage, making the Ebro River in northern Spain the boundary between the two states' spheres of influence. This arrangement did not

10. A map of the Carthaginian Empire. The islands of Sicily, Sardinia, and Corsica had been lost by the time the Carthaginians conquered Spain. Photo: The Punic Wars, 264–146 BC by Nigel Bagnall, © Osprey Publishing Ltd.

prevent but rather led to war. Hannibal Barca, Hamilcar's son and now the Punic commander in Spain, decided to capture the town of Saguntum. Whether or not Saguntum was a Roman ally is still debated, but there is no doubt that the later Roman claim that the city lay north of the Ebro River, and was thus in their strategic zone, was false. When Saguntum was captured, the Romans demanded that Hannibal be turned over to them for punishment. The Carthaginians' refusal to do so led to the Second Punic War (218–201 BCE).

Rome planned a two-pronged strategy. One consular army would march through southern Gaul to Spain and another would make an amphibious assault on North Africa. It was an ambitious and sophisticated plan, illustrating the increased capabilities of the Roman military and Rome's broader strategic vision. Hannibal, however, did not wait for the Romans to attack. He marched across southern Gaul, outmaneuvered the Roman force there, crossed the Alps, and swept into Italy. The Romans were forced to cancel their elaborately laid plans and rush all their forces to face the invader. Hannibal was as brilliant a tactician as he was a strategist and defeated P. Cornelius Scipio at the battles of Ticinus and Trebia in 218. The next year, the forces of Gaius Flaminius were decimated at Lake Trasimene. The Romans, terrified, appointed a dictator, Q. Fabius Maximus, the grandson of Rullianus. Another defeat on the battlefield could mean the end of Rome, as the Italian allies, on whom it depended, might well defect. Fabius adopted a delaying strategy, following Hannibal's army close enough to threaten possible defectors but far enough away to prevent being drawn into battle. This so-called Fabian tactic was very successful but also frustrating for the Roman nobility, who thought it dishonorable to avoid battle. Fabius' enemies in the Senate called him "Hannibal's Pedagogue," a biting reference to the slave who followed a young boy to school carrying his books. After Fabius' six-month term as dictator ended in 216, the two new consuls, Gaius Terentius Varro and Lucius Aemilius Paullus, immediately planned to face Hannibal in a decisive fight. They got their battle at a southeastern Italian town named Cannae, where Hannibal won a stunning victory that virtually annihilated the Roman army.

Historians still argue about whether Hannibal should have immediately attacked the city of Rome after Cannae and why he decided not to do so. Whatever the reason, he continued his strategy of trying to win over and detach Rome's Italian allies. If he had succeeded, the Romans would have faced disaster. Two factors saved them. First, as in the First Punic War, the Romans refused to even consider surrender. Second, although some allies did go over to Carthage, most of them stayed loyal. This gave the Romans the manpower they needed to keep fighting. Oddly, as in the First Punic War, no reinforcements or supplies came from Carthage during this crucial period. Perhaps it was because Hannibal failed to capture a large enough port, or because the Romans maintained naval superiority, or because an anti-Hannibal faction at Carthage prevented it. Whatever the reason, it meant that the Romans, now using Fabian tactics again, could wear down Hannibal while avoiding a battle that might lead to their defeat.

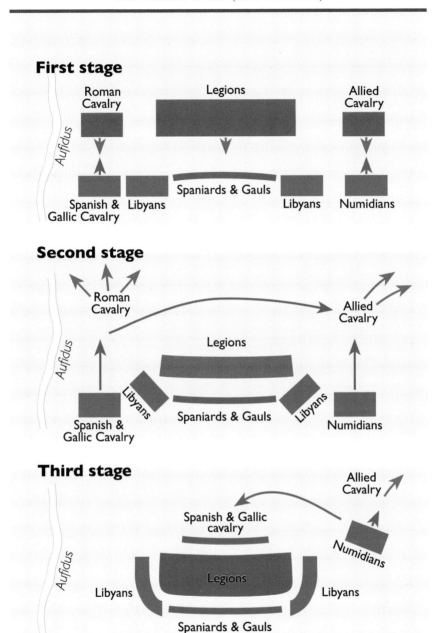

11. Three stages of the Battle of Cannae, fought between the Romans and Carthaginians in 216 BCE. Photo: The Punic Wars, 264–146 BC, by Nigel Bagnall, © Osprey Publishing Ltd.

The Battle of Cannae (216 BCE)

Even today the Battle of Cannae is studied in military academies as the classic example of a smaller force defeating a larger one. We know that the two consuls, Lucius Aemilius Paullus and Gaius Terentius Varro, had combined their armies, though modern estimates of their total force vary from 50,000 to 80,000. It is fairly certain that Hannibal had around 40,000 men, most of them less well trained and armed than the Romans, though he outnumbered his enemy in cavalry. Depending on our estimates of the Roman army's size, Hannibal either faced twice his number or was slightly outnumbered. In any case, given the better quality of their army, the Romans should have won.

The consuls set up their troops as always – with the light troops in front, Roman legions in the center, Italian infantry and cavalry on the wings. The Roman practice of regular deployment meant that each unit instantly knew its place in line. The Romans also had a standard tactic: the legions would smash through the enemy center, with the allies and the cavalry holding the flanks. This pattern had worked consistently. Hannibal, however, was well aware of Roman practice and had the skill to exploit it to his advantage. The Carthaginian general placed his Gallic and Spanish infantry in the center, with his excellent cavalry on the wings – the Gauls and Spanish on the right, the Numidians on the left. As expected, the Roman center pushed the Punic forces back, but the Carthaginian left and right held. Hannibal's superior cavalry drove off the Roman horse, and as the legions pressed relentlessly forward they eventually found themselves hemmed in on three sides. Soon the Romans were completely surrounded and pushed so tightly packed together that they could not fight effectively. A slaughter ensued. The consul Paullus, two proconsuls, both quaestors, 29 of 48 military tribunes, and 80 senators were killed, and so many equestrians died that their gold rings filled several baskets. Only 15,000 Romans escaped death or capture. It is true that Carthaginian losses were not light – estimates range between 5,700 and 8,000 – but Hannibal's victory was complete.

Cannae did result in some Carthaginian successes: Philip V, the king of Macedonia, became an ally, as did the cities of Capua in southern Italy and Syracuse in Sicily. Hannibal also captured Tarentum, located at Italy's tip, though the Roman garrison in its citadel held out. Starting in 212, however, the tide of war turned. The Romans recovered Syracuse in 211 (the famous Greek mathematician Archimedes died in the aftermath of the siege). Capua was retaken the same year and severely punished for its disloyalty to Rome. It took until 209 for Tarentum to fall, but by this time Hannibal was on the run, concentrating on surviving rather than conquering.

In 210 the Roman Assembly, bypassing the Senate, elected the charismatic but inexperienced Publius Cornelius Scipio to be commander in Spain. On his arrival there, Scipio retrained his army, instilling not only discipline but a fighting spirit as well. Polybius tells us that the 18-inch (45 cm) Spanish thrusting sword, called the *gladius*, was introduced during the Second Punic War, and this may have occurred at this moment, though some modern historians think that it came into use somewhat earlier. Whatever the case, this sword was a deadly weapon in Roman hands. Designed to be thrust upward into an enemy's midsection rather than downward against the head and shoulders, the *gladius* targeted the bowels, causing mortal wounds. The iron rim and iron boss of the *scutum* were also used as weapons, the former against an enemy's chin or face, and the latter to punch him backward, creating an opening for a killing thrust with the *gladius*.

In 210 BCE, Scipio's careful preparations paid off. He set out with an army of 25,000 infantry and 2,500 cavalry on a surprise attack against the Carthaginian base at New Carthage (Nova Carthago, now Cartagena in Spain). The Carthaginians were caught completely off guard, with most of their forces being too far away to render assistance to the city. While exploring the city's defenses, Scipio discovered that its seaward walls were accessible via a lagoon. Personally leading a force of five hundred men wading up to their necks, he took New Carthage. Subsequently, at the Battle of Baecula (208), Scipio defeated Hannibal's brother Hasdrubal, though he failed to prevent him from slipping

Publius Cornelius Scipio Africanus (236–183 BCE)

Publius Cornelius Scipio Africanus was born in 236 BCE into the *gens Cornelia*, one of the most noble of the patrician clans. In 218, he served in the cavalry and, according to a popular story, saved his father's life at the Battle of Ticinum. A military tribune during the disastrous battle at Cannae, Scipio is supposed to have rallied survivors at Canusium. In 213, he was elected curule aedile, normally a purely civilian post, but during the Punic Wars the holder of this office was responsible for defending the city of Rome itself. In 210, the Assembly voted Scipio consular *imperium*, although he was only twenty-six. He was awarded the province of Spain, where he whipped an undisciplined army into shape through vigorous training. In 209, this paid off. He made a forced march on the Punic supply base of New Carthage, now Cartagena, and took the city. The next year he defeated Hannibal's brother Hasdrubal at Baecula by adopting the Carthaginians' flanking tactics. In 206, he beat Hannibal's other brother Mago at Ilipa, north of modern Seville. Scipio was elected consul in 205, although he was only thirty-one, well under the traditional minimum age. Invading North Africa in 204, he defeated the Carthaginians in two great battles, Campus Magnus in 203 and Zama in 202. In the latter battle he faced and defeated Hannibal. Carthage surrendered and Scipio received the *cognomen* Africanus and a great triumph.

Scipio became a censor in 199 and was elected consul a second time in 194. In 190, his brother was elected consul and assigned the war against King Antiochus III. Scipio went along as a mere legate, but most historians believe he was actually the commander and responsible for the Roman victory at Magnesia in 189. His extraordinary successes led to the legend that he was the son of the god Jupiter. Although there is no evidence that he used this prestige to gain power at Rome, it caused envy and resentment. Scipio and his brother were brought to trial and accused of embezzlement and corruption. Although he was undoubtedly innocent of these changes, Scipio chose to go into retirement in Campania in 184 rather than face trial. He died there the next year.

12. A terracotta statuette of an elephant carrying a castle with two shields hanging on it and an African driver, illustrating either the Punic Wars in the third century BCE or the Roman wars against the Hellenistic monarchies in the second. Photo: Scala/Art Resource, NY.

away with most of his force and marching across Gaul to bring help to Hannibal. Scipio did not follow Hasdrubal but remained in Spain, winning the Battle of Ilipa (206), which put the entire country in Roman hands.

Meanwhile, Hasdrubal had moved into northern Italy, where he faced one of the consuls, Livius Salinator. In the south, the other consul, Claudius Nero, checked Hannibal's army. The Romans intercepted a message telling Hasdrubal to meet his brother in Umbria. Claudius Nero came up with a bold plan. Leaving a small number of troops facing Hannibal, he forced-marched the bulk of his army 240 miles in six days, arranging for supplies to be left along the route to speed the troops' movements. With a united army, the two consuls surprised and crushed Hasdrubal at the Battle of the Metaurus River (207). Another of Hannibal's brothers, Mago, led a desperate invasion of Italy in 205 but was defeated in 203.

Elected consul in 205, Scipio advocated an invasion of Africa, arguing that in this way Hannibal would be forced to leave Italy to defend his homeland. This "indirect approach" was strongly opposed by the more senior senators such as Fabius Maximus and Fulvius Flaccus, who considered it too risky. As a compromise measure, the Senate awarded Scipio the province of Sicily with the option of invading Africa, although he was not assigned any troops to do so. Remarkably, Scipio was able to raise an army consisting entirely of volunteers, including four thousand of his own clients – those citizens for whom he was a patron. Allying himself with the Numidian prince Massinissa, he besieged the city of Utica, and when Hannibal indeed returned to Carthage, he met his nemesis at the Battle of Zama (202). Here the two greatest generals of their generation, perhaps of all time, fought it out. Scipio and the Romans were victorious, ending the war. Carthage was forced to pay an even higher indemnity than in the First Punic War. In addition, Carthage had to give up virtually its entire fleet and was banned from employing its army outside its borders. The Romans took over Spain, dividing it into two provinces. Rome was now the dominant force in the western Mediterranean.

During the Punic Wars, both sides regularly fielded armies of 50,000 and fleets with crews of 70,000. The ability of the Romans to repeatedly raise such forces is a testament to the increasingly sophisticated infrastructure of their state and economy. At some point during this period the Romans made a key reform in the organization of the legion, changing it from a phalanx of tightly packed soldiers in ranks and files to a more open formation in which each soldier fought individually. Some historians date this modification to the early third century, others to a later date. Whatever the date, the Romans now deployed, not in a solid line, but in a checkerboard fashion called the *quincunx* because it resembled the arrangement of the five pips on dice.

Throughout the Punic Wars, the legion retained its fourth-century divisions. Although we hear of a legionary "cohort" for the first time in 212, this seems to be an ad hoc grouping of maniples, which remained the basic tactical units. Roman equipment, however, gradually changed. The *hastati* seem to be have been the first to adopt the javelin (*pilum*) in place of the spear (*hasta*). Eventually the second line or *principes* joined them, and by 223 BCE only the *triarii* apparently still had their spears, although they too switched to the javelin at some point. The most important innovation was the adoption of the Spanish sword, or *gladius*, and the *scutum*, the concave, oval shield. The new armament made the legion a much more flexible and powerful military unit. The "wall of shields" effect was lost, but individual soldiers were better protected by their *scuta*. The new shield, the short sword, and the javelin would remain the legionaries' main armaments for hundreds of years.

Battles generally opened with the light infantry (now called the *velites*) skirmishing to the army's front. Armed with javelins, slings, and swords, they harassed the enemy until the two main battle lines joined. Once the light infantry had cleared the field, the heavy infantry marched forward, hurling their *pila* at 50 to 100 feet from the enemy line, and then sprinted forward to close with the sword. The *hastati* in front started the battle, backed up by the second-line *principes*. The *triarii* generally stayed in reserve: to "get to the *triarii*" meant the same as our expression "to come down to the wire." The cavalry, almost always placed on the wings, engaged the enemy's horsemen and tried to drive them off the battlefield. If they succeeded, they could attack the opponent's infantry in its vulnerable flank. Battle was generally decided, however, by the engagement of heavy infantry in the center of the battlefield.

We know that on the individual level Romans now fought "man-to-man," each soldier trying to kill the enemy in front of him. The *gladius* was a very effective weapon in this sort of fighting, providing half again as much thrusting power as a spear; but, due to its short length, it had to be used at very close quarters. What is unclear is how the Romans fought in units. They probably deployed their maniples some twenty men across and six deep, three deep in the case of the *triarii*. The big question is whether the Romans rotated men into the front rank (and if so, how they managed this while fighting) or, alternatively, if a soldier in the second rank waited until the man in front of him died or fell, then took his place. The mechanics of Roman battle remain obscure, but it is clear that whatever they did, they did it very well.

The Roman practice of daily camping probably dates to the late fourth or early third centuries, but it is in the time of the Punic Wars that it was perfected as a technique. The Romans would build an identical rectangular camp each day, with both the exterior and interior elements highly standardized. They did not take advantage of natural features of the terrain for defense or convenience, but the practice meant that every soldier knew his place in the layout, and that he understood exactly what he needed to do. Thus, a fortified camp could be built with astonishing rapidity. Measurements were standard, so the camp could be expanded simply by multiplication to contain any size force. Specialists in measurement (*mensores*) traveled with the army to handle this.

The commander's headquarters, or *praetorium*, stood at the center, flanked on the right by the *quaestorium*, where supplies were stored and administered, and on the left by the *forum*, where troops could be assembled. A road called the Via Principalis ran through the camp, dividing this administrative area from the tents of the legionaries. Though a wall surrounded it, with a gate on each side, the camp was not intended to be able to withstand a siege. Rather, the Romans used it

13. Three legionaries of the Second Punic War: a *hastatus*, a *triarius*, and a *veles*, as reconstructed by Angus McBride. Photo: The Punic Wars, 264–146 BC by Nigel Bagnall, © Osprey Publishing Ltd.

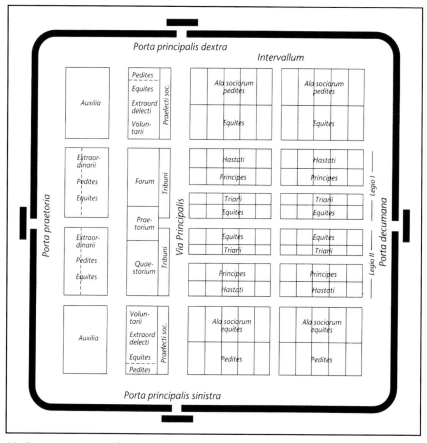

14. A reconstruction of the layout of the Roman daily marching camp as described by Polybius, a Greek historian living in Rome.

as a base to sally forth to meet any threat. The camp did, however, provide excellent security from surprise attacks.

By the end of the third century, the Romans were regularly moving provisions long distances from Etruria, Sardinia, and Sicily to armies operating not only in Italy but also in Spain, Macedonia, and Africa. Large Roman fleets carried more than just supplies; they also transported troops. When Scipio Africanus invaded Africa in 204, 16,000 infantry and 1,600 cavalry traveled in 400 transports. During and after the Punic Wars, Roman armies also used overland supply lines, moving provisions over considerable distances, employing magazines and supply depots. To facilitate these movements, the Romans continued to construct a sophisticated network of roads throughout Italy.

During the epic struggle with Carthage, several substantial armies were kept in the field simultaneously and significant garrisons maintained. Thus, the number of legions and of soldiers serving in the army increased dramatically. Indeed, during the long years of war, virtually every able-bodied adult Roman male saw military service. In addition, a substantial proportion of the Italian population was recruited. The alliance system set up in the fourth century was sorely tested in the third, and passed with flying colors. The Italians, whose manpower was vital to Rome, remained loyal at the crucial hour. Nevertheless, it was probably during the Punic Wars that the Romans first used mercenaries, primarily to provide light infantry and cavalry. Noteworthy were the Balearic slingers who came from the islands now called Majorca and Minorca off the coast of Spain, and archers from Crete.

The war made enormous demands, not only on Roman manpower, but on Rome's ability to provide military leadership. Many individual units were Italian or foreign, but virtually all officers, and certainly all commanders, were Roman aristocrats. The demand for officers meant that almost all male adult members of the Roman nobility spent long years fighting in wars. This resulted in a highly militarized elite class. The combination of experience in war, diplomacy, and statesmanship among Roman leaders of this period was certainly a factor in Roman success.

Links: Livy 22.35.1–49.18 (Battle of Cannae), 28.12.13–16.13 (Battle of Ilipa), 30.32.1–35.11 (Battle of Zama).

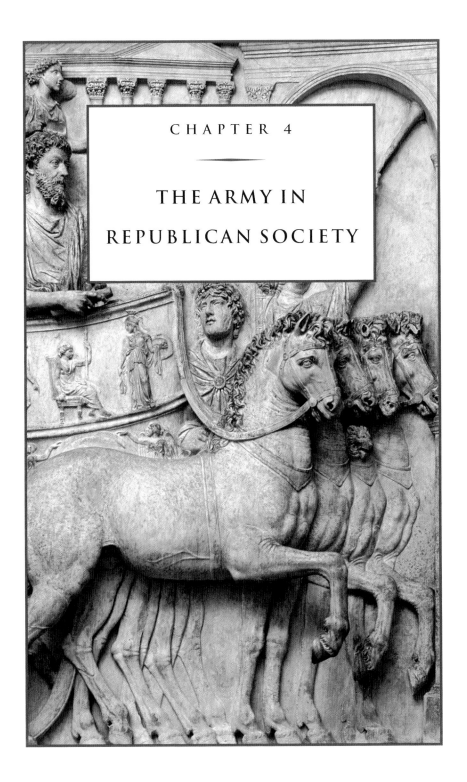

CHAPTER 4

THE ARMY IN
REPUBLICAN SOCIETY

The Romans had organized a remarkably successful imperial republic, and over the course of the third and second centuries BCE they became the rulers, directly and indirectly, of virtually the entire Mediterranean region. Today's historians, of course, are interested in *how* the Romans managed to create their great empire, but they also ask *why* the Romans engaged in this long and difficult course of conquest. This is the question of Roman imperialism. Some scholars think that the Romans were drawn into ever more distant campaigns by a fear of hostile neighbors. In this view, called the "defensive imperialism" theory, the Romans always believed that they were defending themselves, even when they were marching to war outside their borders. Other historians disagree: they see the Romans as aggressive conquerors. According to this view, Rome was a warlike society, considering the Roman domination of others a good thing. This latter view seems to be the more compelling.

Whatever the truth, we know that Roman society was organized around a ritual calendar of which war was a key part. When the consuls assumed office, their first job was usually raising troops. During the Republic, the year began in March, which meant that wars would begin in April. As time went on, though, wars were fought farther and farther afield. In 153 BCE, January 1 became the date consuls took office, so that Roman armies could take the field earlier in the year. Naval operations generally still began on March 10, the start of the sailing season. Campaigns normally ended by October, as most Roman Republican soldiers were farmers and had to get back to their fields. To allow the army to fight over the winter, pay was introduced to the Roman army, traditionally at the siege of Veii. If a war did not end by the fall, the army would retire into winter quarters (*hibernacula*) until the spring. Under the pressures of frequent wars, Romans more commonly continued fighting after the onset of winter. Nevertheless, the traditional idea of the campaigning season remained the norm for Romans throughout the period and beyond.

The Romans believed that Jupiter, the king of the gods, determined victory and that a war had to be just in order for him to grant them success. This did not mean they fought only defensive wars, of course, otherwise Rome would never have grown into an empire. Nevertheless, special individuals called fetial priests were consulted to make sure that a war was just. In his first book, Livy describes these priests' elaborate rituals, which included a formal complaint about grievances; then, if they were unsatisfied after thirty-three days, a declaration of war was made by hurling a spear into enemy territory.

The Campus Martius, the place where the army mustered, was named for the Roman god of war, Mars. Whenever a new army was raised there, or if two armies joined together, priests performed a special cleansing ceremony, called a lustration, in which they circled around the army carrying torches and leading sacrificial animals. Commonly a pig, a sheep, and a bull were slaughtered in a sacrifice called a *suovetaurilia*. The ceremony was always performed before, not after, battle; thus it was not intended to purify soldiers after killing. Its purpose seems to have been to drive away evil and ensure that the army had divine sanction. Such ceremonies helped to bind soldiers together psychologically, and thus aided them in fighting more effectively.

Religion also followed the Romans into the battlefield. Various omens were used to determine if the gods approved of when and where a battle was to be fought. The army brought sacred chickens along with it. Before a battle the commander would offer the chickens food in a ritually prescribed manner. If they ate, then battle would be joined; if they refused, it meant the gods were warning that defeat loomed. The origin of this custom is not known – it may be Etruscan. The Roman fleet also took the sacred chickens to sea when at war. Livy writes that when P. Claudius Pulcher faced the Carthaginians at the Battle of Drepana (249 BCE) he consulted the sacred chickens, but they refused to eat. Anxious to engage the enemy, Pulcher quipped, "If they will not eat, let them drink" and had the birds thrown overboard. He lost the battle. Whether or not the story is true, it illustrates how seriously the Romans took such omens.

Ritual sacrifices, often of a bull or ram, might be offered before a war was undertaken or a battle commenced. The Romans believed that their gods operated according to a formula known as *do ut des*, that is, "I give in order that you might give." Offering an animal as a sacrifice was supposed to obligate, or at least encourage, a god to reciprocate by granting the sacrificer's prayer. In addition to the standard ceremonies, a general might promise elaborate offerings to a god, and even the con- struction of an entire temple at enormous expense, as an incentive for the divinity to grant him victory. In the heat of a battle, when things were going badly it was believed that a tremendous sacrifice might induce the gods to give the Romans victory. A Republican commander might dedicate himself in a special ritual, offering his own life as a sacrifice in order to bring victory to Rome. Covering his head – a sign of piety – he would ride headlong into the midst of the enemy, seeking death at their hands. Decius Mus "devoted" himself thus at the Battle of Sentinum in 295. A more direct form of human sacrifice, sometimes the burial of live victims, was also practiced by the Romans; but it was very rare, and only three cases are known.

The Romans drew no distinction between military and civilian power, and their elected officials generally served in both capacities. All Roman magistracies lasted only one year, and in between terms of office a senatorial noble would usually serve as an officer in the army. A young and ambitious Roman aristocrat would first spend time as a military tribune in one of the legions. If he distinguished himself, he would try to be elected a quaestor, accompanying the army in a financial capacity. After this, he stood for either aedile or plebeian tribune, both with mainly civilian duties, although occasionally they had military functions. After all this experience, he would run for the praetorship, a post that brought him *imperium*, the right to command Roman citizens in battle. A very few achieved the highest office, that of consul.

Having only four officials per year with the *imperium* to command armies was sufficient in the fifth and early fourth centuries, but as Rome expanded and fought more wars, the practice of prorogation arose. The Senate would prorogate – that is, extend – the command of a general in the field. Former consuls were called proconsuls and former praetors, propraetors. Q. Publilius Philo was made the first proconsul in 326, and by the third century the practice had became common. Eventually proconsuls and propraetors were being called back to duty years after their original election. This gave Rome a large pool of experienced general officers.

Roman commanders lacked any formal training in warfare and therefore some scholars refer to them as amateur generals. Although it is true that the Romans had no equivalent to our military academies or officer training programs, there were informal ways in which military knowledge was passed on. Young aristocrats learned about war from relatives and family friends who had served in the army. Discussions during dinners, feasts, and drinking parties played an important role in teaching nobles. War, and how to fight it, must have been a common topic of discussion. Poems and songs also instilled a martial spirit and even taught tactical lessons. In the end, Roman nobles served long years in the military and learned how to fight "on the job."

In all military systems, politics is part of choosing a commander, and Rome was no different in this respect. Indeed, due to the dual political and military nature of Roman offices such as consul or praetor, the potential for military politicking was more pronounced than in other societies. Senatorial nobles manipulated the Roman assemblies in various ways, including patronage and even bribery, but Roman voters were skillful at matching the character of a commander to the task at hand. Soldiers and officers were also voting citizens, and this discouraged unnecessary risk taking among Roman commanders. A reputation for not considering the lives of one's troops could jeopardize a political career. The way in which the Romans chose commanders could be messy, but on the whole the quality of Roman generals was high. Of course, since noble birth and wealth played an important part in political advancement, there were always some inept Roman commanders. In part to compensate for this, Roman warfare took on its characteristic standardization.

Military Legends and Stories

The Romans found ways to inculcate martial virtues such as courage (*virtus*), honor (*honos*), discipline (*disciplina*), and obedience (*pietas*) into their boys and young men. These ideas are reflected in Roman mythology, poetry, and history. Livy's history of Rome and Virgil's epic poem *The Aeneid* tell the tales of Rome's heroes – Aeneas, Romulus, and others. The way they behaved, and in particular the bravery and loyalty shown in battle, were meant to be models for the young Roman nobles who heard and memorized these stories. The stories of Cincinnatus, who assumed the office of dictator but laid it aside immediately after defeating the enemy, and Regulus, who voluntarily accepted death by torture rather than recommend negotiation with the enemy, were intended as powerful lessons. In ancient religions, important ideas were sometimes personified as gods, and the Romans worshipped Courage, Discipline, and Duty in temples built in Rome.

There was, however, a countertradition that poked fun at war and the military. The Latin plays of Plautus, although based on Greek originals, make light of the arrogance of Roman soldiers. The triumph, though an important religious event, included the singing of satirical and often obscene songs by soldiers. These songs, a few verses of which survive, often made fun of Roman commanders and of the army. They demonstrate that in Rome, as everywhere and in all times, many ambiguous and often contradictory ideas were held simultaneously.

Measured marches, the custom of building fortified camps daily, and conventional tactical patterns made it easier to run the army. Command could be assigned to elite young men with less danger that incompetence would lose a war. Standardization did mean that, occasionally, the Romans missed the opportunity for a quick decisive stroke, but overall the system worked well. Despite their commitment to system and tradition, the Romans were not set in their ways. They learned from their defeats and were perfectly willing to borrow from their enemies.

Although there are notable exceptions, as a rule Roman generals did not fight in the ranks but commanded from the rear. Glory and honor were important to Roman nobles, but these came from victory in battle, not hand-to-hand combat. Nevertheless, the old ideas of courage (*virtus*) and strength (*vis*) survived. Lower officers, such as tribunes and prefects, frequently led from the front, as they knew that soldiers respond much better to examples of courage than to exhortations delivered from the rear. Thus, the casualty rate among young nobles was very high.

The Senate at Rome was made up of its most powerful nobles. Senators handled the political aspects of war, deciding whom to fight, the size of armies, and logistics. Having two consuls with equal powers of command could be troublesome, although in practice they were often each leading an army in separate theaters. When there were disputes, the collective influence and prestige of the Senate helped keep the command system working. The Romans did not have a war department or a general staff, but the Senate, made up of former, present, and would-be generals, functioned as a sort of strategic command. Rome, however, usually gave the general in the field a great deal of control in terms of military action through the method of *imperium* (absolute authority) within a *provincia* (area of operations), which prevented too much political interference in military operations.

The centurion was long a position in the Roman military, and his importance steadily grew over time. Originally, like Greek hoplite officers, he served in combat only as a marker for the troops to form up on, to keep them in line, and to lead by example. As the legion became more flexible, and its organization more open, the centurion took on more and more importance as a low-level commander. Although patronage always played a role, and those from "good families" always had an advantage, common soldiers could be, and were, promoted to this rank due to skill, courage, and strength. Thus, the centurionate turned into an important means of social advancement as well as a backbone of the Roman fighting forces.

Roman historical writing, literature, and art pay the most attention to aristocrats and Senators, who were both the authors and the audience for such works. Nevertheless, wars were fought, won, or lost by the common soldier. There was no basic training in the Roman army, so the first time a young man of seventeen served must have been a frightening – and exhilarating – experience. Virtually all young Romans, however, had male relatives who had combat experience. Thus, like nobles, commoners would have heard about, and learned about, war from a very early age. As is the case today, many games and sports prepared young men for warfare, both physically and psychologically. We have no firsthand accounts from the Romans who fought in the ranks, so we must use our imaginations to understand what it was like to fight as a Roman soldier. It would have involved the fatigue and deprivation of long marches, the boredom and anxiety of waiting for battle, intervals of confusion and fear, and brief bursts of intense energy. Unlike the relative ease of killing or wounding an enemy with a gun or bomb, the use of a spear or sword required determination, skill, courage, and considerable physical strength. During the Republic, many Roman men served in the military for much of their adult lives. Soldiers often fought for year after year, frequently, though not always, in the same legion.

By law, legions were raised at the beginning of each campaigning season and dissolved at its end, though many soldiers remained in the same legion year after year. An oath (*sacramentum*) was taken to the commander, who held authority only while the legion was in existence. Within each one there were five traditional standards – an eagle, horse, bull, wolf, and boar. As in all ancient societies, the Romans did not separate "church and state": military units, like all elements of society, were imbued with religious institutions, rituals, and beliefs. The standards were not assigned to subunits but seem to have represented different divine spirits (*numina*) that were part of the legion. After Marius, a legion retained only one standard – the eagle – but it still had religious significance.

The Romans made a sharp distinction between life at war (*militiae* or *armata*) and life at peace, literally "in the home" (*domi* or *togata*). This was represented by a literal division, as the army was not allowed within Rome's sacred boundary, called the *pomerium*, and were enrolled in the Field of Mars (Campus Martius) outside the city. The only exception was the triumph, one of the oldest and best known of Roman institutions. Only a commander of troops who held *imperium*, and whose army had killed over five thousand foreign enemies, could celebrate a triumph. This rule led to the Roman tendency to try to annihilate rather than simply defeat its enemies. In the triumph, a victorious army marched through the streets of the city, with cheering crowds lining the route. The *triumphator*, dressed as the god Jupiter Optimus Maximus (Best and Greatest), rode in a four-horse chariot. Behind him marched important prisoners, dressed for execution, indeed, many were strangled that very day; the lucky ones were sold into slavery. Then came plundered treasures piled high on wagons and captured animals, such as oxen, destined for massive sacrifices in Rome's temples. In the later Republic, dioramas illustrating the war were also pulled along in wagons. Slaves or soldiers carried signs identifying various elements of the parade or bearing mottoes of the triumphator, such as Caesar's pithy claim: *veni, vidi, vici* ("I came, I saw, I conquered"). The legionaries sang as they marched – often vulgar ditties parodying their generals in the light-heartedly cruel manner common to soldiers throughout time.

Other honors were given to successful generals. There was a lesser form of triumph, with fewer requirements, called an ovation. After a victory, assembled Roman soldiers might acclaim a general "*Imperator.*" Soldiers also awarded the *corona obsidionalis* (literally the siege crown) for liberating an army trapped in a siege, and the *corona graminea*, or grass crown, giving for saving a legion. A Roman commander who killed an enemy commander in battle was given a very high distinction: the *spolia opima*. This was a very rare prize, awarded only three times in Roman history. There were also awards given to any Roman for valor: the *corona civica*, made of oak leaves, was for saving the life of a fellow soldiers; the *corona muralis*, for being the first to get over the walls in a siege; and the *corona navalis* for special valor in a sea battle.

15. Emperor Marcus Aurelius enters Rome in triumph. Although this relief dates from the second century CE, the ritual had changed little from Republican times. Photo: Nimatallah/Art Resource, NY.

Although war's purpose is the defeat of the enemy in combat, much of the experience of war does not involve fighting. To get to battle a Roman soldier had to march many miles and spend long hours in camp. Early in Rome's history, soldiers would have fought only a few days' or weeks' march from the city, but as time went on the distances grew. By the third century BCE, Romans were traveling hundreds of miles by boat and/or on foot to the field of battle. In the Early and Middle Republic, soldiers generally did not carry their own food or gear – their personal slaves accompanied the armies to do the cooking and cleaning, and to carry equipment. Despite the help of slaves, however, Roman soldiers did a lot of hard marching and hard labor. Roman armies marched from the early morning to the early afternoon, and then spent several hours building their camp. Each soldier knew his place and his job: erecting tents, building the perimeter, or digging trenches. When the camp was finished, soldiers stood guard. Long hours were spent on watch, and the penalty for sleeping on guard duty was severe – being beaten to death by one's fellow soldiers. Roman discipline was strict. Although a citizen had the right to a trial when a civilian, while he served in the army, a commander with *imperium* could punish him, or even execute him, at will.

Common soldiers ate a version of the normal diet for peasants. Wheat was eaten in the form of *puls*, a kind of wheat-meal mush, or as flat bread (*panis*). Barley was considered fit only for animals and Greeks. Various beans and peas, onions, and other vegetables were added, but there was little meat, at least by modern standards, although the Republican soldier was no vegetarian, as was once thought. Olive oil was an important part of the diet, as was wine. Officers ate much better, of course. In fact, while soldiers were said to "take food" (*cibum capere*), an officer would "dine" (*epulare*). Even Cato the Elder, renowned for his parsimony, took a baker and a cook with him on campaign.

Both soldiers and officers received a regular ration, and Roman law strictly controlled "personal foraging." Nevertheless, soldiers would naturally do whatever they could to supplement their diet. For example, we hear of an incident in 107 BCE in which a soldier gathered snails to eat. There were generally two meals a day, breakfast (*prandium*) and a main meal (*cena*) eaten in the evening. Military manuals stressed the importance of having the soldiers eat before fighting.

We think of the Romans mainly as soldiers, but many served in the navy as well. Steering ships called for experienced officers and rowing required well-trained and motivated crews. Despite what one sees in movies, the Romans never used slaves or criminals to row in the navy: free men manned their warships. In addition to a crew, a seaworthy ship required hides, rope, pitch, and above all, timber, the last a product in short supply in the Mediterranean. Therefore, controlling one or more regions with large forests was an absolute necessity. The Romans benefited from the presence of such woodlands in Italy, and this was an important factor in their wresting control of the western Mediterranean from the Carthaginians. Ancient warships had very shallow drafts and were vulnerable in storms. There were times when entire fleets were destroyed by heavy winds and tens of thousands of sailors drowned in a single day.

Under the Empire, Rome developed the most advanced military medical practices of premodern times, but during the Republic, military medicine was primitive. The Romans did carry their wounded along with them after battle, although it is questionable whether this practice raised or lowered death rates. Of course, both military and civilian deaths also occurred off the battlefield. Roman historians conscientiously recorded deaths in battle but almost always ignored the losses suffered from exposure, accident, desertion, and disease. One traditional means of taking cities, by starvation, could entail enormous death rates on the besieged cities, and a large percentage of these would have been civilian deaths. Blockades or a breakdown in logistics could lead to malnutrition among soldiers as well. On the other hand, some of the epidemic diseases that caused enormous losses in later armies – such as typhus, bubonic plague, and cholera – were not present in the Mediterranean world in Roman Republican times. (The same is probably, though not certainly, true of smallpox.) In contrast to accounts of medieval and early modern warfare, deaths from epidemic diseases are rarely mentioned in Roman sources. On the other hand, dysentery, a fatal and highly contagious disease caused by infected fecal matter, did exist and was always a danger to armies, especially during sieges. Although the Romans did not know how such diseases were actually spread (this was only discovered through modern science), their belief that "bad water" and "bad air" generated illness led to their promotion of sanitary practices, such as latrines, for the army. This certainly reduced the spread of diseases such as dysentery among Roman soldiers.

War could be quite profitable, and this helps to explain the Romans' enthusiasm for fighting. Nevertheless, when an enemy camp or city was plundered, soldiers were not legally entitled to keep valuable objects for themselves; everything had to be turned in to the army's commander on penalty of death. The Romans' strict discipline extended to looting. The items and people (who were to be enslaved) seized by the army were generally sold to waiting merchants and the resulting money shared among the soldiers and officers. Of course, the distribution was not equal – equality was not a Roman notion. The amount received by an individual depended on his rank. However, as most of the soldiers were subsistence farmers, for them war represented one of the only ways to obtain significant amounts of money and the social advancement that went with it. Nobles were generally already quite wealthy, but a particularly profitable war could make the difference between rich and superrich, and for the politically ambitious, a move up the ladder of offices.

War is always horrific, and ancient war was particularly so. The looting of captured cities was routine. Rapes, beatings, and killings of civilians were normal. Prisoners who were not killed outright were often enslaved or consigned to work in mines. The Greek historian Polybius noted that the Romans were especially cruel in war, frequently mutilating the corpses of enemy soldiers, and were even known to cut dogs in half while pillaging cities. At times, Roman generals might try to control their soldiers' violence; for example, after the capture of Syracuse, Claudius Marcellus ordered that free citizens of the city not be killed during plundering. Such orders were not always obeyed; indeed, the famous Greek mathematician Archimedes was slain by a soldier despite Marcellus' order.

Links: Livy 1.10.3–11.9 (Romulus), 1.24.4–9 (Fetial priests); *CIL* I^2.6.7, 8.9 (Scipionic elogia), Plautus, *Pseudolus* 574–594; Suetonius, *Julius Caesar* 49, 51.

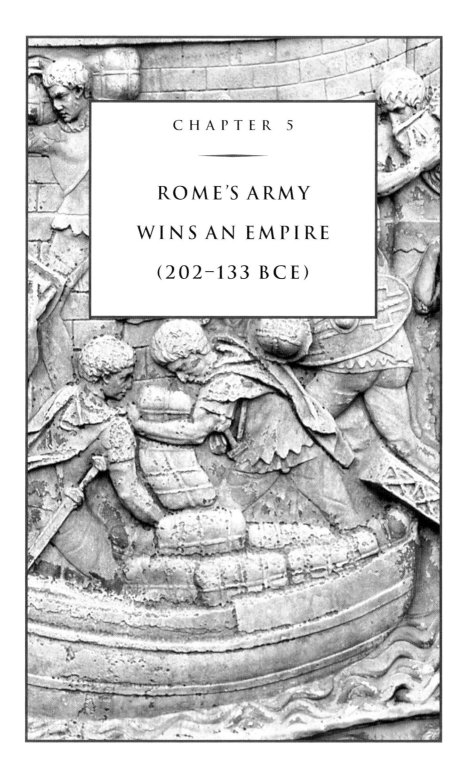

CHAPTER 5

ROME'S ARMY

WINS AN EMPIRE

(202–133 BCE)

Although still organized as a citizen militia, the Roman legions now had the effectiveness of a professional army. This was due more to experience than training or organization: virtually every Roman officer and soldier spent years in service. Romans marched hard and fought hard, and were highly skilled in siege warfare. The army now included engineers and architects, who planned and directed the building of siege ramps, movable towers, and torsion artillery. The legionaries themselves did the construction. For hundreds of years, the Roman army was the most skilled in siege warfare that the world had ever seen. Attitudes changed – where once fighting hand-to-hand was seen as more honorable than a long siege, now a Roman general remarked that it was better to win battles with the shovel than with the sword. The Romans had also learned logistical skills: the ability to gather, transport, and distribute these enormous amounts of supplies meant the Romans could project their power over long distances. Sometime in the second century BCE, the "Servian" walls, now some two hundred years old, were repaired and casemates added to accommodate torsion artillery.

Some scholars date the addition of the cohort to the Roman legion's organizational structure to a reform of Scipio Africanus carried out during the Second Punic War. Others argue it was introduced a century later, in the time of Marius. Quite possibly, the cohort gradually developed during the period between Scipio and Marius, the time covered in this chapter. In any case, the new "cohortal legion" (as opposed to the old "manipular" one) was divided into ten cohorts, each made up of six centuries. The exact number in each subunit still depended on the number of troops assigned to the legion as a whole by the Senate. The development of cohorts allowed for the more flexible use of the legion's forces, and even for parts of legions to be deployed independently. Now that all legionaries were armed alike with a short sword (*gladius*) and javelins (*pila*), the old subdivisions – *hastati*, *principes* and *triarii* – were mostly abandoned, though in battle the legion still used the "triple line" (*acies triplex*) derived from the former organization. In practice this meant there were four cohorts in the front line and three in second and third, resulting in an open formation that remained typical of the Roman battle line well into the imperial period. The legion's standards were arranged behind the first line, so the four cohorts in the front were called *antesignani* ("those before the standards"). There is some evidence that these troops continued to be identified as *hastati* and may have been more lightly armored than the other legionaries in order to facilitate quicker movement, but this remains unclear.

During the Punic Wars, the Gauls had allied themselves with Hannibal but had done little to trouble the Romans. In 200, however, two years after the Carthaginian defeat, three Gallic tribes, the Insubres, Cenomani, and Boii, attacked the Roman colonies of Cremona and Placentia. In 197 they were crushed by a two-pronged attack of both consular armies, and the next year M. Claudius Marcellus smashed the Gauls near Lake Como, and the Insubres and Cenomani sued for peace. The Boii remained hostile, but in 191, the Romans finally settled their account. P. Cornelius Scipio Nasica defeated them, and the entire tribe migrated north to what is called Bohemia after them (now in the Czech Republic). On the conquered and now empty Boiian lands, the Romans formed new colonies: Bononia (now Bologna), Mutina (Modena), and Parma, but most of the land was distributed to individual Roman citizens, who became eligible for military service. A number of military roads, including the Via Aemilia, were built and the area rapidly became Romanized.

In 201 Philip V of Macedonia went to war with Pergamum, Rhodes, and Athens, small states in the eastern Mediterranean. These sought help from the Romans. The next year, one of the consuls, Publius Sulpicius Galba, proposed a declaration of war to the Centuriate Assembly. A tribune of the plebs, however, argued against it – the war with Carthage had just ended, why start another? Remarkably, the assembly voted against the consul's proposal! This had never happened in Roman history and shows the level of war-weariness in Rome. But Galba called another assembly, promising that no veterans would be drafted, only first-time soldiers. The people then voted for war. When Galba began the campaign, however, he seemed to be more interested in gathering plunder than attacking the Macedonians. Little was accomplished until a new consul, T. Quinctius Flamininus, who was only thirty years old, arrived in 198. The Romans pushed south into central Greece, defeating Philip at the river Aous. Meanwhile, Flamininus waged a propaganda war, claiming he was liberating the Greeks from Macedonian rule. Most of the Greek city-states, as well as the Achaean League, went over to the Romans.

Philip sued for peace, but when Flamininus learned he had been reassigned the war in Greece as a proconsul, he made sure that the negotiations failed: it would be more politically advantageous and more profitable for him to end the war by conquest. In 197, Flamininus defeated Philip at the Battle of Cynoscephalae in Thessaly. After the battle, Philip surrendered unconditionally. The next year, Flamininus announced to an enthusiastic crowd that Greece would be "independent, ungarrisoned, and tribute-free." What was the Romans' purpose in granting this freedom? Why did they give up a potentially valuable conquest? This decision is the crux of a debate on the nature of Roman imperialism. It is important to note in this context that Greeks and Romans defined "freedom" differently. To the Greeks it meant they did not have to support the Romans financially, militarily, or politically. For the Romans it meant precisely the opposite: just as a freed slave (*libertus*) in Rome had obligations to a former owner, so the newly "freed" Greeks were expected to support the Romans with troops, money, and supplies.

In any case, the political instability of Greece made it difficult for the Romans to leave. In 195, King Nabis of Sparta tried to reestablish his city-state's traditional domination of the Peloponnesus. The Romans could not allow this, but Flamininus took the trouble of calling a council of the Greeks and asking their permission before crushing Nabis' forces. After this war was over, the Romans withdrew their troops – making a dramatic gesture out of it. Even by temporarily occupying Greece, however, the Romans had been drawn into eastern Mediterranean

The Battle of Cynoscephelae (197 BCE)

Titus Quinctius Flamininus commanded the Roman forces that invaded Thessaly. The Romans had about 33,000 men: three Roman legions, plus Italian and Greek infantry and cavalry. They brought with them twenty elephants, which had probably been taken from the Carthaginians. During the Macedonian Wars the size of the Roman legions had grown from 6,000 to 6,200 men, with 200-man centuries. The reason for these larger-size units is unclear, but may have had to do with the challenge of fighting the Macedonian phalanx. King Philip had a smaller force, some 25,000 men, and in advancing seems to have been unaware that he was facing the entire Roman army, a sign of poor scouting. Admittedly, the Romans did little better, as both armies marched past each other on either side of a set of hills, unaware of the enemy's presence.

Conditions were wet and misty, which both cut down on visibility and was a disadvantage to the more heavily armored Macedonians. Nevertheless, the Macedonians had the better of it during the opening of the battle. They seized a strategic hill and defeated the Romans sent to take it; thus the Macedonians held the high ground as the battle began. The Macedonian right and center were successful, but Philip's left wing was not yet in position and struggled up the hill in some disorder. Flamininus threw in reserves at this weak spot. At this point a tribune, commanding forty centuries of *triarii*, saw an opportunity and attacked the unprepared left wing from its rear. The Macedonians broke and were massacred. This battle illustrates the primacy of the more flexible legion over the Macedonian phalanx.

politics. The Seleucid King Antiochus III was moving to reassert control over Asia Minor, which had been lost by his kingdom in the previous century. The Romans sent a series of embassies, basically telling him to back off. It is clear that, although they had "freed" Greece, the Romans

Spurius Ligustinus (ca. 217–ca. 178 BCE)

In Livy's history we read a speech supposedly given by a common soldier named Spurius Ligustinus to the Roman assembly, setting out his service to the state. Although it was Livy who actually composed the speech, the details of Ligustinus' life might well be real. He was a Sabine, and in 200 B.C.E. had entered the army, probably at the age of seventeen. Ligustinus fought for two years in Macedonia and participated in the decisive battle at Cynoscephelae. By the end of the war he had been made a centurion in the tenth century of the *hastati*. To obtain this promotion Ligustinus must have been brave, steady in battle, and intelligent. He may also have had an important patron. Ligustinus returned to Italy, but soon he volunteered to join Cato's expedition to Spain. He apparently performed as well in this war as in the last, and was promoted to first centurion in the *hastati*, the lead centurion in the legion.

When the war against Antiochus III broke out in 192, Ligustinus again volunteered, and perhaps due to the need for experienced combat officers, Manius Acilius Glabrio made him first centurion of the *principes*, although he was only about twenty-five years old. Ligustinus subsequently served in a number of campaigns, including two in Spain, under Q. Fulvius Flaccus in 181, and the next year under Ti. Sempronius Gracchus. Although less than forty years old, he had now achieved the highest rank possible for a Roman citizen outside of the noble class: the first centurion in the *triarii*. Indeed, he held this rank four further times. He was rewarded thirty-four times for his courage and received six civic crowns, the award for saving the life of a Roman citizen. Ligustinus owned a small farm, which presumably had been worked by his wife and children during his long absences.

considered it part of their sphere of influence, and perhaps even their empire. They would not tolerate any outside interference – other, of course, than their own.

In 192 BCE, the Aetolian League made a grab for power in Greece, and, despite Roman warnings, King Antiochus sent ten thousand troops to help them. If the Aetolians and the Seleucid king had thought the Romans were making empty threats, they were wrong. In 191, Manlius Acilius Glabrio met Antiochus at Thermopylae, where the Greeks had held off the Persians three hundred years earlier. Just as in that battle, the defenders were outflanked, and Glabrio annihilated Antiochus' army. Despite this victory, the next year the Senate replaced Glabrio with Lucius Cornelius, Scipio Africanus' brother. Africanus went along as a legate – and probably the strategic "brains" of the operation. Although Antiochus' army had 72,000 men, more than twice the size of the Roman force, it was generally of poor quality, and the Romans decisively defeated the Seleucids at the Battle of Magnesia in 190. Then the Scipios began raiding Galatia, in central Asia Minor. Though carried out mainly to extort money from the locals, this expedition drew the Romans further into Asia.

In 179 King Philip V of Macedonia died and his son, Perseus, replaced him. Despite Perseus' obviously peaceful intentions, the Romans made a unilateral decision to attack the new king. The Senate sent a legate to negotiate, but Rome was not seriously seeking peace, only cynically drawing out talks while it prepared for war. The Third Macedonian War technically started in 171, but there was little fighting until 168. In late June of that year, Lucius Aemilius Paullus defeated the Macedonians at the Battle of Pydna. The Romans abolished the Macedonian monarchy but did not annex Macedonia as a province. Instead, they divided the region into four small puppet republics. A pretender to the throne named Andriscus tried to restore the kingdom, but Caecilius Metellus defeated him handily and Macedonia became a Roman province. In 146, the Achaean League, in another bid for power, had declared war on Sparta, a Roman ally. Rome responded by crushing them in what is known as the Achaean War. Although Greece, which the Romans now called Achaea, was not made a province until a century later, much of its territory was turned into Roman public land and distributed to Roman citizens.

At the same time that the Romans were operating in the East, they were fighting a long series of wars in Spain. After the Second Punic War, the Senate had created two provinces there, Hispania Citerior (Nearer Spain) and Hispania Ulterior (Farther Spain), with a combined garrison of only eight thousand allied troops. In 197, two revolts broke out, one in the extreme southwest and another in the north of the country, the small garrisons barely holding their own. In 195, the Romans finally sent a consular army of fifty thousand under M. Porcius Cato, who put down the revolts. The wars, however, were not over. The Celtiberians, who controlled the center of Spain, carried on fighting, and the Lusitanians, who lived in the far west of the peninsula, joined in. Each time the Romans defeated a Spanish tribe, they were drawn into more conflicts farther inland. Seeking to secure stability, in 193 and 192 the Romans conquered the Meseta, Spain's central plateau. Far from giving them more peace, however, the occupation of this region gave the Romans lots of trouble in the following decades. In 185, the Celtiberians and the Lusitanians joined forces in a major revolt. The Romans defeated them in a series of campaigns, but it was only in 179 that a peace settlement was achieved. This was done partly through force, and partly through the diplomatic skill of Tiberius Sempronius Gracchus, who gained the trust of the Spanish tribes. The Romans now controlled all of Spain except for the Atlantic coastline – but they faced ongoing insurrections.

In 154, the Lusitani, who lived along the Atlantic coast, invaded Roman territory, and the next year the Celtiberians in the center of the country seized the opportunity to take up arms once more. M. Fulvius Nobilior campaigned in central Spain in 153–152, but was defeated at the town of Numantia. Despite, or perhaps because of, this victory, the Celtiberians decided to surrender themselves "into the good faith of the Roman people" in 151. The next year, the Romans defeated the Lusitanians. During the peace negotiations, however, in a misguided attempt to finally end the rebellions, the Roman commander, Sulpicius

Galba, treacherously ordered the slaughter of the Lusitanian emissaries. In 147, one of the survivors of this massacre, named Viriathus, began a renewed campaign against Rome. His strategy was to make small attacks on isolated groups of Roman soldiers – what we would call guerrilla warfare. The Senate began assigning consular armies against Viriathus, but without success. Starting in 143, the Celtiberians renewed their uprising, their resistance again centered on the town of Numantia. This caused difficulties for the Romans, although there was apparently no coordination between the Lusitanians and the Celtiberians. In 141, Viriathus succeeded in surrounding the army of the proconsul Fabius Maximus Servilianus: the Roman commander had to agree to a peace treaty to prevent his army from being destroyed. The Roman Senate, however, disavowed this agreement, and hostilities continued. Ultimately, the Romans gained victory by treachery, bribing some of Viriathus' followers to murder him in his sleep. The loss of their leader led the Lusitanians to make peace in 139.

Resistance continued in Celtiberia, however, where in 140 another Roman proconsul, Quintus Pompeius, had been defeated at Numantia. He was also forced to make a peace treaty, but the Senate repudiated that one too. A similar situation occurred at Numania in 137, and the Roman army was saved from destruction only by the intervention of the young Tiberius Sempronius Gracchus, whose father (of the same name) the Celtiberians still remembered for his justice. Again, the Senate overturned the treaty and continued the war.

Due to the ongoing fighting in the far-flung areas of Spain, Greece, and Asia Minor, the Roman system of supply grew more and more sophisticated, allowing them to keep several armies in the field for long periods. In this period Romans routinely moved thousands of tons of food supplies by sea for hundreds of miles. The large Roman expeditionary forces sent to Greece consumed enormous amounts of food. After the Second Macedonian War (200–196 B.C.E.) the government had sold off 1,000,000 *modii* (6,700 metric tons) of *surplus* grain.

In addition to sending foodstuffs over long distances by ship, the Romans also relied on local resources. For example, Cato seized the

16. A relief on Trajan's column shows a barge, part of a convoy carrying soldiers, being loaded with tents in the harbor of a fort serving as a supply depot. Photo: Scala/ Art Resource, NY.

supplies of grain merchants in Spain, saying that the war should feed itself, meaning that Spain should pay the costs for its own conquest. Indeed, this idea of passing the cost of war onto the conquered was routine for as long as the Republic survived. Normally, this was done through war indemnities, large payments made to reimburse the treasury in Rome. Macedonia, for example, paid 1,000 talents (about 30 tons) of silver in 196. In addition, of course, the plunder of cities and the enslaving of conquered peoples continued to enrich the state and many individual Romans.

In addition, of course, the Romans would forage while on campaign. This was not done by individual or small groups, but rather as an organized military operation. Forces, sometimes as large as several cohorts, were assigned to collect grain (either from storage facilities or by harvesting it), fodder, water, and firewood. Other units, often cavalry or light infantry, provided security from attack. Horses and other military animals were fed from a combination of pasturing (when possible) and with fodder.

In the 150s, while the Romans were bogged down in Spain, Roman relations with Carthage were becoming strained. Although the much reduced city of Carthage, now without army or navy, posed no real threat to Rome, leading senators started advocating a war to destroy it. Some were certainly using this issue for their own political advantage, and others wanted to eliminate economic competition and gain access to North Africa's rich grain-growing regions. Nevertheless, it is clear that, despite the reality of Carthage's military weakness, there were Romans who actually felt threatened by their old nemesis. When we are speaking of the origin of a war, perception is as important as, or more important than, reality.

Rome's hostility led to the overthrow of a pro-Roman oligarchy in Carthage and its replacement by an anti-Roman democracy. The Romans then prepared a major expedition, some eighty thousand infantry and four thousand cavalry, for an invasion. When it arrived in North Africa the Carthaginians negotiated a surrender, agreeing to turn over two thousand hostages and all of their military equipment, including two thousand catapults. But when the Romans demanded that the Carthaginians move their entire coastal city ten miles inland, the outraged inhabitants declared war. The Romans vastly outnumbered the Carthaginians, and their army was generally accepted to be the best in the world. They were in for a shock. Carthage held out against the Roman siege for three years, while a Carthaginian field army harassed

17. A Roman silver denarius from the end of the third century BCE shows the two gods Castor and Pollux, called the Dioscuri, dressed as Roman cavalrymen. Photo: Bildarchiv Preussischer Kulturbesitz/Art Resource, NY.

the besiegers. As the war dragged on, the Roman people's dissatisfaction grew. Finally, in 147, the Senate assigned the campaign to Cornelius Scipio Aemilianus, who drove his troops relentlessly until they pierced Carthage's defenses. It took six days of intense fighting for the Romans to reach the citadel, where the last defenders, including nine hundred Roman deserters, were holding out. After their victory, the erstwhile Carthaginian state became a Roman province called Africa.

After the end of the Third Macedonian War in 167, the traditional Roman military system began to show increasing signs of strain. Wars were now being more commonly fought in poor, undeveloped regions, offering little in the way of plunder, though Rome's need for military manpower remained enormous. When revolts broke out, legions had to be sent to suppress them, but unlike wars of conquest, such fighting brought little reward. More and more propertied Romans resented having to leave their increasingly comfortable lives to fight in distant wars, and significant draft avoidance began occurring at Rome for the first time since the Conflict of the Orders.

In order to increase the number of men eligible to serve in the legions, Rome steadily reduced the necessary property qualification. This meant that many Romans who had previously been exempt from service now spent long and unprofitable years in the army. Tensions grew between the consuls, on the one hand, who wanted a large army, and the tribunes of the plebs, on the other, who wished to keep voters out of the military service. On two occasions, the plebeian tribunes actually arrested the consuls when the latter tried to levy new troops in Rome. Desertions apparently became a more serious problem: in 138, deserters from the army in Spain were whipped in the Forum. Of course, the annual draft of allies also continued. Increasingly, the Italians resented the prospect of difficult and lengthy military service taken on Rome's behalf, without the privileges that came along with Roman citizenship. Auxiliary soldiers, many of whom were mercenaries, were increasingly drawn from outside Italy, especially to provide specialist troops such as light infantry and cavalry.

Meanwhile, the hundreds of thousands of captives taken in Roman wars had swelled the population of slaves. This was especially true in the province of Sicily, where wealthy Romans had invested their war booty in large plantations worked by slave labor. In 135 a major slave revolt broke out in Sicily. Some sixty thousand slaves, as well as poor free Sicilians, joined the rebellion. They defeated first the local garrison and then a series of Roman forces sent to suppress the revolt. This First Servile (or Slave) War raged on for three years, as rebel armies roamed through the countryside, killing and looting.

The seemingly endless wars in Spain also continued. In 134, the Senate assigned the Spanish war to Scipio Aemilianus, the victor of the Third Punic War. He did not order a levy of Romans or Italians, but rather traveled to Spain bringing only volunteers with him. In Spain he assembled an army of some sixty thousand – one-third Roman and Italian and two-thirds Spanish. The Roman army in central Spain had been demoralized by the long series of defeats there, so Scipio began by disciplining and training them. He then marched into Numantine territory. There were relatively few defenders – perhaps as few as four thousand – but Scipio did not risk his soldiers' lives in an assault. Surrounding the town with a circumvallation of some six miles (9.6 km) with seven siege camps (whose remains can still be seen) he starved Numantia out. As in many cases of such blockade sieges, there are horrific stories of cannibalism. The survivors were sold into slavery and the town razed to the ground. This was the end of the Celtiberian War. On their way home, some of Scipio's well-trained troops were sent to Sicily, where they suppressed the slave revolt there with great brutality.

Links: Livy 33.11.1–12.10 (Battle of Cynoscephelae), 37.38.1–44.7 (Battle of Magnesia), 42.34.1–15 (Spurius Ligustinus); Frontinus, *Stratagems* 2.8.7, 4.1.1, 4.7.27 (Siege of Numantia).

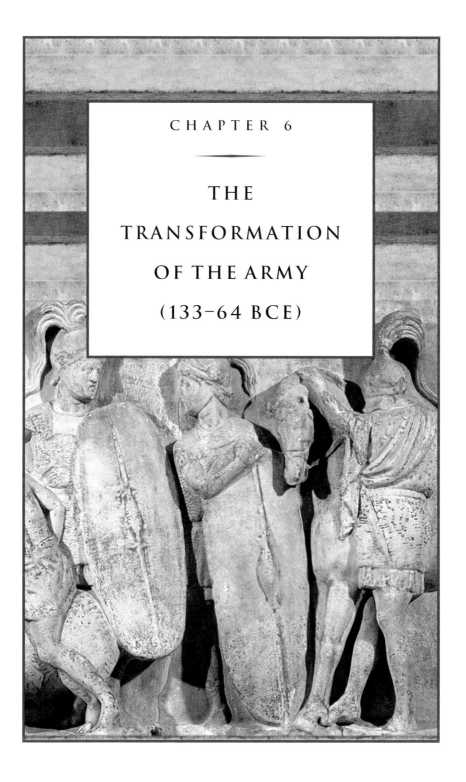

CHAPTER 6

THE
TRANSFORMATION
OF THE ARMY
(133–64 BCE)

Rome had now grown to be a great empire – though it was still ruled as a republic. In 134, a tribune of the plebs, Tiberius Sempronius Gracchus, son of the hero of the Celtiberian War, started pushing through a number of reforms, many of which would affect the Roman military. He banned the conscription of underage Romans, as the consuls had been drafting youngsters under the age of seventeen, and also provided state support for the purchase of military clothing. The latter move indicates that the property qualifications had dropped so low that some recruits had difficulty in this regard. Principal among the reforms was the attempt to give public land to proletarians in order to provide them enough wealth to qualify for military service as *assidui*. Wealthy landowners with financial interests in leasing public lands dominated the Senate. Most Senators resisted any attempt to distribute land, considering it a radical and dangerous proposal. The political struggle soon turned violent, and ended in Tiberius Gracchus' murder at the hands of an aristocratic mob. Ten years later, his brother Gaius Gracchus tried land reform again, with some initial success; but he too was ultimately assassinated. Some measures survived, but serious land reform to support Rome's traditional military system failed, and the Gracchi's deaths set off a violent conflict between two camps: the Populists (*populares*), who appealed to the poor and disenfranchised, and the Optimates, who represented the landed aristocracy.

Despite the civil strife and pressures on the army, Roman dominion continued to grow. In 133, the king of Pergamum willed his kingdom to Rome, and after the Romans suppressed a revolt there, it became the province of Asia. Between 125 and 121, the Romans subjugated Liguria (including today's Italian Riviera), which resulted in conflict with two nearby Gallic tribes, the Allobroges and Averni. Domitius Ahenobarbus used war elephants to crush the Allobroges and shortly after, Fabius Maximus defeated the Averni. Avernian and Ligurian territory became a new province: Gallia Narbonensis. The Romans also annexed the

18 (*above*). A stone relief illustrates two Roman soldiers being enrolled at a military census. It is from the so-called Altar of Domitius Ahenobarbus, dating to around 100 BCE. Photo: Erich Lessing/Art Resource, NY.

19 (*left*). A scene from the same relief shows an officer, possibly a military tribune, watching a sacrifice being carried out during the military census. Photo: Erich Lessing/Art Resource, NY.

Balearic Islands (now Majorca and Minorca), attaching them to the province of Nearer Spain.

Soon, a long and fateful conflict in North Africa began. Rome's ally King Micipsa of Numidia died, and his ruthless nephew, Jugurtha, seized power, capturing the capital, Cirta. During the looting of Cirta, Jugurtha's troops massacred hundreds of resident Romans. Jugurtha claimed, probably truthfully, that he had not ordered the killings, and tried pacifying the Senate with large amounts of cash (as reparations or bribes, depending on one's point of view). The senators were satisfied, but the Roman public demanded revenge. In 111 and 110, Optimate generals led remarkably unsuccessful campaigns: in one incident, a Roman army under Aulus Postumius was forced to pass under a yoke of spears by the Numidians. The Populists accused the Optimate generals of taking bribes from Jugurtha to lead the army to defeat. True or not, three former consuls were exiled.

This political challenge had to be met, and in 109 the leading Optimate, Caecilius Metellus, was elected consul and assigned the task of defeating Jugurtha. Metellus put his army through rigorous training, then took several cities by siege, including Cirta. The forty-day siege of Thala, a town in the midst of the Sahara desert, is a tribute both to Metellus' skill and to the sophistication of Roman logistics. After Jugurtha lost two more battles, he offered to surrender but would only negotiate by messenger, quite reasonably fearing being seized or assassinated during peace talks. The Romans refused, so the war continued. Jugurtha hired the Gaetulians, a desert tribe, as mercenaries and allied himself with King Bocchus of Mauretania.

In 108, Gaius Marius, Metellus' second-in-command, returned to Rome and ran for consul as a Populist, claiming that Metellus was incompetent. The charge was untrue, unfair, and highly effective. Marius won the election, but an outraged Senate refused to assign Marius the Jugurthine War. The Plebeian Assembly, however, passed a special law granting him the command. The Senate then denied Marius sufficient troops for the campaign (as they had done a century earlier to Scipio Africanus), so Marius then took a bold step: he allowed proletarians (the

Gaius Marius (ca. 157–86 BCE)

Marius was born in Arpinum (now Arpino) in Italy, probably a member of the town's elite, though the family had only recently become Roman citizens. He entered military service under Scipio Aemilianus and distinguished himself at Numantia in 134. Returning to Rome, he was elected a military tribune and may have served in Manius Aquillius' Asian campaign of 129. Around 123 BCE, Marius was elected as quaestor, which made him a Senator. He was called a "new man," as he had no ancestors who had been members of the senatorial nobility that dominated Rome. Marius became tribune of the plebs in 120, and after failing in two unsuccessful tries to become an aedile, in 116 won election as praetor. Usually the latter involved a military command, but Marius served as a judge. In 114, he went to Further Spain as propraetorian governor and led his first army. He must have done a good job, as Caecilius Metellus made him his senior legate in the Jugurthine War.

When Marius returned to Rome, he was elected consul for 107 BCE and given Metellus' army to command. After his defeat of Jugurtha, Marius held an unprecedented five consecutive consulships from 104 to 100 and fought successfully against the Teutones and Cimbri. Ancient sources attribute many army reforms to Marius, though modern scholars debate this point. After 100 BCE, Marius' political star faded. Sulla drove him out of Rome, but soon he joined Cinna to seize the city. Marius was again elected consul for 86, for the seventh time, and assigned command of the forces in the East. However, he died only seventeen days later.

propertyless poor) to volunteer for service. A regular salary and the chance of booty were powerful incentives, and Marius soon had more than enough men. Technically, the propertied *assidui* were still liable for military service, but since they were no longer needed, the Roman army was quickly transformed into a quasi-professional one. Few proletarian recruits had military experience, so gladiators were hired to teach them sword fighting. Many historians think that the army had long been moving toward a professional force, so the "Marian reform" was more a recognition of long-existing reality. This is still under study, but the possibility of a rapid change attributable to Marius himself should not be rejected out of hand.

Marius is also credited with introducing the *furca*, a forked stick to help the soldier carry his equipment more easily. A pack was made up of the *sagum* or military cloak (also used as a blanket), shaving gear, spare straps and other items, a *patera* or mess kit, a kettle or pot, and some rations. This was tied to the end of the *furca*. The forked stick was then draped over the top of the shield, which was strapped to the soldier's back. This distributed the weight of the equipment to the hips, like a modern backpack, and allowed the legionaries to carry more for longer periods. It is not surprising, therefore, that the soldiers jokingly gave themselves the nickname "Marius' Mules." From a practical perspective, the use of the *furca* meant the soldiers themselves transported more of their own supplies, which in turn meant fewer wagons, fewer pack animals and fewer slaves, reducing the size of the army's train. Marius drove his men hard, but he only expected from them what he could do himself. Personal toughness and the ability to "soldier hard" became a new model for Roman generals.

There were other changes, too. Marius replaced the legion's traditional five standards with a single one – a silver eagle – which would remain the proud symbol of the legions for centuries to come. A new style of *pilum* was also introduced. Wooden pegs replaced the iron rivets that attached the iron head to the javelin's haft, so that it broke on impact. This prevented an enemy from pulling it out and hurling it back at the Romans. The *pugio* or dagger was added to the legionary's standard equipment around this time. Since weapons and armor had to be distributed to the proletarians because they could not afford to buy their own, standardization certainly increased. The position of legionary armorer (*custos armorum*), well known in Imperial times, probably dates to this period. The job of manufacturing and repairing weapons was contracted out to private companies, the so-called publicans. It may also be due to the Marian reforms that the legionary light infantry disappeared from the legion. There are sporadic mentions of *velites* over the next century, but probably refers to auxiliaries in these cases. Legionary cavalry also seems to have been eliminated around this time. Subsequently, we find the Romans relying almost exclusively on allies for light infantry, archers, slingers, and cavalry. These were recruited from specific ethnic groups who specialized in particular types of fighting – for example, slingers from the Balearic islands, archers from Crete, and Numidian light cavalry.

In 107, after training his new army, Marius marched into Numidia's interior and captured the town of Capsa. Its population was either killed or sold into slavery. Sallust says this was "against the law of war," which seems an odd statement, given that is was a common Roman practice. Nevertheless, it is clear that to some Romans such practices were repugnant.

Marius then marched six hundred miles to capture the Numidian royal treasury, crippling Jugurtha's war effort. Both Jugurtha and Bocchus launched desperate, but unsuccessful, counterattacks. The proletarian army had proved itself. The war, however, ended not through battle but though treachery. Marius' quaestor, Cornelius Sulla, undertook a dangerous mission, crossing the desert to convince King Bocchus to betray Jugurtha to the Romans. This ended the war. Marius returned to Rome from Africa and celebrated a triumph, after which Jugurtha was strangled.

Meanwhile, two German tribes, the Cimbri and the Teutones, had migrated into southern Gaul, defeating several Roman armies along the way. In 105, the Germans faced two Roman forces, one led by a member of an old noble family, Servilius Caepio, the other by a "new man," Mallius Maximus, the first in his family to be elected consul. Caepio refused orders to join up with his "social inferior" Mallius. As a result, at the Battle of Arausio (105), the Germans destroyed each army in turn. In the worst defeat since Cannae, eight thousand Romans died. Furious Populists blamed the defeat on Optimate arrogance: Gaius

20. A silver denarius minted in 103 BCE shows a Roman defending a wounded fellow soldier in a sword fight with a barbarian. Photo: Bildarchiv Preussischer Kulturbesitz/Art Resource, NY.

Marius, still in Africa, was elected to a second consulship. The Cimbri had wandered into Spain and the Teutones into northern Gaul, but the Populists used the voters' fear of the German menace to reelect Marius consul in 104, 103, and 102. In that year the Germans returned to southern Gaul. Seeing that the tribes moved separately in order to live off the land, Marius first defeated the Teutones near Aquae Sextae (not far from modern Aix-en-Provence) and the next year crushed the Cimbri at Vercellae (now Vercelli, Italy). This was the last battle in which legionary cavalry is known to have fought. In fact, it may have been his triumphant victory that gave Marius the political muscle to abolish the *equites*, a jab at his aristocratic enemies. In any case, it is certain that the jubilant Roman people elected Marius to an unprecedented sixth

The Battle of Aquae Sextae (102 BCE)

Aquae Sextae (now Aix-en-Provence in France) was the site of a Roman fort built in 123 BCE, so the Romans were very familiar with the area. The German forces, perhaps as large as 110,000, included many numbers of women and children. They were under the command of King Theobod. Gaius Marius commanded an army made up of his new volunteer proletarian legions, backed up by auxiliaries, including Ligurian light infantry. As the two forces neared each other, a skirmish broke out between the Ligurians and one of the German tribes, the Ambrones, which the Roman allies won.

For the decisive battle, Marius chose a position on a hill and remained on the defensive. He hid a force of three thousand men to launch an attack on the enemy's rear when the opportunity arose. Marius used his cavalry and light infantry to goad the enemy into an uphill assault. The Germans, overconfident after their previous defeats of the Romans, attacked, led by the Ambrones. Marius launched his ambush from the rear. Ninety thousand Germans were killed and twenty thousand captured, including King Theobod. This victory showed that the quality of the new proletarian legions was up to the traditional Roman standards.

consulship. Meanwhile, another slave revolt had broken out in Sicily (the Second Servile or Slave War). Many who joined this revolt had been born free, kidnapped by pirates, and illegally sold as slaves. For several years the slaves maintained their rebellion, until Marius sent troops to Sicily under his co-consul Manius Aquillius, who defeated the slaves.

After the end of the German wars and the slave revolt, Marius' troops were discharged. A problem then arose – what to do with proletarian veterans. Military pay was too low for soldiers to save much money. Previously this had not been a problem, as a legionary had to have a farm or a business to qualify for service in the first place. Now, unless a proletarian soldier had been in a lucrative campaign (and there were few in this period) he could look forward to a miserable existence. Marius tried to obtain land for his men, but the Senate refused to cooperate. A riot broke out over the issue and Marius' veterans took part in a pitched battle in the Forum. It was a minor affair, but it foreshadowed the increasing use of military force in Roman politics. Overall, however, the 90s were a time of relative quiet for Roman armies: there was a revolt in Lusitania and another in Celtiberia, but both were quickly put down. However, this was the calm before the storm: for the next sixty years Rome would be almost constantly at war.

In 90 the Social War broke out. Italian allies had been dying in Rome's wars for centuries and had long sought Roman citizenship, but both the Senate and the assembly had consistently refused. Discrimination against Italians seems to have been the one issue on which both Optimates and Populares agreed. Frustrated, the Italians revolted, seeking not citizenship, but independence. The Marsi and the Samnites, two of Rome's ancient enemies, were the uprising's mainstays. The threat was serious: the rebel soldiers were experienced and led by skilled officers, and many angry Marian veterans, though ethnic Romans, joined the revolt. The Italians established a capital at Corfinum (near the modern Corfinio), which was renamed Italia. The new state had a federal senate and elected two commanders-in-chief. Control of the war was supposed to be coordinated by the new federal government, but in practice each rebel nation fought on its own. Not all Italians participated in the revolt. Many allies stayed loyal: the Etruscans and the Umbrians in the north, the Campanians and the Greeks in the south, and the Latins around Rome itself.

The Italian forces numbered some one hundred thousand men, but the Romans were able to raise one hundred and fifty thousand soldiers by enlisting freed slaves and proletarian volunteers, and adding auxiliaries from Gaul. Factional strife was put aside for the moment and veteran generals from both Optimates and Populares served. The Italian revolt was not the only threat: simultaneously, King Mithridates of Pontus invaded Bithynia and Cappadocia, both Roman allies in Asia Minor.

The Senate dispatched Manius Aquillius as proconsul – rebellion or no, Rome still had an empire to rule. The Social War was fought on two fronts. In the north, the Marsi, led by Pompaedius Silo, won an early victory but were soon besieged at Asculum by Pompeius Strabo. In the south, Lucius Julius Caesar (a distant cousin of the famous Caesar) fought the Samnites under Papius Mutilus to a stalemate in Campania.

In 89, fearing the revolt would spread, the Romans granted citizenship to any Italian nation that surrendered. This drove a wedge between various rebel groups. In the north, Asculum surrendered, finishing the rebellion there. In the south, Cornelius Sulla took over from Lucius Caesar and drove the Samnites out of Campania. Sulla showed not only military skill but personal bravery. He won a "grass crown," given to those who saved a Roman army, an honor awarded by the soldiers themselves. Around the same time, the Romans granted citizenship to all Italians, essentially putting an end to the war. One Italian nation fought on – the Samnites. It was another year before they were crushed.

Italian citizenship eliminated the category of "allied troops," vastly increasing the manpower available for legionary service. Roman citizens, new and old, served almost exclusively as legionaries. Over time, various specialists had developed in the legion: artillerymen (who manned catapults and *ballistae*), engineers, medical personnel, and so forth. Unlike the practice of modern armies, however, such individuals were not organized into separate units but were part of the rank-and-file. When a battle came, these specialists fought just like any other legionary. This had some advantages, as each legion had the ability to undertake a siege without the addition of separate noncombatant or specialized units. Of course, the downside was that a valuable technician might be killed in battle. In contrast to earlier times, Roman armies now remained abroad for years at a stretch. Soldiers thereby developed a strong sense of loyalty to a single general, loosening their allegiance to the state. The old idea of the dual citizen-soldier died out, and legionaries increasingly saw themselves as a separate class from the rest of the Roman population and acquired a disdain for civilians (*quirites*). Conversely, civilians began to look on soldiers (*milites*) with fear and contempt.

In 89, King Mithridates of Pontus suddenly attacked again, driving a Roman army out of Bithynia and invading the province of Asia itself. The province's Greek population rose in support of the king, massacring tens of thousands of Romans and causing an uproar in Rome. The Senate appointed Cornelius Sulla, an Optimate and Gaius Marius' former second-in-command, to defeat Mithridates, but the Plebeian Assembly passed a law giving command to Marius himself. Furious, Sulla took a fateful step. He marched on Rome with the six legions he had led in the Social War and forced the assembly to assign him the war against Mithridates. In addition, Sulla made them reassign Pompeius Strabo's army – stationed near Rome – to his friend Pompeius Rufus. Sulla then marched east.

Almost immediately, violence replaced political authority at Rome. Unwilling to relinquish his command, Pompeius Strabo simply murdered his replacement Rufus. Factional fighting broke out in the capital. In 87 BCE, the Optimate consul Gnaeus Octavius drove his Populist colleague Lucius Cornelius Cinna out of the city. The latter, along with Gaius Marius, then marched back to Rome with an army of former Italian rebels, including many Samnites, as well as discontented veterans. Octavius repaired the city's fortifications and appealed to Strabo for troops, but the latter demanded a consulship in exchange for his help. The delay allowed the Populists to surround Rome and starve it into submission. The city was sacked, and looting ended only when Cinna sent disciplined troops against the plunderers. Cinna and the aged Marius made themselves consuls for the year 86 BCE (it was Marius' seventh term), but the old man soon died. Cinna appointed Papirius Carbo as his consular colleague, and these two illegally reappointed themselves consuls for another year, ruling Rome as virtual dictators. The legal command, or *provincia*, of the war against Mithridates was taken away from Cornelius Sulla and he was declared an outlaw. Naturally, Sulla paid no attention to orders from the new government. The complicated coups and countercoups show how rapidly Roman political control over military institutions collapsed as the use of force replaced debate and voting.

While this infighting was going on in Rome, Mithridates had invaded Greece. Many city-states overthrew their pro-Roman governments and massacred local Roman residents. Sulla's arrival had been delayed by his takeover of Rome, but finally he landed in Greece with some thirty thousand men and took Athens by siege in 86. Despite the city's status as a cosmopolitan cultural center, Sulla brutally sacked it. Soon Sulla had taken all of Greece, wrested control of the seas away from Mithridates' navy, and invaded Asia. Sulla was anxious to return to Rome and gain control of the government, so he negotiated a peace with the Pontic king. Since he was not receiving any funds from Rome, whose government had outlawed him, Sulla demanded enormous sums from the cities of Asia as a penalty for their killing of Roman citizens. The resulting treasure supported Sulla's armies for the rest of the civil war.

Back in Italy Cinna had raised an army to fight Sulla, but his soldiers mutinied and killed him. In 83, Sulla landed in Italy with his own forces. Carbo, now ruling alone, had a hundred thousand men, but they were mainly raw recruits. Sulla led thirty-five thousand veterans, joined by three legions raised in Italy by the twenty-three-year-old son of Pompeius Strabo, named Pompeius Magnus or Pompey the Great. In two successive battles, Sulla defeated Carbo and entered Rome. When a force of Samnites desperately tried to retake the city, Sulla defeated them at the city's Colline Gate. Most of the Samnites died fighting and Sulla slaughtered the few who surrendered. Sulla then made himself dictator and moved to seize control of the western provinces. He sent Pompey the Great to seize Sicily and Africa for the Optimate cause, which he did without trouble. Another Optimate general, Metellus Pius, was sent to Spain as governor, but a Populist general named Quintus Sertorius continued resistance there. Sertorius would be a thorn in the Optimate side for years to come. Sulla retired in 79 and died shortly afterward. He had hoped to restore the old political order, but Roman leaders had seen clearly that swords spoke louder than debates in the Senate.

In 78, two senators raised an army in an attempt to take control of the government by force, and the Senate dispatched Pompey to suppress them. After he had defeated the rebels, however, Pompey forced the

Senate to give him proconsular powers to fight Sertorius. By this time, Sertorius controlled most of Spain and the surrounding waters, and had confined the governor Metellus to the extreme south. At first, Pompey, anxious to take personal credit for a victory, refused to cooperate with Metellus. Over the next several years, however, Sertorius beat Pompey in three battles. At this point, the Senate sent reinforcements and a fleet to take control of the Spanish seas. Pompey now cooperated with Metellus, and together the two pushed Sertorius into the Ebro valley. The war was concluded not by battle but through treachery. In 72, an Etruscan named Marcus Perperna assassinated Sertorius and seized control of his army. Pompey quickly defeated Perperna. Although Metellus had done much of the fighting, Pompey took all the credit for the victory.

In 74, Mithridates again invaded Asia (in what is called the Third Mithridatic War). Licinius Lucullus, a brilliant commander, won a series of victories against the king, first destroying a Pontic army besieging Cyzicus, then defeating the enemy fleet at the Battle of Lemnos (73). Lucullus then invaded Pontic territory. Mithridates skillfully managed to avoid battle for three years. Eventually, with the help of a chief of the Galatians (who lived in what is now central Turkey) named Deiotarus, Lucullus smashed the Pontines at the Battle of Cabira (70). All of Asia Minor then fell into Roman hands, though Mithridates escaped and took refuge in Armenia. The Senate had not authorized an invasion of Armenia, but Lucullus pursued Mithridates anyway, and although badly outnumbered, beat him at the Battle of Tigranocerta (69). Lucullus drove on toward the Armenian capital, Artaxata (near modern Yerevan); his soldiers, however, used to the loose discipline of Fimbria and Sulla, resented his strictness, so they mutinied and refused to advance. Lucullus had to retreat into winter quarters in Nisibis (now Nusaybeh in southeastern Turkey).

Meanwhile, Rome was threatened by the outbreak of another slave war, this time in Italy itself. Led by Spartacus, a Thracian slave who once had been a Roman auxiliary soldier, a group of slave-gladiators escaped from barracks in Capua and fled to nearby Mount Vesuvius. Tens of thousands of runaway slaves, as well as poor Roman citizens, rushed to join them. Spartacus organized both slave and free into military units and had his gladiators train them to fight. Over the next two years, the slave army defeated a series of Roman forces, roamed around Italy, and plundered at will. Finally, in 71, Licinius Crassus, with an army of forty thousand, defeated the slaves. Spartacus died in this battle, but some six thousand survivors were crucified along the Appian Way as an example to rebellious slaves. At the same time, Pompey returned from Spain with his army. Camping near Rome, he demanded permission to run for consul, although he was not technically qualified. Licinius Crassus had sufficient forces to defend the city, but he decided to join with Pompey. Although Pompey and Crassus disliked each other, they formed an alliance and received the two consulships for 70.

Throughout this period of rising political violence, a pirate menace had burgeoned in the Mediterranean. In the course of their conquests, the Romans had suppressed those naval powers, such as Rhodes and Carthage, which had traditionally controlled piracy in the Mediterranean, neglecting, however, to take on the job themselves. As long as it was foreign ships that were being seized, the Romans looked the other way and even bought and sold those hapless persons kidnapped into slavery. When, however, the wealthy island of Delos was sacked, the grain ships that fed Rome were captured, and two praetors were kidnapped from the coast of Italy, the Romans finally took action. In 67 BCE the Plebeian Assembly passed a law giving Pompey an extraordinary *imperium* to destroy the pirates. Pompey raised a force of 270 ships and 100,000 soldiers, dividing them into thirteen commands covering the entire Mediterranean. In less than three months, the last pirate base in Cilicia had fallen by siege. In a short, ruthless, and brilliant campaign, Pompey solved the Mediterranean's pirate problem.

Back in the East, Lucullus could have won the Mithridatic War if he had been given sufficient reinforcements, but his political enemies desired his failure. The government at Rome actually authorized soldiers to leave his army if they wished to (and many did). The assembly then awarded Pompey control of all the Roman forces in the East. Pompey

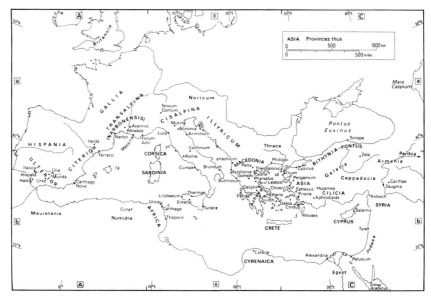

21. A map of the Roman Empire around 60 BCE, the period of the Roman Civil Wars. Photo: Copyright Cambridge University Press.

began his offensive in 66, with a force of some fifty thousand men. Mithridates, with only a small army, tried guerrilla tactics, but Pompey hemmed him in with a series of fortifications and then destroyed his forces at the Battle of Nicopolis (66). The king himself again managed to escape. Pompey then invaded Armenia, which lost no time in surrendering. Moving north, he defeated the Albanians, who lived in the Caucasus, and after negotiating a peace treaty with the Parthians, chased Mithridates through Iberia (modern Georgia). Skirting the Black Sea, he marched farther east than any previous Roman force had ever done.

In 64, Pompey marched south and invaded Syria. He extinguished the puny remnant of the Seleucid Empire that had survived there. Farther south, in Judaea, two brothers, Hyrcanus and Aristobulus, were fighting over the throne of the Jewish kingdom. Both appealed to Pompey. The Roman general picked Hyrcanus, but Aristobulus seized Jerusalem anyway. Pompey captured the Jewish capital after a three-month siege and made Hyrcanus the king of the Jews. Anticlimactically, the problem of Mithridates solved itself. His son Pharnaces revolted against him and Mithridates committed suicide in 63. In that year, Pompey settled the affairs of western Asia: Syria became a Roman province, but the rest of the region remained in the hands of friendly "client" kings, such as Hyrcanus. Pompey then returned to Rome and celebrated an enormous triumph.

Links: Sallust, *Jugurthine War* 44–45 (Metellus trains his army), 75–76 (Siege of Thala), 92–94 (Siege of Mulucha); Frontinus, *Stratagems* 1.5.20–22, 1.7.6, 2.5.34 (Spartacus).

CHAPTER 7

CAESAR'S WARS

(64–44 BCE)

Pompey's conquest of the East brought enormous wealth to Rome, but the Senate still refused to grant land to his veterans. Pompey was the most powerful general in Rome and an Optimate. In order to obtain what he wanted for his men, however, he now formed a political alliance, called by historians the First Triumvirate (60 BCE), with two Populist leaders Licinius Crassus and Julius Caesar. When the Optimates blocked another attempt to give Pompey's veterans land, Caesar called in soldiers to force the Senate to pass the bill. At the same time, he obtained a five-year command in Cisapline Gaul and Illyricum. A last-minute change fatefully added Narbonese Gaul, which bordered unconquered, or what the Romans called "long-haired," Gaul.

Caesar had certainly already seen his share of military action, winning a civic crown at the siege of Mytilene in 80 BCE and probably taking part in the war against Spartacus. He had raised a naval force to punish a pirate fleet and commanded a group of auxiliaries in the Pontic War in 74. As governor of Baetica in 61, he had led a force of thirty cohorts on a successful campaign against two Spanish tribes. Nevertheless, when he took command in Gaul, few Romans would have guessed that he would become one of the great military leaders of all time. Caesar was, however, a quick learner, had personal courage, and was a natural risk taker. He developed the habit of moving his forces rapidly, not waiting for complete preparations. His speed, or *celeritas*, led to many victories but also to near disasters, and in such cases Caesar often had to rely on his famous luck (*fortuna*) to save the day. Also a brilliant politician, Caesar realized that winning the war was generally less important than winning the peace.

Caesar's army both looked back to the Republic and forward to the Empire. Officers still came mainly from aristocratic families, with the top ranks dominated by senators. Although Caesar was himself a patrician and had the prejudices of his class, he valued talent and loyalty regardless of class background. Under him both common Romans and foreigners

22. This idealized marble portrait of Gaius Julius Caesar originally would have been painted in lifelike colors. Photo: Scala/Art Resource, NY.

Gaius Julius Caesar (100–44 BCE)

Julius Caesar came from a patrician family – indeed, the Julian *gens* claimed descent from the goddess Venus. Caesar was a complex and paradoxical character, both as a politician and a military man. Historians still debate vigorously about his career. Often ruthless and opportunistic, he could also be beneficent, even idealistic. He was calculating but also a risk taker, at times to the point of recklessness. Remarkably, we possess a great deal of writing by Caesar, principally in the form of his Commentaries (on the Gallic War and the Civil War), but also some of his letters. This is virtually unique for such a great character in antiquity; yet he was such a guarded and careful writer that his own words are not very revealing about his character and psychology.

Most Romans in the Republic had a great deal of military experience from their youth. Those who made a special career of military service tended to rise steadily in the ranks until they received command of an army. Caesar was very unusual in this regard. He was not totally without experience in war – he had served as a tribune in his twenties, led a small fleet against pirates, and during the Mithridatic War had raised volunteer Roman troops to defend Asia. As governor of Spain, he led the equivalent of three legions on two campaigns of conquest. We lack clear details of any of these operations, but it is clear

gained promotion. An example is Cornelius Balbus, a Spaniard of Phoenician ancestry who rose to the rank of consul. Caesar's capable officer corps was a great asset, and most of his soldiers saw continuous action for decades and became highly skilled. Due to years of fighting together, there was strong unit cohesion in the Caesarian legions.

At the time of Caesar's invasion of Gaul, the independent Gallic tribes had been waging incessant warfare with each other for centuries. Some tribes had kings, but aristocratic councils ruled most of them. Human sacrifice, particularly of captives, was common. The Gauls, also called the that, unlike most of his rivals, Caesar did not hold a major military command until he was almost forty years old. In contrast, before Pompey was thirty, he had become one of Sulla's chief generals, conquered Sicily and Africa, and celebrated a triumph.

The details of Caesar's military career are covered in this chapter, but his political achievements are equally important. Family connections were very important in Caesar's choice of politics. Though he came from a patrician family, Caesar's uncle was Gaius Marius, and as a result he was a member of the Populist party. A skilled orator and statesman, he instituted a number of major reforms, the most lasting of which was the solar calendar that is still in use today (July is named for him). Caesar was married three times, to Cornelia, Pompeia, and Calpurnia. Only the first marriage produced a child, his daughter Julia, who married Pompey (at a time when they were friends and allies) but who, like many women in ancient times, died in childbirth. Caesar had no sons, nor any nephews or brothers, so he made his grand-nephew, Gaius Octavius, his heir and adopted him posthumously. (Subsequently, Octavius was known as Octavian, and later as Augustus Caesar.) Julius Caesar's followers had been almost fanatically devoted to him, and when he was assassinated, they raised a shrine and worshipped their murdered leader as a god. The ruins of the temple to the Divine Julius, built on the site of the impromptu altar, can still be seen in the Roman Forum.

Celts, were skilled sword makers, and their cavalry, made up of nobles, was highly effective. Their infantry, however, consisted of poorly armed retainers. In the 60s BCE, Germans, attracted by Gaul's wealth, started moving across the Rhine. One German tribe, the Suebi, under their king, Ariovistus, had become involved in a war, helping two Gallic tribes, the Averni and the Sequani, defeat a third, the Aedui, after which Ariovistus seized a large piece of Gaul (much of modern Alsace) for himself.

In 58 BCE, when the Helvetii, a tribe in what is today Switzerland, began moving west into Aeduan territory, the Aedui appealed to Caesar for help. He responded by invading with six legions, including two newly recruited ones, with the Aedui providing auxiliary cavalry. In the Battle of Bibracte (near modern Autun, France) Caesar decisively defeated the Helvetii, who agreed to return home. The Aedui now wanted help in their fight against Ariovistus. This was awkward: the Senate had made Ariovistus a "friend of the Roman people." Caesar tried negotiating, but the German king insisted on his right of conquest. In the early autumn of 58, the German and Roman armies met at the Battle of the Vosges, in modern Alsace. The battle was won through the initiative of a legate, Publius Licinius Crassus, son of the triumvir. The Suebi broke and ran, ending Ariovistus' plans of domination in Gaul.

After his victory Caesar annexed the lands of the Aedui and Sequani, who realized too late that to the Romans the term "allied" meant "subject." The next year, fearing – with reason – that Caesar intended to conquer all of Gaul, a coalition of Belgic tribes in the northwest of the country challenged him. Caesar skillfully avoided battle, forcing the Belgae to stay mobilized longer than their primitive logistics allowed. Their coalition fell apart and Caesar struck into their territory. The Roman siege equipment terrified the Gauls and they surrendered. Caesar then moved against the Nervii, south of modern Antwerp in Belgium. The Nervii ambushed the Romans near the Sabis (Sambre) River, almost overwhelming them, but the legions' discipline and Caesar's presence of mind turned the tide. Meanwhile, Publius Crassus conquered the Veneti and other Gallic tribes along the Atlantic coast, today the Bay of Biscay. By the end of 57, Caesar had conquered the west, north, and east of Gaul – the south was already in Roman hands – completely surrounding the interior.

At this point, Caesar obtained a five-year extension of his *provincia*. In the same year the recently conquered Veneti revolted. They fought from fortresses in tidal estuaries, which were virtually impossible to take by land. Caesar built a fleet from scratch, then defeated and punished the Veneti with mass killings and enslavements. All of southwest Gaul down to the Pyrenees was annexed. Then Caesar moved into the northwest, into what is today the Netherlands, but the Usipetes and the Tencteri, two German

23. A silver denarius issued by Julius Caesar in 48 or 47 BCE shows a trophy with arms and equipment captured from the Gauls. Photo: Bildarchiv Preussischer Kulturbesitz/Art Resource, NY.

tribes, were migrating into the same region. Caesar opened peace negotiations, but when the Germans let down their guard, he seized their leaders and massacred their warriors in a surprise attack. Caesar then hunted down and killed the tribe's defenseless women and children.

At this point, Caesar considered conquering Germany and built a bridge over the Rhine for a brief invasion. We do not know why, but he eventually decided not to proceed north but instead to invade Britain. This campaign nearly ended in disaster. Caesar's fleet was wrecked in a storm and an assault by the Britons came close to overwhelming his two legions. Caesar managed to make it back to Gaul, then returned to Britain in 54 BCE with a larger force of five legions. This time he stayed for two or three months, fighting with a British chief named

Cassivellaunus, who had established a large kingdom on the island. Caesar captured Cassivellaunus' stronghold, but gained only cattle as booty: Britain's valuable tin mines were far inland. Caesar decided to withdraw, giving the Britons another century of independence. His two invasions of Britain were bold to the point of recklessness: both were "rolls of the dice" for Caesar, and dangerous ones, considering how precarious was his hold on Gaul.

Remarkably, Gaul had remained quiet despite the fact that Caesar had only established a few isolated garrisons there. The Romans, however, requisitioned supplies ruthlessly, forcing the locals into auxiliary service. Finally, in 54 one tribe, the Eburones, lured fifteen cohorts out of a camp and wiped them out in a narrow valley in the Battle of Atuatuca. At the same time, the Nervii besieged a legion under Quintus Cicero (the famous orator's brother). At the beginning of 53, Caesar relieved Cicero, and then, over the summer, defeated the rest of the hostile Gauls. Later that year, a more serious revolt broke out. King Vercingetorix of the Averni put together a massive Gallic coalition and cut off the Roman garrisons in the northeast. Caesar made a dangerous winter march through enemy territory and besieged the enemy stronghold of Avaricum. He threw a circumvallation around the town, but Vercingetorix surrounded him in turn, and the besiegers found themselves besieged. Caesar built a second ring of fortifications to protect his troops. It was Roman determination and skill in siege craft that allowed them to break into the city before their own supplies gave out.

Caesar now took an enormous risk by dividing his army in the face of the enemy. Four legions under Titus Labienus marched north, defeating the Gauls at Lutetia (now Paris). With his remaining forces, Caesar himself tried, and failed, to take another fort, Gergovia. This setback encouraged more tribes, including the Aedui, to revolt. Caesar, however, slipped around the Gauls and united his forces, recruiting German cavalry to replace the Aedui. Vercingetorix then made a bold move of his own, invading the province of Narbonensis and threatening Italy. Caesar, however, defeated him at a hard-fought battle near the modern city of Dijon. At this point Vercingetorix commited a fatal error

24. A painting by Peter Connolly reconstructs the Roman circumvallation at the siege of Alesia in 52 BCE. Moats, obstacles, and double walls with wooden guardtowers made for a formidable defense against attempts to break in or out. Photo: akg-images/Peter Connolly.

by retreating into a fortress-city called Alesia. The Gallic king hoped to pin the Romans down and then have his allies strike at the enemy from the rear. Just as at Avaricum, however, Caesar built a double circumvallation, and although at times pushed almost to the breaking point, his forces held. Alesia was too small to hold sufficient supplies. To rid himself of "useless mouths," Vercingetorix sent the old men, the women, and the children out of the city, but Caesar refused to allow them to cross his lines, so they starved. Ultimately, the food in Alesia ran out and Vercingetorix surrendered. The Gallic coalition collapsed. A combination of Caesar's skill, the superiority of the Roman forces, bad decisions by Vercingetorix, and downright luck, had led to a decisive victory.

In 55, with Caesar in occupied Gaul, Pompey had been offered a command to reinstate the Egyptian king, Ptolemy XII Auletes, to the throne after an anti-Roman party in Alexandria had deposed the king. Pompey turned down the opportunity. If he had accepted, he might well have, with Egypt's wealth, become Rome's ruler rather than Caesar – but the old soldier was not interested. (The task was accepted by one of Pompey's friends, Aulus Gabinius, governor of Syria, who received 10,000 talents, some 300 tons, of silver for his pains.) Meanwhile, the third triumvir, Marcus Licinius Crassus was planning to conquer the Parthian kingdom, located in present-day Iraq and Iran.

The Parthians were an Iranian-speaking tribe who had taken over Mesopotamia and Persia from the Seleucids around 250 BCE. Nobles played a significant role both in Parthia and its military, serving as cavalry of two types. One were the cataphracts, who wore scale armor, were armed with long lances and bows, and rode the large Nisaean "blood-sweating" horses, prized as far east as China. Horse archers rode smaller horses and were highly skilled at shooting while riding. Lightly armed serfs, following their noble lords, served as infantry. Like the Hellenistic kingdoms, the Parthians used settler-soldiers who, in exchange for a farm, did military service in the king's army. Many non-Parthians, including both Greeks and Jews, served as settler-soldiers, and as officers, in the Parthian army.

The Parthians used a decimal system of organization common to central Asia – and utilized centuries later by the Mongols – with units of 100, 1,000, and 10,000 men. Little is known of Parthian tactics except for the famous feigned retreat: cavalry would charge and then withdraw, firing backward, the so-called Parthian shot (corrupted in English to "parting shot"). When the enemy followed, they would suddenly turn around and attack their pursuers. The Parthians lacked siege equipment, which hampered their offensive operations.

In 53, Crassus invaded Parthia with a force of thirty-five thousand, almost entirely legionary heavy infantry, except for a small force of auxiliary cavalry from Gaul led by his son Publius Crassus. The Romans met a Parthian army of ten thousand cavalry under the command of a noble named Rustam Surena. Surena's force included a thousand camels carrying a huge supply of arrows. At Carrhae (now Harran in southern Turkey), the Parthians, alternately charging and retreating, unleashed hails of arrows. They first demoralized, then broke up, and finally totally destroyed the Roman legions. Crassus and his son were killed, and the eagles of four legions lost. Less than one-third of the Roman force escaped death or capture. King Orodes II rewarded Surena by killing him – a too successful general was always a threat to a monarch. In 51, Orodes invaded Syria, but was beaten off by Crassus' former quaestor, Cassius Longinus. Oddly, the Parthians made no further offensive moves for more than a decade, even while the Romans were locked in civil war.

Crassus' disaster in the East contrasted with Caesar's success in the West. Victory in Gaul brought Caesar enormous wealth and prestige as well as a large, experienced, and fiercely loyal army. Pompey, although still technically Caesar's partner, was alarmed. So were many other powerful Romans. Caesar's *provincia*, his legal command in Gaul, was scheduled to end in 48. This meant giving up his army – a dangerous prospect. Caesar made an offer: both he and Pompey would demobilize simultaneously. Caesar's enemies, however, sensing weakness, refused. Twelve of Caesar's legions were spread out through Gaul and the Balkans, and only one was in northern Italy. Pompey naturally thought Caesar would gather all his forces before attacking, allowing him ample time to organize a defense. Characteristically, however, Caesar decided to strike with only a single legion, the Thirteenth. In January 49, he crossed the Rubicon River, the border between Cisalpine Gaul and Italy, dramatically exclaiming, "The die is cast" (*alea iacta est*), knowing that once done, this act of civil war could not be undone.

Caesar's rapid advance stunned Pompey, who fled to Greece with five legions. Caesar had gambled and won. He quickly moved to solidify his advantage. Caesarian troops soon took Sicily and Sardinia, providing Rome with much needed grain. Another force besieged Massilia (now Marseilles), an ally of Pompey, which resisted fiercely. Caesar himself went to Spain with an army. Two of Pompey's best generals, Lucius Afranius and Marcus Petreius, dug in at Ilerda (modern Lleida). Their defensive line was strong, but Caesar skillfully cut off their supplies with his Gallic cavalry. Caesar then maneuvered Afranius and Petreius onto a waterless hill, forcing their surrender. Panic-stricken, all the Pompeian forces in Spain then gave up. The campaign illustrates both the sophistication of Roman warfare in this period and Caesar's brilliance as a commander. Massilia also soon capitulated. Caesar then consolidated his forces in Italy in order to invade Greece and confront Pompey directly.

The Battle of Pharsalus (48 BCE)

This decisive battle of the Civil War was fought not far from Cynoscephelae, site of the Roman victory of 150 years earlier. Pompey had eleven legions plus allied forces, some 35,000 to 40,000 men. They outnumbered Caesar's eight legions, and far fewer auxiliaries, which totaled approximately 22,000. Pompey also enjoyed a seven-to-one advantage in cavalry. Pompey held the high ground, and his left flank was protected by the Epineus River. Caesar had two advantages: the greater experience of his men and his own military genius.

Pompey planned a massive cavalry attack on the Caesarian right, which would then roll up the enemy line, driving it into the Epineus. Caesar guessed Pompey's intention and stationed legionaries hidden behind his right. Although Pompey succeeded in routing Caesar's Gallic cavalry and light infantry, the Caesarian legionaries launched an ambush. They had been trained to use their *pila* like modern bayonets against Pompey's cavalry, which they drove off the field. The legionaries pressed on and struck against Pompey's light infantry on the flanks. When the rest of Caesar's legions surged forward, Pompey panicked and fled the field. This caused a general rout that ended the battle.

Pompey did not think his enemy would make a dangerous winter crossing from Italy, but Caesar did just that. With only seven legions, he boldly besieged Pompey's eleven at Dyrrhachium (now Durres in Albania), but lack of supplies forced the Caesarian army to withdraw into Thessaly. This placed Pompey between Caesar and Italy, but he did not take the opportunity to recapture Rome. Rather, he pursued Caesar. This made some sense: control of the seas meant that he could hem Caesar in and let starvation do its work. The Pompeian generals, however, wanted a more aggressive approach, and finally convinced a hesitant Pompey to engage the Caesarians in the field. At the Battle of Pharsalus (48) Caesar won a stunning victory.

Pompey fled to Egypt. Caesar, accompanied by only three thousand men, followed in hot pursuit. The king of Egypt, Ptolemy XIII, had the old general murdered, but instead of thanking him for this, Caesar joined forces with Ptolemy's sister (and wife), Cleopatra VII, who was trying to seize the throne. This Alexandrian War proved surprisingly difficult, and Caesar was almost overwhelmed by Egyptian forces. He was saved by the intervention of several client kings, one of whom was Hyrcanus II of Judaea. With these reinforcements, Caesar defeated and killed Ptolemy XIII and made Cleopatra queen of Egypt.

The Pompeians, including the general's son Sextus Pompey, still controlled Asia Minor, parts of Spain, and North Africa. In the summer of 47, Caesar marched to Asia Minor and, in a quick but hard-fought campaign of only five days, defeated the Pompeian ally King Pharnaces of Pontus (Mithridates' son). This was the inspiration for Caesar's famous boast: *veni, vidi, vici* – "I came, I saw, I conquered." Caesar put his own ally, King Mithridates of Pergamum (no relation to the former king of Pontus), in charge and returned to Rome. Once there, Caesar had to deal with increasingly undisciplined soldiers in Italy. One of his legions had threatened to march on Rome if not paid a large donative. Caesar is supposed to have put down the mutiny simply by addressing the troops as "citizens" (*Quirites*) rather than "soldiers" (*milites*), shaming them into compliance. Whether or not the story is true, Caesar did not feel it necessary (or perhaps possible) to punish the mutineers.

In early Janury 46, Caesar launched another midwinter campaign, risking a dangerous crossing to Africa to gain the element of surprise. His army was again outnumbered by the Pompeians, but at the Battle of Thapsus he allowed the enemy to "trap" him on a sliver of land surrounded by water. Its narrowness meant that the Pompeian advantage in numbers was neutralized. The more experienced Caesarian troops crushed the enemy. Caesar then moved on to Spain in the winter of 46 and, in March 45, met another of Pompey's sons, Gnaeus Pompeius, at the Battle of Munda. The Caesarians charged uphill against the enemy, and after fierce fighting the Tenth Legion broke the Pompeians' flank. Caesar's cavalry then struck the enemy's rear and a rout resulted.

Victorious on all fronts, Caesar returned to Rome and mounted the most lavish triumph ever seen. The four-day affair officially celebrated the victories over the Gauls, Pontines, Numidians, and Egyptians, as it was not considered proper to triumph over fellow Romans. Caesar's veterans, however, were probably thinking of their victories over Pompey and his generals as they marched through the streets of Rome. Caesar gave each soldier a generous bounty and permanently raised legionary pay to 900 sesterces a year. He settled tens of thousands of veterans, both his own and Pompey's, in new Roman colonies around the Mediterranean and granted Roman citizenship to entire units. For example, every soldier in the Fifth Legion Alaudae, which had been recruited from Gauls, was made a Roman citizen. Given the savagery with which the Civil War had been fought, Caesar showed remarkable clemency toward former Pompeians: Junius Brutus, who had opposed him at Pharsalus, and Gaius Longinus, a Pompeian admiral, became praetors.

During the winter of 45 to 44, Caesar began building up an enormous force in Greece. He planned to attack the Dacians (in modern Romania), and then to march through the Balkans and Anatolia to strike against Armenia. Then, turning south, he would invade Parthia. The entire operation would take two years. However, this campaign never occurred. Preoccupied with his military planning, Caesar paid insufficient attention to his enemies in the Senate. Remarkably, he chose this moment to dismiss his personal bodyguard of Spaniards. This slip allowed a conspiracy of senators to assassinate him in the atrium of Pompey's Theater on the Ides of March, 44 BCE.

Links: Caesar, *Gallic Wars* 1.21–28 (war with the Helvetii), 4.17–18 (building a bridge across the Rhine), *Civil Wars* 3.82–99 (Battle of Pharsalus); Lucan, *Pharsalia* 3.375–508 (Siege of Massilia).

CHAPTER 8

DEATH THROES
OF THE REPUBLIC
(44–30 BCE)

Caesar's assassination divided Rome into two factions. The Caesarians, led by Mark Antony, Aemilius Lepidus, and quickly joined by Caesar's grandnephew Octavian, sought to avenge Caesar's murder and replace him with a new strongman. Republicans, such as Junius Brutus, Decimus Brutus, and Cassius Longinus, desired a return of control to the Senate run by the traditional elite. Considering how important warfare was to such Romans, it is almost incredible that Caesar's assassins did not immediately move to seize control of Rome's military forces. This mistake allowed Mark Antony, once he realized that the Republicans had also neglected to order him killed, to gather a private bodyguard of soldiers. More important, a legion under the command of Aemilius Lepidus lay just outside the city. As the Republicans made no effort to control or neutralize it, the Caesarians moved these troops into the city. However, Antony and Lepidus, unsure of their ability to maintain control, negotiated a truce with the Republican leaders.

Antony himself made some remarkable missteps, allowing Republican leaders to proceed to the provinces that Caesar had assigned them, and even giving them military commands! Decimus Brutus took Cisalpine Gaul, and Gaius Trebonius the important province of Asia. Antony did retain Macedonia and its legions, and another Caesarian, Publius Cornelius Dolabella, took a vital post as Syria's governor, with the largest army in the East. The biggest problem faced by the Caesarians, though, was the fact that they had two leaders who despised each other. Mark Antony, long one of Julius Caesar's key subordinates, was known for his physical strength and bravery, if not for his intelligence. He had a long military record and enjoyed the loyalty of many officers and men. Caesar's grandnephew, Octavian, was brilliant and showed personal courage on several occasions. He was, however, only eighteen years old, rather sickly, and had no military experience. But Octavian had one great advantage: the dictator had adopted him posthumously,

25. On a denarius issued sometime between 32 and 29 BCE, Octavian is called "Caesar son of the god (Caesar)." He is shown as a general directing his troops and carrying a spear, his military cloak or *pallium* billowing out behind him. Photo: Bildarchiv Preussischer Kulturbesitz/Art Resource, NY.

so he was now the great man's son and heir and possessed the magical name "Caesar."

The armies in this round of civil wars were the product of a century of almost constant warfare. In many respects, the Roman army was at the height of its military capabilities, so it is not surprising that there were few drastic reforms. One slight, but important, change in equipment occurred sometime in the last half of the first century BCE. The oval top and bottom of the *scutum* were straightened, making its iron rim an even more effective weapon when jammed against an opponent's chin. A new type of helmet, which historians call the Coolus type, was introduced. Derived from a Celtic style, it had a flat neckguard per-pendicular to the helmet's back, as well as cheek guards.

Another more subtle change was that, due to the constantly shifting political and military situations, units developed more of a self-identity, and even a sort of self-government. For example, we find legions deciding on which side they would fight at a particular moment in a civil war. The mechanism for this sort of decision making remains obscure, however.

Mark Antony was a brave and tenacious fighter, but he was not a very astute or creative strategist. He had a tendency to follow Caesar's practice, for example in his decision to concentrate a large army in Gaul to use as a base to control Italy. This show of force led to a breakdown of the fragile truce. Brutus and Cassius immediately moved east to join a growing Republican force in Greece. At the same time, Octavian began to raise an army, although he had no legal right to do so, as he held no office with *imperium*. His being a Caesar, though, proved to be a magnet to soldiers, and thousands flocked to Octavian's service. Significantly, of the four legions Antony was moving from Macedonia to Gaul, two defected to Octavian.

Marc Antony's rather lethargic leadership sharply contrasts with his patron's boldness. In December of 44, fully nine months after Caesar's assassination, Antony moved cautiously into northern Italy. Rather than marching, as Caesar had, directly on Rome, he initiated a months-long siege of Decimus Brutus' forces in the town of Mutina (now Modena). It was the Republican government in Italy, now under the leadership of Cicero, who made a daring move. They allied themselves with their ideological enemy Octavian, giving him legal authority to raise troops (though he had already done so anyway) and instructing him to join the new consuls Aulus Hirtius and Vibius Pansa in a strike against Antony. Marching north, the coalition army under Hirtius, Pansa, and Octavian defeated a counterattack by Antony at Forum Gallorum. In April of 43, they won a victory outside the walls of Mutina, driving the Antonian forces back into Gaul.

The overwhelming victory for the Republicans, however, quickly turned into disaster. Both Hirtius and Pansa died of battle wounds suffered at Mutina, leaving Octavian in sole command of the army. Offering his soldiers a large donative, which the Senate foolishly refused to match, he induced the Republican troops to defect to him. In July 43 BCE, Octavian, not yet twenty years old, seized control of Rome.

Antony was still in the game, however. He returned to Gaul, and by offering Aemilius Lepidus a joint command, obtained seven of the Caesarians' best legions. The governors of Gaul and Spain were also induced to join up, and so by the time Octavian entered the capital, Antony had twenty-two legions at his disposal. Despite Octavian's relative military weakness, however, he had a trio of brilliant friends, Gaius Maecenas, Salvidienus Rufus, and Vipsanius Agrippa, who would be instrumental in his ultimate victory. It is striking, although completely in keeping with Octavian's (and Julius Caesar's) practice, that the latter two, Rufus and Agrippa, came from very humble backgrounds. They rose to prominence on the basis of their talent and loyalty to Octavian and the Caesarian cause.

Brutus, the most able of the Republican leaders, had seized control of Macedonia and convinced a Caesarian army in Illyricum to join him. He took time out from the civil war to defeat a Thracian tribe, the Bessi, and was hailed as *imperator* by his troops. Cassius Longinus, meanwhile, had gone to Syria to take this valuable province. The Caesarian governor of Syria, Cornelius Dolabella, summoned the Roman garrison of Egypt, but they defected to the Republicans. Cassius besieged Dolabella at Laodicea (now Latakia, Syria). Cassius and Brutus both sent forces to seize the rest of Asia Minor, and the Republicans were now in command of the entire East. Their powerful fleet also controlled the waters between Italy and Greece.

The Republican side was successful in attracting most of the Senatorial Order, including many talented military officers, to their side. There also seems to have been significant rank-and-file devotion to the Republic, contrary to the view of Roman soldiers of the time as being

Marcus Vipsanius Agrippa (ca. 63 BCE–12 CE)

Marcus Vipsanius Agrippa came from an obscure family, and his rise to power was due almost exclusively to his tenacious loyalty to the man who became emperor. We know little of his early life, but he was about the same age as Octavian. In 44 BC, in Greece, Agrippa probably helped the eighteen-year-old Octavian make the momentous decision to go to Rome. In the confused months that followed, Agrippa assisted Octavian in raising and leading his private army of Caesar's veterans. During the subsequent campaign against Antony's forces at Mutina, Agrippa, although only a teenager, commanded Octavian's part of the Republican army.

In 43, Agrippa became a tribune of the plebs and entered the Senate when perhaps only nineteen years old. He became a praetor at well below the legal minimum age, and was governor of Gaul in 38 when only in his twenties. In this capacity, he put down a revolt in Aquitania and led an expedition across the Rhine. He was only about twenty-six when he became consul in 37 BC. Although he apparently had had no previous experience at sea, he won three major naval battles: those at Mylae, Naulochus, and Actium. In fact, Agrippa is often referred to as Octavian's or Augustus' "admiral," although no such rank existed in Latin.

When Augustus, never a healthy man, fell seriously ill in 23, he gave his signet ring to Agrippa. Augustus recovered, but he still gave Agrippa proconsular power over the entire eastern Mediterranean and married his daughter Julia to him. In 20, Agrippa was again governor of Gaul, and in 19 he went to Spain and put down a rebellion. In 18 and again in 13, he was granted tribunician power for five years, the same power that Augustus possessed. In essence, this was making him co-emperor. In 12 BCE he went to Pannonia, where there were rumblings of revolt. Upon his return he died; he was not yet fifty-two. Agrippa was buried in the mausoleum of Augustus, the round marble tomb that still rises above the Campus Martius in Rome.

easily bought and sold: Republican soldiers, and legions, tended to be loyal to their cause without the inducement of the large donatives the Caesarians had to pay. Brutus and Cassius both proved to be skilled generals, but the Republican side suffered from poor strategic thinking overall. Had Brutus and Cassius attacked Italy between July and November of 43, they might have been able to defeat the mutually hostile Octavian and Antony separately. As it was, they waited too long. This delay had a dramatic impact on Roman history.

In November 43, Octavian, Antony, and Aemilius Lepidus agreed to share power in the Second Triumvirate. The next year their combined forces, under Antony and Octavian's command, slipped past the Republican navy in the Adriatic and crossed into Macedonia. The Republican fleet remained, however, creating problems for the Caesarian supply lines. Brutus and Cassius entrenched themselves in the city of Philippi and waited for the lack of food to destroy the Caesarians. The Republican plan foundered, however, on poor placement of troops, which allowed Antony to build fortifications between the Republican lines and their supply base, forcing them out of a strong position. In October of 42, two battles were fought outside Philippi. In the first, Antony defeated Cassius, who killed himself in despair, although on the other flank Brutus had routed Octavian. Three weeks later, at the same place, Antony and Octavian decisively defeated Brutus, who also took his own life. The surviving Republican troops were incorporated into the Caesarian army. About a third of the Republican fleet escaped to join Sextus Pompeius in Sicily.

After its defeat of the main Republican army, the triumvirate received a shock. In 41, one of Antony's brothers, Lucius Antonius, aided by his wife, Fulvia, made an attempt to seize power from Octavian. Lucius and Fulvia made a dash on Rome, but Octavian's soldiers stood by him, and the two retreated to Perusia (now Perugia). Antonian relief forces dithered, and Octavian starved the city into submission. After the fall of Perusia, Antony himself moved on Italy, but it was much too late. In 40, he landed near Brindisium and besieged the city. Had Antony pressed the issue, he still might well have defeated

Octavian, but he allowed Octavian's side to convince him to make peace and end the so-called Perusine War. According to the deal, Antony would retain control over the eastern provinces, and Octavian hold Italy, Spain, Gaul, and Illyricum. In 36 BCE, Octavian made a bold move, marching virtually alone into Aemilius Lepidus' camp. The name of Caesar led to mass defection of Lepidus' troops. This eliminated one of the triumvirs: Lepidus was allowed to keep Africa, but he was no longer a contender for power. Antony, as always a capable soldier but a poor strategist, had been outmaneuvered and lost his best chance to gain overall victory.

Even so, Antony had reason to be confident. He controlled the wealthier eastern part of the empire, and like Julius Caesar he had allied himself, politically and romantically, with Egypt's Queen Cleopatra. Instead of taking on Octavian immediately, Antony decided to carry out Caesar's planned invasion of Parthia. He reasoned that a victory would not only bring him enormous plunder but also a great deal of glory (*gloria*) and military prestige. He could then turn his attention to the upstart in the West. The failed Perusine War, however, delayed Antony's invasion. This allowed Parthia's King Orodes II to strike first.

The Parthian invasion of Roman territory began in 40 BCE. If it had succeeded, it certainly would have changed the course of Western history. The Parthians, led by the king's son, Pacorus, were joined by Quintus Labienus, the son of Titus Labienus, who had been one of Caesar's best generals. Labienus and Pacorus defeated a Roman army under Antony's general Decidius Saxa in open battle, largely due to the Parthian cavalry's skill. It is noteworthy that the surviving Romans, most of whom had served the Republicans, joined the Parthians rather than fight for the Caesarians. This combined Parthian-Roman force then took Apamea. Pacorus moved south and invaded Judaea. He removed the puppet king, Hyrcanus II, killed his minister, Antipater (the real ruler), and placed a pro-Parthian king, Antigonus, on the throne. Herod, Antipater's son, fled to Rome, where the Senate appointed him king of the Jews. King Antiochus of Commagene now joined the Parthian side. Labienus moved north, took Antioch, defeated the Romans again in Cilicia, and seized Asia Minor. Most of the East lay in Parthian hands.

Antony sent Publius Ventidius to meet this threat. Again, defense of the empire took precedence over victory in civil war. In 39, Ventidius won victories at the Cicilian Gates and Mount Amanus, and Labienus died in battle. Ventidius then defeated Pacorus near Antioch in 38. Here the Parthian cavalry, grown overconfident, had not used their bows but charged into the lines of legionaries and were slaughtered. Pacorus escaped, but was subsequently killed riding into a Roman camp he mistakenly thought was empty. Antony now joined Ventidius, and together they besieged Samosata, the capital of Commagene (now in southern Turkey). King Antiochus defended the city so vigorously that he was able to negotiate a settlement that kept his kingdom independent for another century. Antony dispatched Herod to Judaea and gave him Roman troops under Gaius Sosius, the new governor of Syria. The Romans took Jerusalem and established Herod as king of the Jews.

Meanwhile, Octavian and his supporters had been busy. In 38 Agrippa had suppressed an uprising by the Aquitanians, the only tribe in Gaul that still resisted Rome. Agrippa also led an expedition across the Rhine, settling the German tribe of Ubii near what would become the city of Cologne in exchange for their service as auxiliary troops. In 35, Valerius Messala operated against the Salassi and cleared the St. Bernard passes over the Alps. The most serious fighting, though, was against Pompey's son, Sextus Pompeius, who controlled Sicily with a powerful fleet. In 38, Octavian launched a two-pronged naval attack, but Sextus defeated each fleet in turn. Octavian then made a deal with Antony, obtaining 120 warships in a trade for twenty thousand Italian soldiers (which he never sent), at the same time extending the triumvirate for another five years. Octavian also brought in Agrippa from Gaul, established a naval base near Naples, called Portus Julius, built more ships, and trained his sailors. In 36, Agrippa won two consecutive naval battles at Mylae and Naulochus. The Pompeian navy was better at maneuver, but Agrippa had developed a new type of grapnel, used to board the enemy ships and engage in hand-to-hand encounters. Agrippa decisively defeated Sextus. Now Octavian controlled the entire West and had an enormous fleet of five to six hundred ships and a huge army of forty-five legions.

While Octavian was fighting Sextus Pompeius, Antony finally had managed to launch his invasion of Parthia. In addition to his legions, he brought light infantry and cavalry, in an attempt to avoid Crassus' fate of eighteen years before. The normal invasion route would have been directly from Syria into northern Mesopotamia, but Antony moved through Anatolia and marched from the north, planning to strike at the Iranian plateau. This uncharacteristically bold strategic move reflects Julius Caesar's plans for his unrealized invasion of Parthia that had been aborted by his assassination. Antony marched through Armenia and Atropatane (modern Azerbaijan), into northern Iran, between Lake Urmia and the Caspian Sea. He laid siege to the fortress city of Phraaspa (near present-day Tabriz). He defeated several Parthian attempts to relieve the city, but a single mishap doomed the invasion. Antony had sent his siege train down a mountain valley where it was ambushed and destroyed by a Parthian force. Without his torsion artillery, Antony could not storm Phraaspa, nor did he have enough supplies to enable him to starve out the defenders. He was forced to retreat. Although he led his columns skillfully, the bad terrain, lack of food, and Parthian attacks cost him twenty-two thousand legionaries.

Octavian must have suspected that a final reckoning with Antony was approaching, but remarkably he did not take advantage of Antony's misfortune. Although civil war loomed, in 35 and 34 Octavian took the time to defend the coastal region of the Balkans from incursions from the Dacians. He personally led a campaign to capture the strategic fortress of Siscia (now Sisak in Croatia). At the beginning of 33, Octavian turned his attention to suppressing piracy in the Adriatic with his powerful fleet. Antony, too, after he had rebuilt his army, did not turn to fighting his rival. Rather, he moved against Armenia, whose king he blamed for the loss of his artillery train. He made that kingdom, briefly, a Roman province. In 33, the king of Atropatene revolted against the Parthians, and Antony moved to the same region he had occupied three years

26. A warship on a relief dating to the late first century BCE. One can clearly see the forward "castle" as well as soldiers ready to board an enemy ship. Photo: Scala/Art Resource, NY.

before. It looked like he would again plunge into Parthia, but he suddenly stopped. He must have sensed that the truce with Octavian was ending and did not want to fight a two-front war. It took another two years, however, for the final reckoning to come. In 31 BCE, Octavian pushed through a declaration of war – not against Antony, but against Cleopatra. By this time, both sides were ready to fight.

It is ironic that the battle to decide the fate of the Roman Empire, whose mainstay was its legions of heavy infantry, was fought at sea. Agrippa, Octavian's commander, skillfully kept supplies from reaching the Antonians both by land and sea. Hunger and disease led to increasing desertion and demoralization. In September of 31, Octavian defeated the combined forces of Antony and Cleopatra at the naval battle of Actium in northwestern Greece. He spent the next nine months marching through the Near East, establishing his authority. In the summer of 30 Octavian marched into Egypt without opposition. Both Antony and Cleopatra committed suicide.

The Battle of Actium (31 BCE)

Antony and Cleopatra had crossed to Greece with about thirty legions, mainly Italians, and a fleet of five hundred, mostly Egyptians. These troops established a base at the Bay of Actium (now Punta in northwestern Greece). These were preparing for an invasion of Italy, but Octavian struck first. Early in 31 BCE, he marched his army, some 73,000 infantry and 12,000 cavalry, overland, and Vipsanius Agrippa sailed a fleet, estimated at from four to six hundred ships, to cut off Antony's supply line to Egypt. Octavian then trapped the Antonian land forces and waited for hunger to take its toll. After several months, Antony and Cleopatra made an attempt to break the naval blockade.

On September 2 the battle began. Antony's fleet, made up of heavy quinqueremes, struck against Octavian's left. Antony and Agrippa fought a running battle, moving north in the bay as each tried to outflank the other. This opened up a gap in the Antonian center. Cleopatra was in command of a reserve of sixty ships. If she had sailed into the gap and checked the attack, the battle, and history, might have turned out differently. She decided to save herself and the large treasure brought to support the army. Cleopatra managed to sail through the Octavian line and return to Egypt. Antony's fleet quickly disintegrated, and he managed to save only a handful of vessels. After some brief fighting, the rest of the Antonian fleet and army surrendered to Octavian, effectively ending the battle – and the war.

Octavian was, in many respects, an unlikely figure to rise to power in the ruthless world of the civil wars. He was a rather sickly and neurasthenic individual, but he managed to defeat Antony, the more robust and stereotypically military figure. Of course, Octavian's brilliant general, Agrippa, played an important role. Octavian experimented with various means of rule, but by 23 BCE had hit on the system that would run Rome for the next three centuries. The Principate was an attempt to make Rome a monarchy while keeping up the pretense of a Republican government. As part of this change Octavian took on a new name: Imperator Augustus Caesar. It is customary to refer to him as Augustus after 29 BCE.

Links: Cicero, *Philippics* 3.29–31 (Romans plunder other Romans), 14.25–28 (Battle of Mutina); Augustus, *Res Gestae divi Augusti* 25–30 (Augustus' military achievements).

CHAPTER 9

AUGUSTUS' NEW
ARMY

After his victory over Mark Antony, Augustus began transforming the Roman military into a unified and professional force. He began with the integration of Antony's army and navy into his own forces. Some units were continued in service, others disbanded. Tens of thousands of troops were demobilized and settled in colonies around the empire. Although the Roman army had long been, in practice, professional, officially it was still the same citizen militia that had fought five hundred years before. Augustus formalized its professional nature, which it retained for next six hundred years, long after the Western Empire had fallen. Many aspects of the Augustan reform drew on elements inherited from the Republican period, but Augustus and the early Julio-Claudian emperors introduced some dramatic innovations. These changes would profoundly affect the course of warfare for the rest of Roman history.

Augustus fixed the four basic branches of the Imperial Roman military. These were the Praetorian Guard, the legions, the auxiliaries, and the navy. The unit organization of the legion and the structure of the officer corps remained the same, as did clothing and equipment, although there was an increased tendency toward standardization. Pay was regularized and a retirement pension established. It seems that, at least in peacetime, the Roman military did not have difficulty filling its ranks with volunteers. According to law, any citizen of good health and five foot seven inches in height could join the legionary forces, although recruits for the cavalry and the elite first cohort had to be as tall as Praetorians. It is likely that a minimum age of eighteen years old was established for recruits. In practice, the military's age and height requirements may have been ignored in order fill the ranks, especially during wartime. On the other hand, we do have evidence that recruits were inspected in a formal medical examination, called the *probatio*.

Roman soldiers had long been paid, but Augustus regularized both pay and deductions for each branch. The legionary soldiers received the same amount as had been common since the time of Julius Caesar, 900 sesterces a month, cash, a third of which was paid every four months. Deductions were taken out for food, clothing, the repair of weapons, a unit fund, and other costs. Soldiers could keep their money in a savings account kept by the unit's standard bearer. Promotion brought with it more pay, and there were ranks identified as "one-and-a-half pay," "double-pay" and so forth. Auxiliary infantry earned less, as did sailors, but the auxiliary cavalryman, though not a citizen, was paid more than a legionary. The pay of the Praetorian Guard was significantly higher, 3,000 sesterces a year. Centurions earned even more: the pay of a *primus pilus* was well over 50,000 sesterces. We know little about the pay of higher officers.

The Republican legion had been variable in its total size, as had the number of troops in its various subdivisions. Now Augustus fixed the number of soldiers to be assigned to the legion. Eight men made up the squad or *contubernium*, eighty a century, and the six centuries a 480-man cohort. There were ten cohorts in each legion. At some point the legion's first cohort was organized into five double-sized centuries, but when this occurred, and for what reason, remains obscure. Of course, the numbers assigned to each unit and subunit were nominal, and in practice legions would generally be understrength, especially in peacetime. The legions were originally recruited mainly from Italy and the Roman colonies strewn around the empire. Later, we find them filling their ranks from provincials and the children of soldiers. By law soldiers could not enter into a legitimate marriage, so their children were not Roman citizens and thus officially ineligible for service in the legions. As time went on, however, it became increasingly common for the illegitimate sons of soldiers to enter the military, and the army turned a blind eye to their questionable citizen status.

The Praetorian Guard was open only to Roman citizens from Italy. Recruits had to be especially tall – five feet ten inches, at a time when the average man was about five feet six (this is in modern, not Roman feet and inches, which were slightly smaller). Service in the Praetorians was very prestigious. Pay was good and service relatively easy. Most,

27. A relief shows a group of Praetorian Guardsmen, probably from the late first century CE. An *aquila* or eagle standard is visible on the left. Erich Lessing/Art Resource, NY.

and eventually virtually all, served in the city of Rome and rarely went to war in the first century. The substantial remains of the large Praetorian camp can still be seen in Rome.

Noncitizens could join the auxiliaries and the navy. Recruits had to be in good physical condition, but we know virtually nothing about the height requirements for these branches. Under Augustus and his immediate successors, each auxiliary unit was usually enlisted from a distinct ethnic group. At times, entire tribes were recruited en masse, and although we have no direct evidence, it may have been only the chieftain who volunteered: the others may well have been obliged to serve by tribal convention or law. Auxiliaries were probably paid less than legionaries, but it was enough to make service attractive to true volunteers. In contrast to legionaries, auxiliaries could marry, and as time went on, the sons of soldiers, now citizens, sometimes followed their fathers into service. When auxiliaries moved to other provinces, the Romans made no attempt to maintain their ethnic composition, seeking replacements from the area surrounding their new garrison. Over time, their ethnic status became only nominal.

Citizens and noncitizens were attracted to military service for a variety of reasons. Life in the thousands of farming villages, where most inhabitants of the Roman Empire lived, was highly circumscribed. Young men may have wished to leave to better their lives or simply in search of adventure. Others may have been fleeing crimes or scandal. Military service offered an escape and a way to see the world. A soldier was paid about the same as a skilled worker and in addition received food and shelter. Cash payment on enlistment was probably a particular incentive to recruits from the countryside. Recruits, called *tirones*, were given travel money, the *viaticum*, to pay for their trip to join their unit. This amounted to a considerable sum and was probably more than most young men had ever seen. The payment served as an inducement, although the evidence is that most of it was spent by the time the soldiers reached their unit. Some was paid for food and lodging, but the experienced soldiers and centurions who accompanied the recruits probably specialized in ways of relieving naive *tirones* of their travel money. Although some young men were, and are, attracted by the prospect of war, military service generally attracts fewer volunteers when the prospect of death or maiming in battle is imminent. Conscription remained a method of filling up the ranks of the Roman army, and those who tried to avoid military service faced severe penalties. It was possible, however, to pay a substitute to go in one's place.

The Roman military continued to use military slaves (*calones*), who provided much of the labor for military units; but slaves, and the worst criminals (*damnati*), were prohibited from serving as combat soldiers in the army upon pain of death. When conscription was used, it was a serious crime to offer slaves as substitutes for oneself. Like all such rules, however, these Roman regulations were probably broken in times of real need. When armies go to war, they need willing soldiers quickly and are often not very choosy. The enlistment period for Augustus' professional army was originally set at sixteen years. The term was the same as that in the Republic, although instead of being the maximum total, it was now served continuously.

As is natural in such a patriarchal society, women could not legally serve in the military, although it is quite possible that a very small number of women did, masquerading as men. This practice of women serving as soldiers in disguise is known to have existed at various times and places. The Chinese story of Hua Mulan may or may not be fiction, but tales of other fighting women are certainly true, such as that of Catalina Erauso, who fought as a conquistador in sixteenth-century Mexico, and of Deborah Samson, who was wounded in action during the American Revolution. About one thousand women fought in the guise of men during the American Civil War.

During the Republic a soldier, whether a Roman citizen or not, could move from military service to civilian life and back. He was only under military discipline while actually serving, and the fact that he had been in the army or even in combat had no legal effect on his citizen status. In the Imperial period, when a soldier entered the military, whether or not he was a citizen, he obtained a special legal status. As a *miles* or soldier, he could only be tried in military courts, even for offenses against civilians. On the other hand, soldiers faced hardships that civilians did not. As under the Republic, a soldier in the Imperial army could be whipped or executed at the order of his commander and without a trial. As noted above, soldiers were not allowed to marry, an abrupt change from Republican military law. This was certainly not due to prudery – there were no rules against sexual intercourse or even long-term relationships. The purpose of the regulation is unclear, but it may well have been to save money: soldiers knew that their pay was not expected to support a wife and children.

After their formal discharge, soldiers were required to serve for four more years as *evocati*. The *evocatus* was relieved from fatigue duties – such as hauling firewood – and was not required to go on expeditions, except in emergencies. They did, however, remain subject to military discipline and had to defend the camp when necessary. Soon, however, Augustus raised the number of years of service to twenty on active duty and five as an *evocatus*. This is what it remained until the end of the empire. In practice, one finds soldiers serving for even longer – sometimes as long as forty years. When a soldier reached the end of his service, he normally received a *honesta missio*, an honorable discharge. The special status of the soldier continued after his discharge – he did not go back to being a civilian, but was classified as a veteran (*veteranus*), a category that gave him special legal privileges. He was free, for example, from certain taxes and duties that were imposed on other citizens. Augustus was also mindful that poor former soldiers had been a major source of discontent and civil war in the late Republic. Therefore, he introduced a regular discharge bonus for legionaries, called a *praemium*, first in land and then increasingly as a cash payment. Because people did not live as long in ancient times, only half of all citizen recruits were likely to live to receive this bonus, even if they never saw combat. For those who did, however, the *praemium*, the equivalent of some twelve years' pay, meant they could retire as wealthy men.

The auxiliaries (*auxilia*) now were recognized as a regular part of the Roman military. In practice, they had long been so and had been occasionally rewarded with Roman citizenship. Under Augustus, the reward of citizenship for the soldier and his family now became a normal recompense for an auxiliary's long years of service, although it was not until the reign of Claudius (41–54 CE) that this was established as a regular rule. The practice of routinely granting Roman citizenship to

28. A bronze military diploma of a Spanish cavalryman, Gaius Valerius Celsus, who served in a Pannonian unit stationed in Britain. Issued in 103 CE, it documents the awarding of citizenship to Celsus, his wife, and his children at the end of his auxiliary service. Photo: © Copyright The Trustees of the British Museum.

auxiliary troops did much to Romanize the empire. Auxiliaries received elaborate bronze diplomas (*diplomata*) that set out their legal privileges. As a matter of course, the diplomas listed every auxiliary unit stationed in a province at the time of a soldier's discharge. They are thus an important source of information for the existence of various auxiliary units and their movements.

There were really only three ranks in the Roman military: one was a soldier (*miles*), the second a centurion (*centurio*), and the third the officer, although there was no one Latin word for this last position. Within each rank there were subdivisions. Soldiers were listed as having double pay, for example, or fulfilling certain functions, like standard bearer (*signifer*). Indeed, there were dozens of various job categories within military units, especially legions, including scribes, medical personnel, engineers, artillerymen, and so forth. Even a legionary cavalryman fit into this model. Such specialists were referred to collectively as *immunes* – that is, they were exempt or "immune" from performing fatigue duties. When in battle, however, all these soldiers fought together without distinction. On one level, this was potentially wasteful. Highly trained personnel, whose expertise was of great value, were put in danger. Looked at another way, however, this was an efficient use of manpower, as the Romans did not have any "noncombatant" soldiers. Each specialist also had a dual function – as a fighting man.

Third in line in the century was the *tessararius*, who was in charge of the unit's daily password and responsible for the soldiers standing guard. Each century had a soldier called the *optio* who served as second-in-command to the centurion and was in line to be promoted. This position was the highest for the *miles*, but there was a giant leap between it and becoming a centurion.

The centurion no longer belonged to a squad but was attached to the century and had his own separate quarters. Low-ranking centurions commanded a single century, but the centurion of the first century of each cohort commanded that cohort as well. The centurion of the first century of the first cohort was also the senior centurion of the legion,

29. A relief from Trajan's Column shows legionaries operating a *carroballista*, a light torsion artillery piece mounted on a wagon for mobility. Photo: Alinari/Art Resource, NY.

called the *primus pilus*, something like "number one spear." The *primus pilus* was highly respected and much better paid, and his lifestyle was more luxurious than that of other centurions. Although some centurions rose from the ranks, others were promoted after service in the Praetorian Guard, or were appointed directly. Such direct appointment, however, was possible only for those of equestrian rank.

Just as the *optio* was a sort of link between the rank of soldier and centurion, the ranks of *praefectus castrorum*, or camp prefect, connected the centurionate with the higher officers. The camp prefect was technically an officer, the third ranking in the legion, but the post was almost always held by an experienced former *primus pilus*. This was solely an administrative, not a command, position – unless the camp itself came under attack. Virtually all the other positions in the officer corps were drawn from the highest classes of a very hierarchical culture: the equestrian and senatorial orders. Each legion had six military tribunes, five of whom were equestrians, most of whom had previously commanded auxiliary units. The sixth, or senatorial tribune (*tribunus laticlavius*), served as second-in-command of the legion, although he was generally an inexperienced young man beginning his military career. This fact illustrates the highly class-conscious nature of Roman society. The legionary commander was called a legate and was virtually always a senator. The only exception was the commander of a legion stationed in Egypt, who was an equestrian and held the rank of Prefect of the Legion. All auxiliary units were officered by equestrians called prefects. The Praetorian Guard was also commanded exclusively by equestrians, and their commander, the Praetorian Prefect, was the highest-ranking equestrian in the empire.

Under Augustus' system, there was very little in the way of military administration or staff above the level of the legion. In fact, there was technically no imperial government at all, as Augustus had pretended to restore the Republic. He held the post of permanent governor of a super-province made up of the majority of provinces (and almost all of those that had legions stationed in them). Augustus, and his successors, appointed deputy governors, called "legates," to actually run these provinces and command the military forces in them. These officials, called *legati pro praetore Augusti*, should be distinguished from legionary legates, the *legati legionis*. However, in small provinces that had only a single legion, the same person would hold both positions (except in Africa). The Senate maintained control of about a dozen provinces, but only one, Africa, had a legion stationed in it. The governors of the senatorial provinces, who variously held the titles of proconsul, propraetor, legate, prefect, or procurator, commanded whatever auxiliary units were in their provinces. One province, Egypt, was run differently. Its governor, called the prefect of Egypt, was from the equestrian not the senatorial order. As noted above, he also functioned as the legionary legate, the only equestrian to do so until the third century.

In the early Principate, the emperor's freedmen, who ran his personal estate and household, also took responsibility for administering the correspondence and pay of the army. Eventually, this work was taken over by the office of the Praetorian Prefect. Since he was the highest-ranking military officer permanently stationed in Rome, it was natural that he assumed the responsibility of transmitting orders to and from the emperor to the units stationed around the empire. During active military operations, a special official was appointed to take care of logistics for the campaign. This emphasizes the rather meager administrative structure of the early empire.

All pay, benefits, promotions, military transfers, orders, and regulations came, officially, from the emperor himself. Of course, neither the emperor nor his Praetorian Prefect could know the capabilities of all the hundreds of officers and men in line for promotion. In practice, the recommendation of a superior officer or influential civilian was very important in obtaining promotion. Indeed, patronage usually counted for more than talent or ability. Some examples of such letters of recommendation from important Senators and other persons have survived, requesting that relatives or friends be given military commands of various sorts.

The military oath (*sacramentum*), taken by every soldier, was sworn to the emperor personally, and not to the Roman state. Although modern historians call Augustus and his successors "emperors," there was in fact no such single office or title: the Romans used the names "Augustus" and "Caesar," as well as *princeps* or "First Citizen." In most languages of the empire, such as Greek and Aramaic, however, he was simply, and more accurately, known as "the king." The "emperor" held a number of Republican offices and powers that combined to bestow on him absolute power. As we have seen, the Latin *imperator*, from which we derived the word "emperor" was an honorary title given to victorious Republican generals. Augustus and his successors took it as part of their personal title, not as the name of a new position in government. Of course, for convenience's sake, we use the term emperor.

When a military campaign was necessary, either to expand the empire, defend its territory, or put down a revolt, either the emperor took personal command or appointed a general who fought on his behalf. Augustus led some campaigns in person, but he and the family members who succeeded him (the Julio-Claudian emperors) relied on others to actually command the army in the field. At times, members of

30. A *sestertius* of Caligula shows the emperor making a formal speech or *adlocutio* to the cohorts of the Praetorian Guard. The troops stand at attention with their eagle standards. Photo: Bildarchiv Preussischer Kulturbesitz/Art Resource, NY.

the imperial family served in this capacity, for example, Tiberius Drusus and Germanicus under Augustus. In other cases, a commanding general from the Senatorial class was assigned to lead a war or campaign. A commander had to take care to have sufficient talent to win wars, but not enough to be able to replace the emperor! Occasionally, particularly in the case of revolts or frontier skirmishes, the governor of a province would command legions and auxiliary troops in the old Republican manner. In all cases, however, campaigns were fought under the auspices (*auspicia*) of the emperor. This meant that, regardless of who did the actual commanding, the emperor was considered to be the victor (although never the loser) of a war. It was the emperor, not the commanding general, who garnered the appropriate honor, such as a triumph, even if the ruler had never left Rome, which was often the case. After the Year of the Four Emperors (69 CE), during which military leaders struggled to replace the urbane but unwarlike Nero, emperors tended more and more to take personal command, at least of major campaigns.

Roman military units, both legions and auxiliaries, were given permanent stations in the provinces, generally along the frontiers. After 30 BCE, Augustus reduced the sixty legions existing at the end of the civil wars to thirty-one, and the three subsequently wiped out at Teutoburger Forest were not replaced. The number of legions remained around thirty for the next three hundred years. Each legion had a number and a title or *cognomen*, for example, the Twentieth Valeria Victrix. Legions from Antony's forces that were merged with those of Octavian retained their numbers, resulting in many legions having the same number. These were distinguished by their *cognomen*, for example the Tenth Fretensis and the Tenth Gemina. Some of these *cognomina* referred to attributes given to the legion, such as *Victrix*, "victorious"; others to where they were raised, for example, *Gallica* or *Macedonica*; and others to the emperor who raised them, which is why so many have the title *Augusta*, as they were raised by Augustus. Remarkably, one legion, the Twenty-second Deiotariana, was named for a foreigner, King Deiotarus, who had organized a legion of his Galatian subjects that fought for Julius Caesar. When Galatia became a Roman province, Augustus added it to his roster of legions, with its unique cognomen. Oddly, when new legions were raised, the numbering always began over again with "one," with the result that there were sometimes as many as five or six First, Second, and Third Legions at the same time.

The historian Tacitus gives us the stations of all the Roman legions in the year 23 CE. Three legions occupied Spain – the Fourth Macedonica, Sixth Victrix, and Tenth Gemina – but there were none in any of the three provinces of Gaul. Much of the Rhine River frontier was divided into the two provinces of Germany. Lower Germany was garrisoned with four legions: the First Germanica, Fifth Alaudae,

Twentieth Valeria Victrix, and Twenty-first Rapax. There were another four in Upper Germany: the Second Augusta, Thirteenth Gemina, Fourteenth Gemina, and Sixteenth Gallica. The Balkan (or Danube) frontier was guarded by six legions: in the province of Dalmatia (modern Slovenia and Croatia), the Seventh Augusta and Ninth Hispana; in Moesia (Serbia), the Fourth Scythica and Fifth Macedonica; and in Pannonia, the Eighth Augusta and Fifteenth Apollinaris. There were no legions in Greece or Asia Minor (modern Turkey). There were four in Syria: the Third Gallica, Sixth Ferrata, Tenth Fretensis, and Twelfth Fulminata. Egypt hosted two legions: the Third Cyrenaica and Twenty-second Deiotariana. The entire border of Roman Africa, some two thousand miles, was guarded by a single legion, the Third Augusta.

Most of the imperial army's cavalry, light infantry, and archers were in the auxiliaries. It is generally assumed that the number of auxiliary troops was about the same as those in the legions. Auxiliaries were divided into cohorts, of either infantry and *alae*, that is wings, of cavalry. In the time of Augustus, most auxiliary units contained about five hundred men; thus we would expect there to have been some three hundred of them scattered around the empire and its borders. In contrast to information about the legions, we have direct evidence of only a fraction of these. Auxiliary infantry units, called cohorts, were identified with the unit type, a number and either an ethnic or tribal identifier, the speciality of the unit, or some other title. For example, the Cohors III Batavorum, Third Cohort of Batavians, or the Cohors I Sagittariorum, the First Cohort of Archers. Auxiliary cavalry wings were originally identified by their commanders, such as the Ala Petriana, named for Titus Pomponius Petra, who led it when it was raised in the early first century CE. This unit, and many others, kept such names for decades, sometimes centuries, after the original commander had died. Later on, cavalry units took identifiers similar to those of the infantry. There were a number of "combined arms" units, made up of 480 infantry and 120 cavalry, called *cohortes equitata*. As their name suggests, these followed the naming conventions of the infantry.

31. A painting by Peter Connolly represents a second-century CE *hippica gymnasia*, a mock battle used to train cavalry in throwing javelins. The elaborate metal masks were worn to protect the face. Photo: akg-images/Peter Connolly.

The mission of the army on the empire's borders, as we shall see, was partly defense against foreign attack and partly for the control of trade. In addition, it functioned to prevent revolt and as a provincial police force. The Praetorian Guard was a garrison and security force for the city of Rome. There were ten cohorts of Praetorian Guards with a thousand men in each, plus a cavalry force, the *equites singulares*, which grew to some two thousand men by the end of the second century. In addition, there were the urban cohorts, originally three, then five, supported by seven cohorts of paramilitary *vigiles*, who served as night watchmen. Although all told the Roman garrison represented almost twenty thousand men, it did not function primarily as a strategic reserve, although the Praetorian Guard did occasionally accompany the emperor to war. They were intended mainly to support the imperial government and keep public order in the capital city.

Links: Tacitus, *Annals* 4.5 (disposition of legions); Suetonius, *Life of Augustus* 49 (reform of the army); Pliny, *Letters* 2.13 (recommendation), 10.29, 30 (recruitment of slaves).

CHAPTER 10

CONQUESTS OF THE
IMPERIAL ARMY
(30 BCE–68 CE)

In 29 BCE Augustus closed the doors of Janus' temple, an act symbolizing that the Roman world was at peace. In fact, it was not: Rome was still almost constantly at war. Although historians tend to characterize the Imperial period as one of tranquility and purely defensive wars in contrast to the expansionism of the Republic, the Imperial Romans continued to conquer and to expand their realm. The notion, expressed by Virgil in his epic poem the *Aeneid*, written for Augustus, was that the gods had given Rome "empire without limit" (*imperium sine fine*). This idea continued to be held by Romans for many centuries, indeed, they never really abandoned it.

Augustus initiated any number of wars after he had declared universal peace. In the early years of his reign, he sent Licinius Crassus to conquer Moesia and made Thrace a client kingdom. Egypt's first governor, Cornelius Gallus, marched into the kingdom of Meroë in Nubia or Ethiopia (modern Sudan) and set up an inscription claiming he had conquered it. (Augustus promptly removed Gallus, either for fighting without permission or bragging about it or both.) A few years later, Ethiopia invaded Egypt, defeating the Romans and carrying off booty. In 26 or 25 BCE Augustus sent Aelius Gallus (no relation to Cornelius) to conquer the Sabaeans in southern Arabia. Sailing from Egypt, eleven thousand Romans and allies (including Jews and Arabs) took the port of Leuke Kome, on the Gulf of Aqaba. Marching south for four months, they arrived at Mariba (now Mareb, Yemen), which Aelius assaulted for six days. Our sources say he gave up due to lack of water, but perhaps the Sabaeans negotiated a peace, allowing the Romans passage into the Gulf of Aden. Shortly after closing the temple doors, Augustus himself led an army against the Cantabri in northwestern Spain. He claimed a quick victory, but fighting went on for years under Agrippa.

There was also fighting in North Africa and Asia Minor. In 19 BCE, Cornelius Balbus occupied an oasis in the Sahara to stop the raiding of the Garamantes, nomads who lived in the Fezzan region of present-day Libya. A few years later, Sulpicius Quirinius undertook a difficult campaign against the Marmaridae southwest of Cyrene, which involved moving supplies over long distances through the desert. Like Agrippa, Sulpicius Quirinius was one of a number of military troubleshooters upon whom Augustus relied, "new men" who rose due to military skill and loyalty. A few years later, the emperor sent Sulpicius Quirinius to Galatia in Asia Minor, recently transformed from a kingdom to a province. Galatia's mountainous border with Cilicia was infested with bandits called the Homonadeis. The Galatian kings had let them alone, reasoning that, after all, the victims were only peasants, but Augustus took it upon himself to protect the Galatians. Sometime after 12 BCE, Sulpicius Quirinius defeated the Homonadeis and settled them in the lowlands, ending the threat.

It is true that there were times when Augustus avoided fighting. In 20 BCE, a rebellion in Armenia gave the emperor the opportunity to avenge the Roman defeat at Carrhae (53 BCE), but he decided against war. He made a deal: Rome would put a client king, Tigranes, on the Armenian throne and the Parthians would return the eagles lost by Crassus. Augustus' propaganda presented him as forcing the Parthians to yield out of fear of Rome's legions, but when Tigranes died in 6 BCE, the Parthians simply took Armenia over again, an aggression Augustus ignored. Historians tend to focus on this action (or rather lack of action) by Augustus, and ignore the many wars he undertook before and after it.

Remarkably, newly conquered Gaul, with the exception of Aquitania, had given the Romans little trouble during the civil wars. The Romans built a military road system converging on Lugdunum (Lyons), but did not find it necessary to station a legion in any of Gaul's three provinces. The route over the Alps was secured, however, and in 25 BCE, Terentius Varro Murena rounded up the surviving Salassi and sold them into slavery. In the year 15 BCE, Augustus ordered his stepsons, Drusus and Tiberius, to conquer Raetia (on the border of modern Switzerland, Germany, and Austria). Each brother led a prong of a pincer movement. Striking over the Brenner Pass, Drusus took over

32 (*left*). A marble statue of Augustus from the first century CE. On his breastplate is a depiction of Parthians returning Roman standards lost at the Battle of Carrhae. Photo: Scala/Art Resource, NY. 33 (*right*). A similar statue, found at Pompeii, represents Marcus Holconius Rufus, an important businessman and civic leader. Although he never served in the army, Augustus gave him the honorary rank of military tribune, so he is portrayed in an officer's uniform. Photo: Alinari/Art Resource, NY.

eastern Raetia, while Tiberius moved along the Rhine Valley to Lake Constance. The two brothers met somewhere near modern Liechtenstein. This sort of two-pronged attack, already known in Republican times, would become characteristic of Imperial Roman strategy.

Around 16 BCE, the governor of Gaul, Marcus Lollius, was ambushed in the Meuse valley by the Sugambri, a German tribe, and a legion lost its eagle. Though there was no real danger, the *clades Lolliana*, or the "disaster of Lollius" caused great alarm in Rome. Augustus reacted by planning to advance the Roman frontier north from the Rhine to the Elbe River. In 12 and again in 9 BCE, Drusus crossed the Rhine and defeated a number of German tribes, including the Sugambri, the Bructeri, the Chauci, the Cherusci, the Suebi, and the Marcomanni. He reached the Elbe where, Tacitus writes, a divine figure stopped his advance. More likely Drusus, or indeed Augustus himself, considered the Elbe a natural northern border for the empire. Drusus built forts on the Elbe, Weser, and Meuse rivers and established a fleet on the Rhine. Clearly the Romans intended to stay in Germany. On the journey home to Rome, however, Drusus died in a riding accident. In his memory Augustus awarded him, and his descendents, the title (*cognomen*) of *Germanicus*, "Conqueror of Germany."

There was also fighting in the East. The death of King Herod in 4 BCE set off a serious revolt in Judaea, which was suppressed by Quinctilius Varus, the governor of Syria. In 6 CE, the Romans, frustrated by the incompetence of Herod's successor, Archelaus, turned Judaea into a province. This set off another unsuccessful revolt. Sometime between these two dates (though almost certainly not in the year 1), Jesus of Nazareth was born in what was now the Roman province of Judaea. (Years later, those hostile to the religion he founded claimed that Jesus' real father was not God, but a Roman soldier named Panthera – "the Panther.")

In 1 BCE, the Sabaeans in Yemen had again imposed tolls on Roman ships using the Gulf of Aden. Augustus sent a naval force that destroyed Aden and settled the issue. Around the same time, an expedition was sent to Armenia under Augustus' twenty-year-old grandson Gaius Caesar, but with little success. In Africa, Cornelius Lentulus defeated the Gaetulians in what is today southern Algeria.

In Pannonia (modern Slovenia and Croatia), Drusus' brother Tiberius had been continuing the campaigns of Agrippa, who had died. From 12 to 9 BCE, he systematically "pacified" the region, enslaving many Pannonians and conscripting others. Meanwhile, a German tribe, the Marcomanni, had migrated into Bohemia (in the modern Czech Republic). Conquering the Boii, they established a state there, with a capital near modern Prague. Their king, Maroboduus, introduced a Roman-style military system: rumors, certainly false, claimed that his German "legions" numbered seventy-five thousand. Augustus saw this as a threat. In 4 CE, Tiberius led a two-pronged invasion from the east and northwest. Maroboduus was trapped and a decisive battle loomed, but in 6 CE a major revolt in Pannonia and Dalmatia forced the Romans to pull back. A subsequent attack on Moesia by the Dacians and Sarmatians also diverted Roman attention. Despite some victories, the revolt spread throughout Dalmatia.

The Pannonian insurrection was the biggest military challenge to Rome since the establishment of the Principate. Augustus may have suspected that Tiberius was not unable, but rather unwilling, to completely pacify the Balkans. Perhaps believing that the veteran legions were loyal to his stepson and not to him, Augustus raised new ones in Italy, putting them under the command of Germanicus, the twenty-two-year-old son of the late Drusus. Italy's youth, however, were used to the "volunteer army" and resisted conscription. Augustus used harsh measures, lopping off the thumbs of draft dodgers. He also offered incentives, donating 170 million sesterces of his own money to establish a military treasury (*aerarium militare*) providing cash bonuses on soldiers' discharge. This fund was subsequently maintained by a sales tax and an inheritance tax. Even with this "carrot-and-stick" approach, Augustus was forced to enlist freed slaves into the new units.

With these new legions, and auxiliaries drawn from Asia Minor, the army in the Balkans reached about a hundred thousand men. Tiberius formed flying columns, which ravaged Pannonia and Dalmatia. Fighting was bitter, rewards were few, and there were murmurs of mutiny. Eventually, though, the Pannonians were pacified, and the Dalmatians trapped in a mountain fortress. A frontal attack suffered heavy casualties but engaged the enemy's attention while a small Roman force slipped through and attacked from the rear. The Dalmatians surrendered.

Balkan success, however, was quickly followed by German disaster. In 9 CE, three Roman legions under the command of Quinctilius Varus were destroyed at Teutoburger Forest (near the modern Kalkriese, north of Osnabrück in Germany) through the treason of Arminius, a Cheruscan nobleman and former auxiliary soldier. The Romans had rebounded from worse losses, but the aged Augustus was psychologically traumatized by the *clades Variana* or Varian disaster. Suetonius reports that the emperor would wander through his palace crying out "Varus, give me back my legions!"

In 14 CE, Augustus died and his stepson Tiberius succeeded to the throne. Mutinies immediately broke out among the Rhine and Danube legions. These probably were not directed against Tiberius personally, as he seems to have been popular with the troops, but were motivated by pent-up anger at Augustus' decision to delay paying discharge bonuses to save money. It is noteworthy that the soldiers waited to rebel until after the old emperor's death – an indication of their personal loyalty to him. The legions along the Danube frontier were brought under control by Tiberius' son, Drusus, and those along the German border by his nephew, Germanicus. Some ringleaders were executed, but in general the soldiers were treated leniently and some of their demands quietly fulfilled.

The emperor had never trusted his nephew Germanicus, though the young man had always showed loyalty to him. Perhaps to test him – or hoping he would not return – Tiberius sent him to avenge the Varian disaster. Between 14 and 16 CE, Germanicus led a series of punitive expeditions into Germany. With a force ranging from thirty to fifty thousand men he devastated the territory of three German tribes and recovered two of the eagles lost at Teutoburger Forest, burying the remains of the Roman dead. Nevertheless, although Germanicus beat Arminius in several battles, he could not decisively defeat him. In 17, Tiberius called off the campaign. Even after the Cherusci overthrew and killed Arminius in an internal power struggle, the Romans took no action. Some forts north of the Rhine were occupied for a while, but soon abandoned. The project of extending Roman control to the Elbe was also abandoned. The Rhine became the permanent frontier, leaving the Germans on the other side free. Five centuries later, they would destroy the western empire. It is impossible to say what would have

The Battle of Teutoburger Forest (9 CE)

The Roman defeat at Teutoburger Forest was long remembered as a "black day" (*dies ater*) by the Romans. The loss was instrumental in the ultimate decision to abandon control of the part of Germany across the Rhine. Until recently we have had to rely on the accounts of Tacitus and other historians, but archaeologists have now found the remains of Roman equipment strewn through the forest. Indeed, they have shown that the battle did not take place in what is now called the Teutoburger Forest south of Osnabrück in Germany, but in the wooded area north of the city. Careful examination of the artifacts has helped reconstruct the course of the battle. Tacitus claimed the defeat stemmed from the fact that the Roman commander, Quinctilius Varus, was an unwarlike lawyer. This was untrue: Varus was an experienced military man who had successfully suppressed a revolt in Judea thirteen years before. When the German Cherusci rebelled, Varus followed standard procedure, taking three legions, the Seventeenth, Eighteenth, and Nineteenth, plus auxiliaries, some eighteen to twenty thousand soldiers, on a punitive expedition. Tacitus notes that a long train of some ten thousand noncombatants, including women and children, slowed down the army. It is unclear, however, if these belonged to the legionaries or, as is more likely, to the German auxiliaries.

Varus relied on his German ally Arminius to plan the army's route through the Teutoburger Forest. Due to his royal birth, bravery, and

happened if the Germans had been pacified and Romanized; Western, and world, history might have been quite different. The decision to abandon Germany is usually attributed to Augustus, but it was Tiberius, who had fought there many times and knew the country intimately, who made the final judgment to leave that country unoccupied by Rome.

Eastern Numidia had been made part of the province of Africa, and the new government, as was by then standard practice, introduced strict long service to Rome, Arminius had achieved equestrian status, possibly commanding an auxiliary unit. It is not surprising that Varus trusted him. However, near modern Kalkriese, Arminius and the tribal auxiliaries turned on the Romans and were joined by rebel tribes, a total of some twenty to thirty thousand men, in an ambush. Varus managed to build a defensive camp the first evening and hold off the German attack. The next day, he decided to try to break out, and burned his train in order to speed up his march. The Roman column, however, began to separate and break up under sustained German attack. It is unclear what happened over the second night, but by the third day the loyal auxiliary and legionary cavalry tried to make it on its own and were massacred. The remaining infantry forces were gradually isolated and destroyed. Varus committed suicide. Those Romans who were captured or surrendered were tortured to death as human sacrifices to the German gods. Only a few escaped to safety. It was a stunning defeat. None of the three legions was ever raised again, and their numbers remained unused throughout Roman history.

property lines according to Roman law. This resulted in greater overall prosperity but infringed on the traditional power and wealth of nomadic tribal leaders. In 17 CE, the same year Tiberius ended the German War, a tribal revolt broke out in Numidia, led by a former auxiliary cavalryman, Tacfarinas, who initially organized his followers in the Roman fashion. When trounced in open battle, though, Tacfarinas turned to guerrilla warfare. In 21, the emperor sent Junius Blaesus, who organized an effective counterinsurgency program. Blaesus first offered an amnesty, drawing away Tacfarinas' supporters. Then he divided Numidia into three military zones, established strong points, and sent out flying columns of small units under the command of experienced centurions. In order to keep up the pressure on the insurgents, the Romans did not go into winter quarters, but fought year round. In 24 CE Tacfarinas was trapped by Roman forces and committed suicide to

34. A bronze statuette from the second century CE, perhaps of a god in the dress of a legionary soldier. The figure wears segmented armor (*lorica segmentata*), the protective leather strips called *pteryges*, and a crested helmet. Photo: HIP/Scala/Art Resource, NY.

avoid capture. Blaesus' strategy became a pattern for successful Roman suppression of revolts in the centuries to come. The rest of Tiberius' reign was relatively uneventful. In 21, a short revolt in Gaul led by two nobles, Julius Sacrovir and Julius Florus, was easily put down. Although Tiberius allowed the soldiers' pay to fall into arrears, this did not lead to serious unrest or mutiny.

It is early in the reign of Tiberius that we first encounter the segmented iron plate armor called the *lorica segmentata*. This is the best known of all types of Roman armor. Its inventor is unknown – perhaps it was first developed for use by gladiators – but it was doubtless the experienced and intelligent soldier-emperor Tiberius who ordered its adoption by the legions. This was the first use of iron-plate armor in history and was revolutionary. *Lorica segmentata* was cheaper, faster to manufacture, and considerably lighter than chain mail, while providing equal or better defense. Common soldiers began using *pteryges* or leather strips that hung down over the groin and hips. This provided some protection without hindering movement. Its name, like the idea itself, was borrowed from the Greeks. In addition, we find an improved type of *gladius* and scabbard being introduced. It is tempting to think that the *pteryges* and the new-style swords were also innovations ordered by Tiberius.

The next emperor, Gaius, had the nickname Caligula, meaning "Little Combat Boots." His father was Germanicus, who routinely brought his family along with him on his military campaigns. Caligula had grown up in camp, often dressed as a little soldier. Despite, or perhaps because, of this upbringing, Caligula was quite unmilitary, though he did lead one "expedition." Increasingly showing signs of mental instability, the emperor once marched with an army across the Rhine and to the English Channel, ordered his soldiers to pick up seashells, and then, declaring victory over Neptune, god of the sea, returned to Rome. Some historians have questioned the stories of Caligula's madness, attributing them to malicious gossip spread by his political enemies. It does seem, though, that the details of this pseudo-military campaign reflect a deeply disturbed mind. The soldiers do

35. The Roman world in the time of Augustus and the Julio-Claudian emperors.
Photo: Copyright Cambridge University Press.

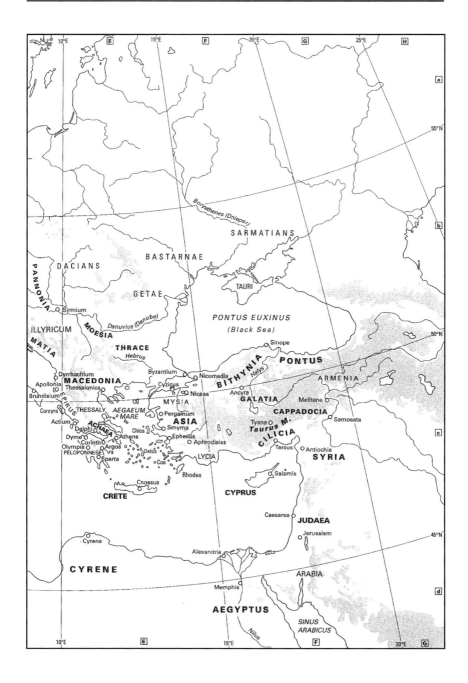

not seem to have minded – a make-believe war was a lot safer than a real one!

Caligula did expand Roman power into the previously independent Berber kingdom of Mauretania in North Africa. Although its king Ptolemy was a loyal supporter of Rome, Caligula had him killed while on a visit to the capital. A revolt immediately broke out under the leadership of a royal freedman named Aedemon. Some of the Berber nobility, such as Sabalus, supported the rebellion, but others, such as Lusius Quietus, fought for Rome. Although Caligula's unprovoked actions had caused the war, he did little to suppress the uprising, which spread throughout Mauretania and lasted four years.

The emperor's increasingly bizarre and dangerous behavior alarmed the elite: eventually, Senators, palace officials, and the Praetorian Guard, normally rivals and even mortal enemies, collaborated in assassinating him. The Guard took advantage of the situation to loot the palace. Praetorians found Caligula's uncle Claudius cowering behind a curtain. Instead of killing him, they proclaimed him emperor.

Lame and a stutterer (probably due to cerebral palsy), Claudius most likely had never set foot in an army camp, but he became a remarkably vigorous commander-in-chief. He sent Suetonius Paulinus to suppress the rebellion in Mauretania, and in the course of the campaign, Paulinus became the first Roman to cross the Atlas Mountains in North Africa. Hosidius Geta, a legionary commander, chased the Berber rebel Sabalus into the Sahara. Lack of water almost led to disaster, but a rainstorm saved the Romans and led to Sabalus' surrender. Mauretanian (traditionally called Moorish) auxiliaries, under the command of Lusius Quietus, played a significant part in the Roman success. After the revolt, Quietus recruited a large number of Mauretanian horsemen, who became an important element in Rome's auxiliary cavalry forces.

Claudius' most important military achievement, however, was the conquest of Britain. Tribal leaders in southern Britain had long called on the Romans to free them from domination by one tribe, the Belgae. Finally, in 54 CE, Claudius sent Aulus Plautius, the governor of Pannonia, with some fifty thousand men to invade the island. The

Romans landed at Rutupiae (now Richmond) and marched inland, defeating the British first at the Medway River and then at the Thames. They were on the verge of victory when Plautius halted to allow Claudius to travel to Britain and take credit for the victory. The emperor led a force, which included camels and elephants, into the British capital of Camulodunum (Colchester). After only sixteen days on the island, Claudius left. Under Plautius and the next governor, Ostorius Scapula, the conquest continued. British tribes in what is now England and Wales were gradually defeated.

Claudius also made improvements in Roman military administration. He appointed freed imperial slaves to manage the army's bureaucracy: an official called the *a rationibus* was particularly important. This administrator was responsible for all of the empire's finances, which of course included its military ones. Although there were famous cases of corruption and resentment at the authority given to "social inferiors," Claudius' bureaucratic reforms probably increased efficiency overall. He also added two urban cohorts, stationed at the ports of Puteoli and Ostia, to control unruly merchant sailors. There was some unrest in the empire: in 42 CE, the governor of Dalmatia, Lucius Camillus Scribonianus, led a military revolt, but after five days the soldiers deserted him and the uprising collapsed. This is a testament to Claudius' popularity with the army.

When Claudius died in 54 CE, his sixteen-year-old stepson, Nero, became emperor. Coins and inscriptions portray Nero as a general, but in fact he showed little interest in the army or in warfare. Nero's powerful mother, Agrippina the Younger, who put him on the throne, had no military experience, unlike her own mother, Agrippina the Elder, who had frequently campaigned with her husband Germanicus. Even the commander of the Praetorian Guard, Afranius Burrus, had never served in the army! Fortunately, Nero had some able generals, as his reign was full of wars.

In 54, Nero ordered Domitius Corbulo to reestablish Roman control over Armenia, and this led to a war with Parthia. The Romans utilized the now routine two-pronged invasion: Corbulo attacking

Gnaeus Domitius Corbulo (ca. 3 BCE–66 CE)

Gnaeus Domitius Corbulo, one of the greatest generals of the imperial period, came from a senatorial family. We know almost nothing of his early career, but Domitius probably followed the normal course of offices, serving as quaestor, commanding a legion, and, like his father, becoming praetor. He was (probably) suffect consul in 39 CE. His rise was partly due to his half-sister, Caesonia, who was the emperor Caligula's fourth wife. Under the emperor Claudius, Domitius was governor of Lower Germany, with the command of four legions. He campaigned against the Chauci, but despite some early successes, Claudius put a stop to the fighting before any part of Germany was reconquered.

Shortly before his death, Claudius gave Corbulo the proconsular governorship of Asia. When Nero came to the throne in 54 CE, he assigned him command over Cappadocia and Galatia as well. His brilliant success against the Parthians, described above, led to his ap-pointment as governor of Syria. Soon he was given overall command in the east, invaded Armenia, and sacked Artaxata. Although he did not win a decisive victory, his skill led to a favorable settlement. Corbulo, however, suffered too much success. His prodigious military skill and popularity with the troops made him a threat to the emperor. When the Jewish revolt broke out, Nero did not assign its suppression to Corbulo. Instead he ordered his best general to Greece and forced him to commit suicide – a victim of too much talent.

from the north and Caesennius Paetus eastward from Cappadocia. Unfortunately for the plan, the two commanders hated each other. When Paetus was ambushed at Melitene (Malatya) just over the border and besieged over the winter of 62/63 CE, Corbulo moved to relieve his rival, but slowly – very slowly. Due to the delay, Paetus was forced into a humiliating surrender, agreeing to give up the Roman claim to

Armenia. Nero disavowed this agreement and gave sole command to Corbulo, who invaded Armenia again in 64 CE with fifty thousand men. Vologaeses offered talks, and Corbulo's chief staff officer, Tiberius Julius Alexander, who came from an important Jewish family in Egypt, negotiated a deal. Although Corbulo and Nero acted as if they had forced the Parthians to surrender, in fact the result was not so different from what Paetus had agreed to under duress. The Romans recognized the pro-Parthian Tiridates as king of Armenia, although he had to do homage to Nero and accept indirect Roman control. This compromise led to fifty years of peace on the eastern frontier.

In 60 or 61, the governor of Britain, Suetonius Paulinus, took the island of Mona (Anglesey in the Irish Sea) and destroyed the druid shrines there. While he was thus occupied, a massive anti-Roman revolt broke out led by Boudicca, queen of the Iceni. Combining several British tribes under her leadership, she sacked Camulodunum (Colchester) and defeated a legion in battle. Suetonius Paulinus swiftly moved south and retook Verulamium (St. Albans) and Londinium (London). With about ten to fifteen thousand men he defeated Boudicca's much larger force, ending the uprising.

Despite the ongoing warfare, Nero himself seems to have been more interested in exploration than conquest. In 61, he ordered a unit of Praetorian Guards to march up the Nile River. The Praetorians reached a point near the modern Ugandan border, one thousand miles south of the Roman frontier. The purpose of this expedition is unknown. Some historians have speculated that it was a response to the rising power of the kingdom of Axum in Ethiopia. It may well have been, however, simply one of Nero's whims. In any case, nothing came of this remarkable African exploration. Another of Nero's military moves seems to have been more practical, although it may or may not have originated with him. The Romans sent forces into the Caucasus, seizing control of the kingdom of Albania – modern Azerbaijan. This was probably due to interest in the recently opened Silk Road to China and the threat posed by the Alans, a powerful Iranian nation that had seized

36. A *sestertius* of Nero shows him and another horseman on a *decursio*, a series of complex and rapid equestrian maneuvers used to train cavalrymen. Nero was an excellent rider and may well have participated in such exercises. Photo: Bildarchiv Preussischer Kulturbesitz/Art Resource, NY.

western Central Asia. After Nero's death Georgia was abandoned, although the Romans seem to have exercised some indirect control in the region for a century or so afterward.

The biggest war of Nero's reign was the revolt known as the Jewish War, which broke out in 66. Its origin is complex, but it was certainly related to the Jews' expectation of a Messiah who would overthrow the Roman Empire and establish a Kingdom of Heaven on earth. A number of individuals over the course of the previous century had been acclaimed as the Messiah, including, most famously, Jesus of Nazareth. However, other factors, such as social unrest, economic dislocation, and political ambitions also played a role in the uprising. At least initially, many Jews in positions of leadership supported the revolt, including a large number of the hereditary priesthood that functioned as the provincial aristocracy. Josephus, the Jewish-Roman historian who later chronicled the war, was among this group. On the other hand, the Jewish king, Agrippa II, and others in the Jewish nobility fought alongside the Romans, considering the rebels to be dangerous fanatics.

At the revolt's outbreak, the governor of Syria, Cestius Gallus, marched into Judaea, but considering speed more important than careful preparation, he did not wait to set up the logistics necessary to besiege a walled city such as Jerusalem. Gallus expected the rebels to open the city's gates as soon as he arrived. When they did not, he assaulted the walls for about a week. Josephus later wrote that the city would have surrendered if pressed longer, but Roman supplies were running out. Gallus made the quite logical decision to withdraw to the coast. The rebels, however, caught the Romans in a defile during the retreat, mauling the army. Nero then appointed an obscure but able general named Flavius Vespasianus (known to history as Vespasian), to suppress the revolt. Vespasian arrived in Judaea in 67 along with his son Titus, taking over an army of fifty thousand. Vespasian swept through Galilee (today northern Israel), the coastal region, and Peraea (now in the kingdom of Jordan).

Josephus' history gives us a clear picture of this Roman army on the march. Auxiliary light infantry and archers led the column, followed closely by a select force of legionaries, mounted and on foot. After them were the surveyors – *immunes* drawn from the legionary ranks – who would mark out the camp built at the end of each day. Then marched soldiers with axes and other tools, who cleared the path for the main body of troops. Leading the main body was the general, Vespasian, and his staff, accompanied by cavalry and an elite guard, called by an old Republican term, the *hastati*. The rest of the legionary cavalry followed, then the torsion artillery, and finally cohort after cohort of legionaries, marching six abreast. The baggage train (*impedimenta*) and military slaves (*calones*) came next, then the auxiliaries and allies. A force of legionaries marched in the very rear to pick up stragglers and prevent desertion.

By 68 CE, Vespasian and his army had isolated Jerusalem and the revolt was on the verge of collapse, but the political situation in Rome preserved the independence of Judaea for two more years.

Links: Tacitus, *History* 5.10–13 (Jewish war); Horace 4.4 and 4.14 (Raetian campaign of Drusus and Tiberius); Seneca, *Natural Questions* 6.8.3 (Nile expedition).

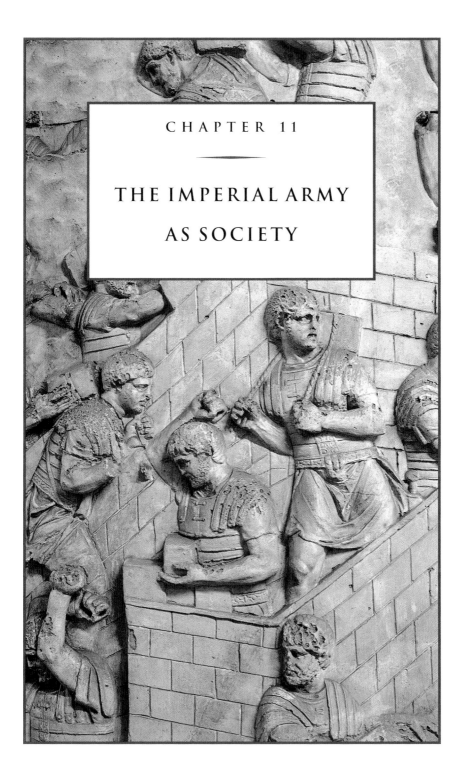

CHAPTER 11

THE IMPERIAL ARMY
AS SOCIETY

For hundreds of years under the Roman monarchy and Republic the army had formed an integral part of Roman society as a whole. Under the Empire, however, the military became a separate institution. Over time it developed a distinct culture, certainly Roman, but different in many respects from the civilian world surrounding it. There were still important interactions in both directions, but one can certainly speak of a military society in its own right under the Empire. The army developed its own identity, and soldiers and veterans became an identifiable class.

Roman imperial soldiers often went for long periods without seeing any major military action. There were certainly many thousands of soldiers during the *Pax Romana* who spent their entire careers in garrison without ever going to war. Every soldier was assigned to a particular military unit, and each unit had a base. This was true for the legions, the auxiliary units, the Praetorian Guard, and the fleet. Many soldiers lived in or near densely populated areas, for example, the fleets in Italy and the legions stationed in Egypt and Syria. Ironically, although they lived in the more advanced areas of the empire, we know the least about them. Few of their camps have been found, having been built over by modern cities, and records are much less likely to survive. The one exception is Egypt, where we have a large number of papyri. Even here, however, they are very few compared with civilian documents. In such locales, soldiers and sailors would have interacted with a highly sophisticated local culture. There were more opportunities for leisure activities, but there is no evidence that units in these regions were less effective militarily. Nevertheless, their access to gladiatorial games, horse races, theaters, and brothels led to the belief among many Romans that soldiers stationed in urban environments were soft and weak.

One reason Augustus stationed most of the army in border regions was that in an age of slow mobility it made sense to place units close to the border. Far from the empire's cities, he doubtless thought, they would be less inclined to corruption. In addition, border units and their generals were far removed from the centers of political power. Whatever the reasons for stationing units so, the practice had a dramatic effect. The money that flowed into border garrisons fueled urbanization and economic growth. Provincials made up an increasing part of the military at all levels, and the army played a key role in their Romanization. The relationships between soldiers and civilians ranged from official ones, such as imposed liturgies (i.e., duties) and policing, to unofficial ones, such as "common-law" marriages and business dealings. Attitudes also varied, from warm appreciation of the army to deep hostility toward it. We should not assume that ethnicity or religion necessarily determined a provincial's point of view toward the army. Some ethnic Romans were antimilitary, as evidenced in poetry and literature, and some non-Romans quite favorable toward it. The very Roman satirist Juvenal hated soldiers, but on the other hand a Greek named Aelius Aristides wrote a speech about Rome in which he praised the army in extravagant terms. Although some Jews (and later Christians) characterized Rome and its military as agents of Satan, others saw the empire as established by God and loyally served Rome as soldiers and officers.

Gradually the legions and auxiliary units began to build permanent camps. Sturdy wooden and stone buildings replaced tents and the camps began to resemble small towns. The layout of Imperial camps was similar to that of Republican ones, with the headquarters (*praetorium*) and parade ground (now called the *principia*) in the center. Two large intersecting streets divided the camp: the Via Principalis (also called the Via Principia, Cardo, or Cardus Maximus), which ran north to south, and the Via Decumana (also the Via Praetoria or Decumanus Maximus), which ran east to west. In addition to barracks, a camp included warehouses, granaries, workshops, baths, and even a hospital (*valetudinarium*). As we have seen, under the Empire, the officer called the prefect of the camp (*praefectus castrorum*) became important and was in charge of administration and management.

Every common soldier belonged to a *contubernium* or squad, normally of eight men in Imperial times. On campaign the squad shared a tent, called a *papilio* as its flaps reminded soldiers of the wings of a butterfly. In garrison, the soldiers' barracks were cramped. It seems never to have occurred to the Romans to increase their size or to have fewer soldiers per room. This may have been because Roman soldiers, like most people around the Mediterranean, spent most of their day outdoors. The crowded conditions were alleviated a bit by the fact that two of the eight barrack mates (*contubernales*) were expected to be on guard duty at any one time.

When in the field the squad pooled its rations, ground its grain in common, and cooked together. Roman military diet, like that of civilians, revolved around wheat, either baked as bread or eaten in a broth or gruel. There is some evidence that the Romans ate grain pasta, but if so, its use was rare, especially in the army. Grain was supplemented by meat, chiefly pork, and by vegetables, including that timeless military staple, beans. A fish sauce, called *garum*, was also used, especially in garrison. Salt and olive oil were used for flavor and for cooking. (Pepper was only for the very wealthy.) Meals were washed down with cheap wine and vinegar mixed with water and known as *posca*. On campaign, diet was simpler (and featured another military classic: hardtack, a very hard and dense cracker).

Food was provided by the army but could be supplemented by personal or unit purchases. Some of the records from Vindolanda, for example, record the buying of food and drink from local dealers. Thus, to some extent a garrison's diet would be similar to that of the local civilian population. There is evidence that those soldiers stationed in beer-drinking regions of the empire, such as Britain and Gaul, drank it in addition to the wine generally preferred by Romans. On the other hand, we know that some items, such as oil, relish, and even grain were shipped from other places, even other provinces, so there may well have been a distinct "military diet" (*militaris cibus*). Hunting would have supplemented meat supplies, especially for officers, and items purchased (or simply stolen) from the local population would have made the monotonous campaign diet more varied.

37. A wooden tablet from the auxiliary fort at Vindolanda, now in England, dating to the late first or early second century CE. Listing the names of soldiers and the prices of various items ranging from bacon to a horse, it may represent the accounts of a private trader. Photo: © Copyright The Trustees of the British Museum.

38. Trajan's Column shows wine barrels being offloaded from a cargo ship. The fort on the river is a supply depot for the Roman army invading Dacia. Photo: Erich Lessing/Art Resource, NY.

Probably a military slave (*calo*) and a mule were assigned to each squad to carry equipment and serve the soldiers. The slave received no wages, of course, but was fed from the soldiers' pooled rations and slept with the unit's mule. In both peace and war armies were often accompanied by sutlers (*lixae*), who sold items to the soldiers, purchased loot, including slaves after campaigns, and provided services, including prostitutes. During sieges, an area was designated for the dwellings of the sutlers that were called *canabae*. The sutlers around a camp or fort often provided the nucleus of what became a civilian settlement, and ultimately a town or city.

One of the most interesting features of the Imperial Roman army was the sophistication of its military medicine. The army had a professional medical service that was attached to every legion (we are, of course, less informed about the auxiliaries). Those who treated soldiers for wounds and illness held the title *medicus*, but this could indicate one of three types: a civilian physician who served in the military; an officer or centurion who had received some medical training; or the *medicus ordinarius*, a soldier who served as what is now called a "medic." Among the last were troops trained in removing arrowheads and bandaging wounds.

Roman treatment of wounds reached a higher level than that of any other ancient culture. For example, they used an arterial surgical clamp that allowed them to cut off blood flow while treating serious injuries. Military doctors also used sedatives such as the opium poppy, henbane, and white mandrake, and they were aware of the dangers of infection. It was standard practice to wash surgical equipment in hot water, and a formula of lint and honey – an antibacterial – was used to dress wounds. The only complete medical text to survive from antiquity was that of Cornelius Celsus, a military doctor who lived during the reign of Tiberius.

While common soldiers lived eight to a small barracks room, centurions lived in relatively large houses. These were quite spacious and housed not only the centurion himself but any number of slaves to serve him, and very likely a "wife" and her children. His pay and rations,

39. A scene on Trajan's Column of Roman soldiers taking care of the wounded. On the right, a cavalryman's thigh is being bandaged, and on the left, a legionary, wounded in the arm or shoulder, is being aided. Photo: Alinari/Art Resource, NY.

40. Surgical instruments found at Richborough, England, the site of a Roman camp. Since there was also a civilian settlement there, it is not certain that these examples actually belonged to an army physician, but similar ones would have been used in military medicine. Photo: © English Heritage Photographic Library.

considerably higher than those of regular soldiers, were intended partly to support this household. Meals were cooked for him and he ate much more sumptuously than the common soldier, though the basic elements of his diet probably did not differ much.

In contrast to soldiers and centurions, officers were allowed to marry and live with their families. Details of the life of the wives and children of officers stationed in garrison towns are illustrated in some papyri and the Vindolanda tablets, as well as evident from archaeological remains. The commander of a unit was almost always accompanied by his wife and lived in a large official mansion and, like all members of the aristocracy, was served by numerous slaves.

Stone or brick walls, some 12 to 15 feet (3.6–4.5 m) high, replaced the earthen ramparts of earlier camps. A defensive ditch, watchtowers, and fortified gates were added. Though better fortified than daily camps, these permanent camps were still not intended to be siege-proof castles but were used as bases for mobile operations. Rome put its trust in the swords of its soldiers, not in high stone walls. Legionary camps were large, around 50 to 60 acres (20 to 25 hectares), but even so, they often spilled outside the walls. Auxiliary forts were smaller, more numerous versions of the legionary ones. Local people settled in the areas around military camps, attracted by the economic activities offered by the soldiers' presence. As the soldiers took wives – legally in the case of auxiliaries, informally for legionaries – these families also settled in the local communities. Veterans often remained in the vicinity of the camp, investing their pensions in land or business and staying in close contact with their former military comrades. As time went on, some of these civilian settlements outside of camps grew much larger than the camps themselves. Many cities and towns of Europe and the Near East began as Roman military bases: Colchester in England, Strasbourg in France, León in Spain, Cologne and Mainz in Germany, Vienna in Austria, and Lejjun in Jordan are examples.

Little is known about the daily routine of the Roman soldier. Since rosters were kept, giving information on where the soldiers physically were at any particular time, there may have been some sort of roll call in

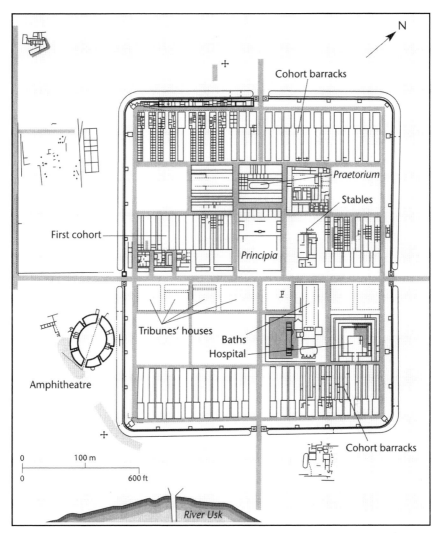

41. A reconstruction of the legionary fortress of the Second Augusta at Caerleon in Wales. Called Isca by the Romans, the modern name of the town derives from Castra Legionis, "camp of the legion."

which a soldier was either "present" or "accounted for." There was some weapons training, or at least practicing with weapons, but how often this happened, and who had to take part, was probably up to the individual unit commander. Vegetius describes practicing sword fighting with wooden equipment and other training exercises. That such weapons training actually occurred is shown by an ox skull found at Vindolanda that had been used for target practice, probably by the crew of a *scorpio* or light ballista.

Entire units sometimes went on training marches, which included building practice camps, some of which have survived. This exercise, called the *ambulatura*, was an important element in the Roman army's training. It is not known, however, whether the frequency of such exercises was set by regulation or how often they actually took place. Soldiers learned how to march at two different rates: a short step, called the "military pace," and a longer "full pace." On flat terrain, troops were expected to be able to march twenty Roman miles, eighteen of our miles (28 km) in five "summer hours" (about seven of our hours), much the same march rate as a modern army on foot. In contrast to other armies throughout history, the Romans do not seem to have used the drum, or indeed any musical instruments, to help them keep pace. The various trumpets, called the *tuba*, the *cornu*, the *lituus*, and the *bucina*, were used only to convey commands, not for marching. It is possible that the Romans did use a form of the modern "cadence" or rhythmic song for this purpose, but there is no direct evidence of this. While we know that generally the *tuba* was straight and the *cornu* curved (shaped like a G), the terms are sometimes used interchangeably and the differences are unclear.

Soldiers were also used for both military and civilian construction projects. Military units built their own camps, and as time went on would improve the border defenses with palisades, walls, and ditches. Hundreds of roads and aqueducts, public buildings, and other structures were built throughout the empire by military labor. Such projects may have taken months, or even years, and involved backbreaking work on the part of most or all of a legion or auxiliary unit. Soldiers certainly were not overly pleased with such assignments, although they do seem to have taken pride in the completed projects. In addition, soldiers might repair, or even manufacture, shoes, clothing, armor, and weapons.

Like soldiers throughout history, Romans had to stand guard duty. Guards watched day and night around the camp walls and at its gates, in

42. Legionaries building a fortification wall as depicted on Trajan's Column. The soldiers are working in armor – does this reflect reality or is it an artistic convention? Photo: Peter Connolly/akg-images.

front of the headquarters, the commander's house, warehouses, and other important buildings. Soldiers also were sent on special duty to guard important places and people outside the camp. In many parts of the empire, the army served as the police force; soldiers guarded, transported, and sometimes executed, prisoners. Roman citizens had the right to appeal death sentences to the emperor, and, as there were no imperial police, soldiers were assigned to escort prisoners, sometimes from one end of the empire to the other. The *Acts of the Apostles* describes the arrest and transport of Paul of Tarsus by soldiers from Judaea to Rome. Physical beatings were a common form of punishment both in the army and in civilian life, and soldiers were assigned to do the whipping. Daily life in ancient times was full of routine cruelty and brutality, and this was certainly true of military life, even during peacetime. Soldiers also carried out capital punishments such as beheadings in the case of citizens (such as Paul) and crucifixion in that of noncitizens (for example, Jesus of Nazareth).

Military life also had its lighter side. Soldiers took part in various festivals and celebrations, both formal and informal. We have a military calendar from third-century CE Dura Europus that lists festivals, mainly connected with the birthdays of emperors and members of the imperial family. These involved sacrifices and a feast in which meat was shared among all the soldiers. There were other holidays, such as the day of discharge (*honesta missio*) and the day of decorating the standards (*rosaliae signarum*).

Despite all their duties and training, Roman soldiers enjoyed a lot of free time. Of course, many had (unofficial) families, and spent their leisure with them. For those without "wives," brothels and prostitutes were doubtless a feature of virtually every military establishment. Men also formed close friendships with their fellow soldiers. Although the Roman society frowned on homosexuality, what we would call "gay relationships" probably did exist among Roman soldiers, as they do in virtually every large-scale all-male institution. There is a sly reference to such a relationship in one of Plautus' plays (*Pseudolus* 1180), so gay soldiers seem to have been well known enough to be a source of humor.

Drinking and gambling were no doubt as popular among soldiers in ancient times as today. The Romans generally drank wine, but there is a good deal of evidence for beer drinking as well. Dice are found in military camps around the empire, and other entertainment included some board games resembling backgammon (though not chess) and ball games, though not those played in teams. Soldiers near larger cities could see gladiatorial games and chariot races, but even in small forts soldiers probably engaged in, and bet on, foot and horse races, dog- and cock-fights, boxing and wrestling matches.

In Roman times, as today, many people were attracted to religion, both out of belief and for its sense of community. Rome had its state gods, of course, such as Jupiter and Mars, but their worship was official and had little to do with personal beliefs. Each unit carried out sacrifices on behalf of the gods and in honor of emperors, many of whom were considered divine. These were certainly festive occasions, with some pomp and circumstance and plenty to eat, as the meat of the sacrificial animal was shared by the troops. The legion's standard, the eagle, was placed in a shrine in the middle of the camp. Alongside the eagle stood images of the emperors and of gods. All these images were treated as divine and sacrifices made to them. The first cohort was responsible for the safekeeping of the legion's shrine and stood a special honor guard over it at all times. Auxiliary units probably followed similar practices, though perhaps less formally.

In addition to the official celebrations, however, there were many other opportunities for religious expression. Certain cults taught devotion to a particular god or goddess, and their temples at times resembled modern churches in their sense of community and ritual. For example, the Isis cult was very popular throughout the empire, including with soldiers. The cult of Mithra, which allowed only male members, was especially attractive to members of the army. All over the empire we find examples of its underground temple, called a *Mithreum*. Soldiers also worshipped the gods of the area in which they were stationed. Of course, for many recruited locally these were their ancestral gods, but for others it simply seemed logical to worship the divinities of the land where they lived. Sometimes these gods were given Latin names, but their original character is usually clear. In other cases, soldiers would bring the worship of their traditional gods along with them as they were transferred around the empire.

New religions also attracted soldiers. According to the New Testament, one of the earliest converts to Christianity was a centurion – a not unlikely scenario. Indeed, there is evidence of both Jews and

43. The tombstone of an auxiliary cavalryman named Longinus Biarta. In the upper register he reclines on a couch in civilian dress; his horse and a military slave (*calo*) are shown in the lower register. Photo: Römisch-Germanisches Museum der Stadt Köln/Rheinisches Bildarchiv der Stadt Köln.

Christians serving in the "pagan" Roman army. We do not know how they dealt with the rituals of military religion, but clearly they did somehow. All soldiers were concerned with how they were remembered after death. Roman practice was to give a great deal of information about a person on his tombstone, and soldiers and officers often listed their highest rank and every unit in which they had served. In addition, a relief was often added, which gives us much information about equipment and arms. The elaborate stones were sometimes paid for in a soldier's will, or by means of a burial society. Often, though, they were erected by those he left behind: a "wife" or children, a slave or freedperson, and in many cases a fellow soldier.

In addition to their military duties, soldiers might also have worked to make extra money. Military pay was good enough that this was not usually a necessity, at least during most periods, but supplementing income was easy and fairly lucrative in the case of specialist soldiers. Blacksmiths and leather workers could fill civilian orders in addition to military ones. Scribes could sell their services to those who could not write. Military bakers might provide bread to the surrounding communities as well as to soldiers. There was certainly illegal activity as well. Bribes changed hands to allow goods to be smuggled, for example, and soldiers in garrison no doubt found various means to extort money from local civilians. Within the camp, soldiers paid money to the centurions to avoid fatigue duty (as is attested in a surviving papyrus letter).

A military unit generally owned the land surrounding its camps. This was intended to provide pastureland for the unit's animals and also to grow food. As time went on, some soldiers, particularly centurions, leased parts of this land to provide extra income. Some enterprising soldiers purchased property and became local landlords even before retiring from military service. Of course, the amount of business being done by soldiers depended to some extent on unit commanders – strict ones would have discouraged the practice, as it undermined discipline and attention to duty. But once such businesses became established, they would have been difficult to suppress.

In Roman law, the army and its officials were entitled to requisition the property and labor of civilians in order to carry out their military duties. For example, a centurion escorting a prisoner might seize a civilian's mule to carry supplies. Although legal, this sort of requisitioning was naturally resented, and soldiers sometimes had to, or wanted to, use force in carrying it out. In addition, the system of requisitioning was open to abuse, and there were doubtless many cases of soldiers stealing under the guise of requisitioning. Apuleius, in his hilarious novel *The Golden Ass*, refers to just such a case, as does Jesus of Nazareth in the Gospels, when he instructed Christians to voluntarily offer more than the soldiers demanded.

As the border fortification system grew in complexity, units, especially legions, were divided into more and more subgarrisons. Although the headquarters continued to be in one place, often the majority of a unit's soldiers were spread out in dozens of small forts and camps throughout a province. In the case of offensive or defensive operations, it was often difficult to move entire legions, as they were needed locally for administrative, customs, and police duties. A detachment, called a *vexillatio*, was therefore used for combat operations. This was a subgroup of a legion, usually made up of several cohorts. Its name came from the flag, or *vexillum*, under which it marched, the legion's eagle staying of course at its headquarters. Such detachments might or might not return to the legion's home station. Thus elements of a legion might become spread out over several provinces. As legions were subdivided into smaller and smaller camps, opportunities for unit training lessened, and both individual training and unit combat effectiveness suffered as a result. Individual soldiers were also assigned – the military term is "seconded" – to many different duties, for longer or shorter periods. Sometimes they would be guarding a prisoner or important traveling dignitary, or escorting a grain shipment. At others they would be assigned to the staff of a governor or to carry out customs duties. Thus they might stay away from their unit for years. A special camp in Rome was set up for soldiers who had been assigned to duties in the capital. Some of these postings lasted for considerable lengths of time.

Flavius Cerialis (ca. 50–after 100 CE)

The biographies of almost all the military figures we know about come from literary sources, primarily the histories of Rome in Greek and Latin. The life of Flavius Cerialis, an officer stationed in Britain, however, has been reconstructed from the Vindolanda tablets. These documents, written in ink on wooden slips, were preserved only because this particular Roman military camp was built, inadvertently, on a bog. When it began to sink, it was abandoned. The bog preserved these records.

Cerialis was a native Batavian, a people who lived in what is today the Netherlands. He was almost certainly a nobleman of his tribe. A Roman citizen as well, he served as prefect in command of the Ninth Batavian Cohort, which occupied Vindolanda after 97 CE. His name suggests that his family received Roman citizenship from one of the Flavian emperors, either Vespasian, Titus, or Domitian. The *cognomen* Cerialis may indicate a connection to Q. Petillius Cerialis, a relative of Vespasian who suppressed a Batavian revolt in 70. Subsequently, Petillius Cerialis brought some Batavian units along with him when he became governor of Britain in 71. It is quite possible that Petilius Cerialis arranged for the father or grandfather of Flavius to receive citizenship from Vespasian, either as part of the negotiations that ended the revolt or as a reward for serving in the army.

Cerialis probably did not rise from the ranks but would have been given his command due to his family background and connections. We know something of Cerialis' social life and administrative duties from the Vindolanda tablets, but virtually nothing about his career. We have no information at all on whether he died in service or retired. He probably died sometime early in the second century CE.

44. A painting of Vindolanda near Hadrian's Wall, around 200 CE, as reconstructed by Peter Connolly. Note the tightly packed barracks, the stone wall, and the town growing up outside the fort's gate. Photo: Peter Connolly/akg-images.

Historians dispute the question of whether there was a sharp division in the upper classes between those who chose a military career (the so-called *viri militares*) and a civilian elite. There probably was not a formal distinction, but it is true that some aristocrats spent most of their adult lives serving in the army. Male relatives of officers were themselves more likely to go into the army, so a tradition of military service would have sprung up in certain families, just as it does today. Although a commander in a provincial garrison lived a relatively isolated life, he would have tried to follow the conventions of upper-class society as far as possible. Indeed, the officers of a military garrison would have been the mainstay of local elite culture. Some leisure time would have been taken up with entertainments such as dinner parties. These were formal affairs, and his fellow officers and the "gentry," that is, the local elite, would be the invited guests. Indeed, it was through such interactions with the local military commander and his officers that much of Roman culture would have been passed on to the wealthy landowners of the border regions.

An example of this sort of social occasion can be seen in one of the Vindolanda tablets, which records an invitation to a birthday party from the commander's wife to an officer's wife.

Another leisure activity of the officers was hunting. This was a favorite recreation of aristocrats, and the stationing of units in the countryside made this an attractive way of passing the time. Those with a more literary bent might spend their time reading, or even writing. Of course, official correspondence took up a lot of time, but Romans also wrote letters as a sort of hobby. The letters of Pliny are a good example. Some engaged in business activities; others recommended friends and relatives for jobs. But it is clear that Pliny wrote for amusement and took great pleasure in his correspondence. A more ambitious officer might even write a book, such as those penned by Julius Caesar and Ammianus Marcellinus.

Links: Epitaphs (*CIL* 13.6898, 13.7029, 13.7041, 13.7255); *diplomata* (*CIL* 16.12, 16.21, 16.35), and papyri (*P. Gen. Lat.* 1); Vindolanda Tablets 156 (work parties), 291 (birthday invitation), 299 (Letter about oysters).

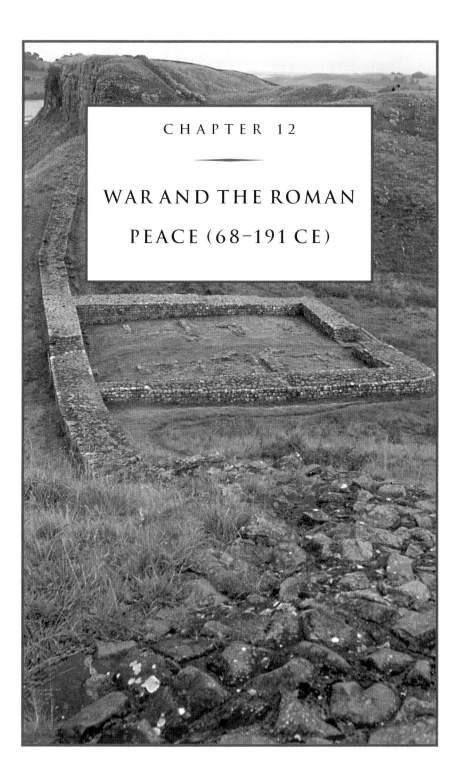

CHAPTER 12

WAR AND THE ROMAN

PEACE (68–191 CE)

The emperor Nero had tried to suppress military dissent by executing his best commanders, but this had the opposite effect. Unwilling to raise taxes, he also delayed paying the soldiers' salaries, increasing their discontent. It is no surprise, therefore, that in 68 CE a military revolt broke out in Spain and Gaul. The troops proclaimed a general, Servius Sulpicius Galba, as emperor. Galba's revolt could have been easily crushed if Nero, or his ministers, had taken decisive action. The emperor dithered, however, and his Praetorian Prefect, Nymphidius Sabinus, decided to support Galba. The Senate followed suit and declared the emperor deposed. Nero soon took his own life.

Galba, with remarkable confidence (or stupidity), arrived in Rome without his army. The new emperor went on to make some serious errors of judgment, pointlessly punishing troops who had stayed loyal to Nero and trying to discipline the unruly Praetorian Guard. On New Year's Day of 69 CE, a revolt along the Rhine raised up a rival emperor, Aulus Vitellius. In Rome, an ambitious senator named Salvius Otho bribed some Praetorians to murder Galba, and in mid-January he too claimed the throne. A civil war now started between the supporters of Vitellius (the Vitellians) and those of Otho (the Othonians). A Vitellian army totaling sixty to eighty thousand marched south into Italy. Otho met them at First Battle of Bedriacum, near Cremona, in mid-April 69. For the first time in a century, legions fought legions, though it was a flank attack by Batavian auxiliaries that ultimately led to Vitellian victory. Otho committed suicide. The Vitellians moved south, sacking every city they took as if they were conquering a foreign country (as in a sense they were), and finally seizing Rome itself.

While the Vitellians and Othonians were fighting it out, another general, Vespasian, was slowing his operations in Judaea nearly to a halt. With aspirations of his own and an army at his disposal, he was in no hurry to finish off the Jewish rebels. Interestingly enough, it was an equestrian Jewish-Roman, Tiberius Julius Alexander, the prefect of

45. A scene on the Column of Marcus Aurelius, dating to 193 CE, shows soldiers looting a village and assaulting women. Such brutality toward conquered peoples was not viewed negatively but as a sign of Roman strength. Photo: Alinari/Art Resource, NY.

Egypt, who first publicly proclaimed Vespasian emperor in July 69. Vespasian planned to conquer Africa and cut off Rome's grain supply, forcing Vitellius to surrender. He also sent an army under Licinius Mucianus to move cautiously toward Italy, avoiding direct confrontations. Vespasian, however, never got the chance to test his careful strategy. A brash Gallo-Roman legate named Antonius Primus disobeyed a direct order and rapidly marched into Italy with five legions. In late October 69 CE, Primus defeated the Vitellians at the Second Battle of Bedriacum, then moved on to Rome, assaulted the Praetorian camp, and took the city. The Senate immediately recognized Vespasian, but Primus' legions sacked the capital anyway. Vitellius was brutally murdered by a mob. Primus was neither rewarded for winning Vespasian the throne nor punished for his insubordination and excesses. Rather, he was quietly retired and lived out his life in obscurity.

Tiberius Julius Alexander (ca. 15–ca. 85 CE)

Tiberius Julius Alexander was born in Alexandria into one of the most important Jewish families in the Roman Empire. A member of the equestrian order and fluent in Latin and Greek, Alexander was raised as a Jew, although he later gave up practicing the religion. His first known office was as governor of Egypt's Thebaid region. In 46, he was appointed prefect of Judaea, commanding the three thousand auxiliaries stationed there. He was strict in keeping the peace and at one point crucified two leaders of the Jewish Zealots. We know nothing of Alexander's career from 48, when he left Judaea, until 63, when he held high rank in Domitius Corbulo's army. He had probably served in some military capacity in the meantime. In charge of logistics, Alexander also handled Corbulo's sensitive negotiations with the Parthians. In 68, he was made prefect of Egypt, commanding two legions. When he suppressed riots in Alexandria's Jewish section, he sent in these legions. Our sources tell us that fifty thousand Jews were killed. In 69, he was the first governor to proclaim Vespasian emperor and supported him throughout the civil war. In 70, Alexander went to Judaea to be chief of staff for Titus. It is likely that he planned the successful Roman siege of Jerusalem. There is some evidence that he was made Praetorian Prefect sometime in the 70s or 80s. If so, this would be the highest military post ever held by a Jewish Roman. The date of Julius Alexander's death is unknown.

The year 69 saw revolt as well as civil war. The Batavians, in modern Holland, rose up under the command of a local chief with the Roman name Julius Civilis. Besieging the two legions at Vetera (Xanten), Civilis declared an "Empire of the Gauls," and some Gauls, Gallo-Roman auxiliaries, and even Roman legionaries joined him. When Vetera fell, some survivors also defected. Ironically, although many Roman soldiers enlisted in Civilis' army, most Gauls did not. Gallic loyalty provided Rome with the opportunity to crush the revolt. Petillius Cerialis moved against the rebels and Civilis was defeated near Vetera. The Rhine frontier was reorganized and the new emperor, Vespasian, instituted a policy of moving auxiliary units far from their homes. He also replaced Romanized native commanders with nonlocal ones. As a result, when Cerialis went to Britain as governor in 71 to put down a revolt of the British tribe the Brigantes, he took four Batavian cohorts with him. A two-pronged attack, one under Cerialis and the other under Julius Agricola, trapped the Brigantes and defeated them.

Vespasian still had unfinished business in Judaea. The new emperor had left command of the Jewish War to his son Titus, who had taken no action during the civil war. The three Jewish rebel factions appear to have hated each other more than they did the Romans. They used this interval not to prepare and strengthen mutual defense, but to slaughter each other in fanatical attempts to wield power over the revolt. Displaying an almost incredible shortsightedness, the factions burned each other's grain supplies in Jerusalem in attempts to take sole control of the city. It is no surprise, therefore, that after the siege began in 70, starvation soon broke out. The Romans took each of the Holy City's three walls in succession and then fought their way into the Temple of God, which the rebels, rather sacrilegiously, had turned into a fortress. Soon, the last vestiges of Jerusalem's resistance were crushed. Titus stationed a legion, the Tenth Fretensis, in the Holy City. Only a few rebel holdouts remained. The siege of Masada in 73 has become famous due to the widely held, and completely false, idea that it held out for months, or even years. In fact, the siege lasted only a few weeks. Its anticlimactic capture ended the Jewish War.

In contrast to Nero, Vespasian took an active interest in the military. Although he himself no longer led armies, he directed his generals to undertake a number of aggressive campaigns. In 74, the governor of Britain, Julius Frontinus, whose book on military maxims is one of the few surviving from antiquity, began the conquest of Wales. Julius Agricola replaced him as governor in 78. We know many details of Agricola's campaigns due to the biography written by his son-in-law, the historian Tacitus. Agricola completed the pacification of Wales and then

46. A scene on Trajan's Column shows legionaries assaulting a Dacian town. The *testudo* or "tortoise" formation, with shields held overhead, protected them from missiles hurled by the defenders. Photo: akg-images.

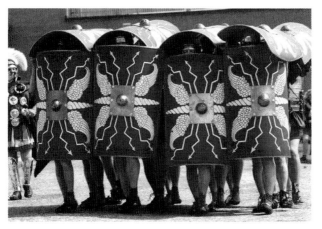

47. Modern-day reenactors dressed as first-century CE legionaries form a *testudo*. Such reenactments can help us to understand scenes such as those seen on Trajan's Column. Photo: www.graeme-peacock.com.

moved on to the Lake Country (in northwest England), conquering the region around the Tyne River. Around the same time, Vespasian ordered the suppression of the Suebi and the conquest of the Agri Decumates (today called the Black Forest), straightening out, and shortening, the Roman frontier. Although relations with the Parthians remained friendly, the eastern frontier was also reorganized to strengthen it. A military zone was created from three provinces in eastern Anatolia (modern Turkey). To guard against the Alans, troops were sent to fortify the Dariel Pass, which guarded two kingdoms, Albania and Iberia (modern Azerbaijan and Georgia respectively) in the Caucasus. It was in this region that a centurion, Lucius Julius Maximus, left the easternmost Latin inscription ever found, in what is today Azerbaijan.

Vespasian also reformed the army, doubling the size of some auxiliary cohorts and *alae* from 480 to 960, as well as at least some legionary first cohorts. These were called millenarian, or "thousand-man" units, and the regular five hundred-man units were now referred to as quingenarian. He also raised more auxiliary cavalry and, in imitation of the Parthians, introduced units of horse archers. In 79 CE, Vespasian died.

The next emperor, Titus, continued his father's expansionist policy, ordering an advance into what is today Scotland: in 80 Agricola built a fortified line from the Firth of Forth to the River Clyde, the site of the future Antonine Wall. Titus died in 81 and was succeeded by Domitian, his younger brother. Domitian showed much less military skill than his father or brother, but he was not afraid to lead armies, and he made some important administrative and security reforms.

In Britain, the new emperor ordered an advance. In 83 Agricola moved into the eastern Scottish Highlands and established the legionary camp at Inchtuthil on the River Tay. He then defeated a confederation of Caledonian tribes at Mons Graupius, near modern Inverness. In 86 or 87, Inchtuthil was abandoned, after only four years. From a strategic perspective, this meant giving up northern Scotland as part of the empire. The reason for this withdrawal is unknown.

Along the Rhine frontier, Domitian attempted to push Rome's borders forward. In 83 and again in 89, he launched campaigns against

The Battle of Mons Graupius (83/84 CE)

This battle, in which Gnaeus Julius Agricola defeated a confederation of Caledonian tribes, was the last of the successful campaigns of conquest by the Roman governor of Britain. The battle is generally placed near modern Inverness in Scotland, though some other sites have recently been suggested. Agricola's legions were accompanied by British allies and auxiliary troops, including several thousand tough Batavian fighters. Probably some twenty thousand Romans faced about thirty thousand Caledonians commanded by Calgacus.

Agricola decided to keep all of his legionaries in reserve, so the entire battle on the Roman side was fought by auxiliary and allied forces. The Caledonians held the high ground, but the auxiliary infantry attacked in the center, pushing back the enemy. The cavalry then succeeded in moving around the Caledonian flank, which led to a rout. Tacitus claims that 10,000 Caledonians were killed at a cost of only 362 Romans.

the Chatti, for which he raised a legion, named the First Minerva. Although he celebrated a triumph for this war, it appears that the Chatti remained unconquered. Along the Danube frontier, the Dacians had developed a sophisticated kingdom in what is now Romania. Their king, Decebalus, reorganized his military along Roman lines. In 85 the Dacians invaded Moesia. The Romans were beaten at the First Battle of Tapae (near modern Bucova), but in 88 they defeated Decebalus at the Second Battle of Tapae. It is clear that Domitian, like his father and brother, was dedicated to the empire's expansion, but the revolt of Saturninus forced Domitian to make peace.

Antonius Saturninus commanded the legions in Upper Germany, and in January 89 declared himself emperor. Swiftly, but unnecessarily, Domitian marched north with the Praetorian Guard: the governor of Lower Germany had taken it upon himself to defeat Saturninus. Since he

48. Roman auxiliaries, probably dismounted cavalry, attack Dacians in a scene on Trajan's Column. Note the characteristic oval shields, as opposed to the rectangular *scuta* carried by legionaries. Photo: akg-images.

was in the neighborhood, Domitian decided to attack two nearby German tribes, the Quadi and the Marcomanni, but the invasion was not successful. The Sarmatian Iazyges, a nomadic Iranian people living in what is today Hungary, aided the Germans and wiped out an entire legion. Details are unclear, but as a result the war ended.

The basic pay of the legionaries, 900 sesterces a year, had not been increased since the time of Julius Caesar. Domitian increased it to 1,200 sesterces, a long overdue raise. In order to pay for this, for an extra legion, and for his wars, Domitian experimented with various fiscal and economic reforms. He changed the silver content of the denarius twice – once up and then down – and tried, unsuccessfully, to increase grain production. He managed, however, to leave Rome with a budget surplus, so his reforms must have ultimately worked.

Domitian also transformed the military zones of Upper and Lower Germany into regular provinces, assigning each a governor. Our literary sources, which are hostile to Domitian, underplay this system's success, but it allowed for the transfer of legions to the volatile Danube frontier. Eventually nine legions were stationed from Vindobona (Vienna) to the Black Sea. If we pay attention to actions and not to the bias of our sources, we can see that Domitian was an intelligent and hardworking military emperor. He built roads along the frontier, with wooden watchtowers, guarded by auxiliaries, at regular intervals. Legions were stationed farther back.

Domitian was assassinated in 98. The plot did involve some Praetorians, but it was initiated by disgruntled palace staff and Senators, not the military. Indeed, the Praetorian Guard, which usually chose the next emperor under such circumstances, had no particular candidate ready, so they left the choice up to the Senate. This body chose an aged civilian politician, Marcus Cocceius Nerva. The frontier armies, however, had not been consulted. The soldiers were angry that someone with no military experience had been raised to the purple. To calm them, Nerva adopted Trajan, the commander of the Upper German legions, as his heir. Subsequently, the adoption of adult generals by emperors became a common custom. Nerva undertook no military campaigns and died in January 98 after only sixteen months on the throne.

Trajan (98–117) had worked his way up from military tribune to the command of Rome's largest army. As emperor, he was the most aggressive Roman ruler since Julius Caesar. First he fought two Dacian wars. There are no written accounts of these campaigns, but their course can be followed on Trajan's Column, still standing in the center of Rome. Trajan attacked Dacia and won a victory at the Third Battle of Tapae (101). He waited, however, until the next year before advancing on, and taking, the Dacian capital, Sarmizegethusa (near modern

49. The emperor Trajan is shown on his column conferring with high-ranking officers. This image emphasizes his actual participation in battle, in contrast with emperors who did not campaign personally. Photo: akg-images.

50. In this dramatic scene on Trajan's Column, King Decebalus of Dacia, threatened with capture, commits suicide. The soldier reaching toward the king is Tiberius Claudius Maximus, an auxiliary officer, who brought the king's head to Trajan. Photo: akg-images/Peter Connolly. Copyright Connolly through akg-images.

Orajstie, in Romania). In 103, Trajan again invaded and won another battle near the Dacian capital. Decebalus surrendered and Dacia was made a client kingdom. Two years later, however, Decebalus revolted, again invading Moesia.

Trajan raised an army of around one hundred and twenty thousand men, the largest single army ever put in the field by the Romans. The war ended with another victory near Sarmizegethusa and the death of Decebalus. The Romans captured 700 million sesterces' worth of booty, the equivalent of 25,000 talents, over 700 tons of silver. This was enough to pay for both wars and still yield an enormous profit. Dacia became a province, and its rich gold mines provided the Empire with an ongoing income. This was the last time that Rome gained such wealth from a conquest – future wars would never be as profitable. Lusius Quietus, a former Berber chief who commanded a force of Mauretanian cavalry, was rewarded with senatorial rank. He became one of Trajan's most skilled and trusted generals.

Between 106 and 114, Trajan transformed the kingdoms of both Nabataea (now southern Israel, Jordan, and northern Saudi Arabia) and of Armenia into provinces. This seems to have been in preparation for his next move – the conquest of Parthia. Unfortunately, we have neither a narrative history nor a column that enables us to follow the course of this campaign. We do know the broad outlines of the invasion, however. Trajan first seized the region around Nisibis and Singara (southeastern Turkey and northwestern Iraq) and created the Roman province of Mesopotamia. In 115, he built a fleet on the Euphrates and moved east into Adiabene (northeastern Iraq), making it into another province, Assyria. Trajan then sent two forces south, one along the Euphrates and another down the Tigris, that joined in capturing the Parthian capital of Ctesiphon. The emperor also reopened the canal from the Nile to the Red Sea, originally built by the Pharaohs, and ordered a fleet to sail around Arabia to Mesopotamia, probably with supplies.

The combined Roman army kept moving southward and took the Kingdom of Characene, on the Persian Gulf. The Parthian King Osroes, however, fought on. In 115, a very serious Jewish uprising in Cyrene, perhaps encouraged by the Parthians and led by a Jewish "king" named Lukuas (perhaps a Messiah figure), spread to Cyprus and Egypt. This forced Trajan to withdraw from Mesopotamia the troops he sent under Lusius Quietus to suppress the revolt. With his reduced forces, Trajan tried, and failed, to take the Mesopotamian desert fortress of Hatra. He was forced to retreat from Parthia, but was preparing for a counterattack when he died in 117. At that moment in time, the Roman Empire had reached its greatest extent.

Meanwhile, the Jewish revolt was foundering and its leader, Lukuas, fled to Judaea. Lusius Quietus, the Moorish-Roman general who had been fighting the rebels in several provinces, was sent to Judaea as governor. He succeeded in capturing the rebel stronghold at Lydda and massacred its inhabitants. The Jews called this the "War of Kitos" – their way of pronouncing "Quietus." It was in the summer of 117 that Trajan, returning to Rome from the east, died in Cilicia. According to one source, he was considering making Lusius Quietus his successor. Whatever the truth of this, it was Trajan's cousin Hadrian who became the next emperor. Hadrian recalled Quietus to Rome, and the next year had him executed.

Hadrian had a great deal of military experience, having served as military tribune, commanded the First Minerva in the Dacian War, and served on Trajan's staff in the Parthian War. Hadrian's approach to empire, however, was very different from that of his predecessor. Seeing the military's role as primarily defensive, he gave up the new eastern provinces of Armenia, Mesopotamia, and Assyria and created a buffer zone with Parthia made up of client kingdoms. A series of legionary forts was built to guard the eastern border with the Parthians. Indeed, Hadrian built fortifications around almost the entire boundary of the empire. On the Rhine and Danube frontier, he had a wooden palisade erected, which eventually became a two-hundred-mile earthen rampart and trench. In Britain, Hadrian ordered the construction of the eighty-mile wall that bears his name.

Hadrian moved the North African border to the Atlas Mountains and began what would eventually become a thousand-mile-long series

51. The foundations of a small stone fort, or mile castle, that served as a base for the soldiers patrolling a section of Hadrian's Wall. The wall was built in the 120s CE to protect the northern frontier of the province of Britain. Photo: akg-images/ Richard Booth.

of fortifications. At first glance, the purpose of these fortifications seems obvious: to defend against invasion. However, they played another, more important, role. Because customs rates were very high in antiquity, there was an enormous temptation to smuggle. A fortified border made sure that merchants paid their taxes. The army also took on police functions along the border, suppressing banditry. Legions and auxiliary units were increasingly garrisoned in small forts spread out along the frontier. This border policy meant that moving entire legions to meet invasion or rebellion would weaken customs collection and local security. The need to keep legions in place accelerated the practice of sending out detachments of legions (*vexillationes*).

By Hadrian's day, legionaries were mainly provincials and often the children of soldiers, despite the fact that soldiers could not legally marry. The western provinces were the main source of recruits, with the Rhine-Danube frontier being second, followed by the eastern provinces. Auxiliary cohorts were now being recruited locally and were losing their original ethnic character. Only the Praetorian Guard was still composed primarily of Italians. Most centurions now worked their way up from the ranks, which increased the army's quality.

For reasons that are not entirely clear, legionary armor shifted from the use of *lorica segmentata* to scale armor (*lorica squamata*) or mail armor (*lorica hamata*). The short, stabbing *gladius* was gradually replaced by a longer, slashing sword, the *spatha*. Around this time, a new type of helmet, called the Weisenau Type, replaced the earlier Coolus Type in use since the time of Pompey and Caesar.

These changes meant that the legionaries and auxiliaries were increasingly armed and armored in a similar fashion. Conversely, a new type of unit, the *numerus*, was raised from warlike tribes. They used traditional weapons and served under their own native chiefs. Hadrian introduced heavily armored cavalry (*cataphracti*), borrowed from the Parthians. He also used soldiers called *frumentarii* as spies and secret police. Training and field exercises were introduced to keep the army in fighting trim. An interesting change among the legions was the new

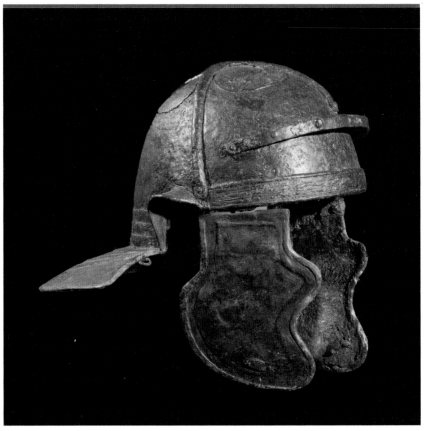

52. This second-century CE bronze helmet of the Weisenau Type was found near Hebron, Israel, then in the province of Judaea. It may date to the Bar Kokhba Revolt of 132–135 CE. Photo: Erich Lessing/Art Resource, NY.

habit of growing beards. Short hair and a cropped beard became the sign of a military man.

Despite his defensive measures, Hadrian's reign was not peaceful. There was another uprising in Judaea, named the Bar Kokhba Revolt. Led by a "Messiah," Simon bar Kosiba, the rebel Jews fought a guerrilla war. The Roman general Julius Severus utilized small units to pacify the countryside village by village. In a strategy reminiscent of modern counterinsurgencies, such as that employed by the Spanish in nineteenth-century Cuba and by the twenty-first-century Sudanese government in Darfur, systematic starvation and massacre were the methods used.

53. A *sestertius* issued by Hadrian shows the emperor at the head of standard bearers. The legend under the soldiers' feet reads *disciplina*, "military discipline," suggesting that this image represents an *ambulatio* or training march. Photo: Bildarchiv Preussischer Kulturbesitz/Art Resource, NY.

Dio Cassius claims that 580,000 Judaeans were killed in addition to those who died of starvation. This is a wild exaggeration, but civilian casualties were doubtless very heavy. After the revolt, a second legion, the Sixth Ferrata, was stationed in the province, now renamed Palestine. Other revolts occurred. One in Mauretania broke out in 123 and may have been related to the execution of Lusius Quietus. Another serious, but undated, rebellion occurred in Britain.

Sometime in Hadrian's reign, an incursion by the Alans was driven back by the governor of Cappadocia. Hadrian's defensive posture was not continued by his successors, who reverted to the idea of an expanding empire. In spite of his own long military experience when he came to the throne, Hadrian chose as his successor a senator who had never served in the army. He was adopted by Hadrian with the name of Lucius Aelius Caesar, but died in 138. Hadrian then adopted another Senator without a military background, Titus Aurelius Antoninus, but on the condition that he in turn adopt Hadrian's nephew by marriage, who became Marcus Aurelius, as well as Lucius Aelius Caesar's son, Lucius Verus.

When Hadrian died in 138, Aurelius Antoninus, known as Antoninus Pius, duly assumed the throne. Hadrian's Praetorian Prefect, Gavius Maximus, continued in the post and directed military policy. The frontier was again pushed forward in Britain and the thirty-seven-mile Antonine Wall built across the island from the Firth of Clyde to the Firth of Forth. Antoninus was proclaimed *imperator* for this campaign, although he never left Rome. The frontier in Germany was also extended. Increasingly, however, the army was becoming preoccupied with frontier incursions and revolts. Between 144 and 152, there was a series of raids by the Gaetulians and other North African tribes, and there was minor action in Dacia. In 154, the Brigantes revolted again in Britain. This uprising was crushed with troops moved from Germany and from the Antonine Wall. One result of the rebellion was the regarrisoning of Hadrian's Wall. There was a threat from the Parthians, but a show of force made them back down. Antoninus' reign is considered the epitome of the Roman Peace, or *Pax Romana*. Although the empire was never entirely at peace and the army was usually fighting a war or suppressing an uprising somewhere, it is true that most regions of the empire saw a remarkable level of peace and security.

On the death of Antoninus Pius in 161, Marcus Aurelius and Lucius Verus became co-emperors. Neither of them had any military background or training and Rome was facing serious, and simultaneous, wars at opposite ends of the empire. In the East, the Parthians, under King Vologaeses IV, invaded Armenia. The war began disastrously with the destruction of a legion, possibly the Ninth Hispana, at Parthian hands in 161 or 162. Vologaeses then ravaged the province of Syria. Also around 162, a serious uprising occurred in northern Britain. Marcus Aurelius sent Calpurnius Agricola to the island, where he spent the next three or

54. The army marches over a pontoon bridge in a scene on Trajan's Column. As an artistic convention, each soldier's pack is shown held high over his head to make it visible, although in fact his shield was strapped onto his back and the pack slung over it. Photo: Alinari/Art Resource, NY.

four years campaigning. Peace was finally achieved there, but the area north of Hadrian's Wall was lost to Rome forever.

In the East, Marcus Aurelius appointed Lucius Verus nominal commander of the Roman counterattack, but operations were actually in the hands of Statius Priscus, the governor of Cappadocia. Priscus defeated the Parthians and pushed them out of Armenia by 163. With the assistance of a brilliant legionary legate, Avidius Cassius, the Romans counterattacked into Mesopotamia. Priscus and Cassius beat the Parthians at Dura Europus (165) and took Seleucia and Ctesiphon, burning both. The Romans continued eastward, in 166 reaching Media between Ecbatana (Hamadan) and Lake Urmia, now in northwest Iran. This is the farthest east a Roman army ever campaigned. At this point, Rome and Parthia concluded a peace. The Parthians recognized both Armenia and Osrhoene as Roman client kingdoms. Lucius Verus was given the triumph, but the real victors were not forgotten. Avidius Cassius became governor of Syria.

Dura Europus became an important Roman border fortress. Modern excavations of the site have revealed dozens of papyri, including military rosters. It is clear that Marcus Aurelius did not seriously entertain the idea of occupying Parthia. He used the victory to extract important border concessions, but the decision to limit expansion to the east had clearly been made. This victory was marred, however, by an epidemic disease, almost certainly smallpox, which spread from China over the Silk Road. The disease swept through the empire and millions of Romans died. The Western world would not recover the level of population it had had in the second century for a thousand years. Some historians consider this scourge a decisive factor in Rome's decline. It certainly exacerbated the empire's increasing social, economic, and especially military, crises.

In 167 or 168, three German tribes, the Marcomanni, the Quadi, and the Vandals, swept into northern Italy. Marcus Aurelius raised money with emergency measures, even selling the silver plate from the palace, and conscripted troops, including slaves and gladiators. Not since the invasions of the Cimbri and Teutones had Rome felt threatened in this way. The emperor established two brand-new legions, the Second and Third Italica. Despite the fact that all the other legions were manned with volunteers from the provinces, these new legions were raised in Italy. It was necessary to use conscription, as sufficient volunteers could not be found. It is telling that the Romans continued the idea, rooted in the distant past, that all legions should spring from the original territory of Rome.

Marcus Aurelius and Lucius Verus both led the armies in the first year, but Verus died in 169. Now the sole emperor, Marcus continued the fight, aided by his generals Helvius Pertinax and the capable Claudius Pompeianus. In one battle a sudden rainstorm turned the battle

55. A relief representing the Roman virtue of clemency (*clementia*) as being exhibited by a conqueror. Here, Emperor Marcus Aurelius spares the lives of two barbarians begging for mercy. Photo: Nimatallah/Art Resource, NY.

to the Romans' advantage. This incident led to the first mention of large numbers of Christian soldiers in the Roman army – they took credit for the rain, claiming that their prayers to God had brought on the storm. Marcus Aurelius himself attributed the miracle to the Graeco-Egyptian god Hermes Trismegistus. The Sarmatian Iazyges attacked Dacia from the east. The next year Marcus Aurelius defeated them. Unfortunately, an unfounded rumor of the emperor's death led Avidius Cassius to revolt. When the general discovered his error, however, he committed suicide, depriving Rome of one of its greatest commanders. In 178, Marcus returned to the Danube frontier – the Quadi and Marcomanni were making trouble again. At the beginning of a new campaign in 180, however, the emperor died.

Marcus Aurelius' son, Commodus, now became emperor. Uninterested in war, he had an obsession with gladiatorial fighting. The new emperor made peace with the Quadi, the Marcomanni, and the Sarmatian Iazyges. But there were other threats. In 180, a serious invasion of Britain from the north took place, and between 180 and 184, the Romans fought in Dacia and on the far banks of the Danube. In 185, there was a revolt in Gaul. All these campaigns were brought to a conclusion due to the skill of Praetorian Prefect Sextus Tigidius Perennis. As a "reward," Commodus had Perennis executed and gave military command to a series of unskilled favorites. Consequently there were increasing numbers of mutinies and instances of soldiers deserting and turning to banditry. Clear details are sparse, but many indications of a dangerous breakdown in discipline exist. Commodus' lack of competence in military affairs, in combination with his cruelty, led to his assassination on the last day of the year 192. An experienced general, Helvius Pertinax, then took the throne.

Links: Tacitus *Agricola* 35–38 (Battle of Mons Graupius); Pliny the Younger, *Panegyricus* (Trajan's campaigns); *CIL* 8.2532, 8.18042 (Hadrian reviews the Third Augusta).

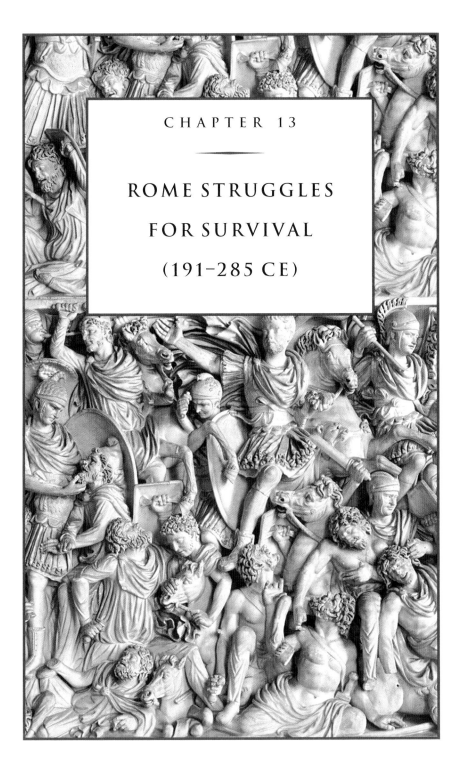

CHAPTER 13

ROME STRUGGLES
FOR SURVIVAL
(191–285 CE)

The new emperor, Helvius Pertinax, was determined to restore old-fashioned Roman discipline to the army. He decided to begin with the Praetorian Guard; but the guard refused to give up its free and easy ways and promptly murdered Pertinax. After this assassination, the Praetorians actually auctioned off the throne, with two Senators competing to offer the largest bribe to the troops. The wealthy Didius Julianus won the bid, but the frontier armies did not accept the choice made by the Praetorians. Didius Julianus lost his life and a three-year civil war ensued, as three leading generals, Septimius Severus, Pescennius Niger, and Clodius Albinus, vied for power.

Septimius Severus, who was from a Romanized Punic family in North Africa, soon seized control of Africa and Italy. Clodius Albinus ruled Spain and Britain, and Pescennius Niger took the eastern provinces. The Severans won a series of battles against Niger's forces in 193 and 194 in Thrace (the southeast Balkans) and Asia Minor. Niger sought help from the Parthians, who saw the advantage of intervening in a Roman civil war, but Severus decisively defeated Niger in 194 at the Battle of Issus (near the modern Turkish–Syrian border). After the battle, Severus drafted three new legions, called the First, Second, and Third Parthica, out of the remnants of Niger's defeated army. Severus then invaded Parthia, but after ravaging some territory and establishing the province of Osrhoene, turned back to deal with Albinus. Severus defeated the western emperor at the Battle of Lugdunum (modern Lyons, France) in mid-February 197.

Meanwhile, the Parthians had again invaded. Severus returned to the East, captured Ctesiphon, and reestablished the province of Mesopotamia. This suggests that the idea of expanding the empire varied with the personal inclinations of the emperor in this period and was not a matter of general Roman policy. In 199, however, Severus, like Trajan, tried and failed to take the desert fortress of Hatra and his war in the East stalled. Not satisfied with having established two new provinces there,

The Siege of Hatra (199 CE)

The city of Hatra, located in the desert of northern Mesopotamia, became an important border fortress in the early second century CE. It was ruled by an Arab dynasty under the loose authority of the Parthian king. A series of important sieges took place there, but they must be reconstructed on archaeological evidence, except for a few brief descriptions. In 197, Septimius Severus, responding to a Parthian invasion, captured and burned Ctesiphon. He reestablished a province called Mesopotamia, in the northern part of that region, but to hold it, or to move south, he needed to take Hatra. In 199, he moved against the fortified city.

Hatra's desert location made it a logistical challenge, even for the well-organized Romans. It was protected by two concentric walls of baked clay brick, some 32 feet (10 m) high and 10 feet (3 m) thick. There were about 40 large bastions and towers, and some 160 small towers around the walls, which allowed the defenders to fire down on besiegers. The Hatrenes were able to hold off assaults with their archers. Recently the remains of clay pots hurled at besiegers have been found at the site. What they contained is unknown – the suggestion that it was scorpions is unlikely – but whatever it was, they could only have annoyed attackers. More important, the Hatrenes made some successful sorties that destroyed the Roman siege engines. The Romans could besiege the city for only twenty days before stiff resistance and the lack of supplies – especially water – forced their retreat.

Severus campaigned in North Africa in 204–205, pushing the southern boundary of the empire farther into the Sahara Desert.

Septimius Severus completely reorganized the Praetorian Guard. All the previous guardsmen were dismissed and entirely new units raised with troops drawn from the legions. The new Praetorian Guard was expanded to forty thousand men and moved from the Praetorian camp in Rome to a new base at Castra Albana, the site of the ancient

Alba Longa (now Albano), 15 miles (25 km) from Rome. The Second Parthica was also stationed there, the first legion to be permanently garrisoned in Italy. The large force of Praetorians and legionaries served not only to secure the city of Rome but was a real strategic reserve that could back up the frontier armies. The Praetorian Prefect now became increasingly an administrative official concerned with legal affairs.

Severus has a reputation as a soldier-emperor and it is true that he understood that real power lay in the military. He advised his sons to "enrich the soldiers and despise everyone else." A legionary's pay was increased from 1,200 to 2,000 sesterces a year, and they were given the right to marry legally. The increase in pay doubtless had something to do with the need of the soldiers to support their wives and children, who were now Roman citizens. There is no question that Severus was very popular with the army. On the other hand, he did not surround himself only with soldiers; both military men and civilians entered the empire's administration in about the same proportion as before.

In 208, Severus went to Britain in response to Caledonian attacks against the province's northern border. Archaeological evidence suggests that he devastated those lands and virtually exterminated that nation. The strategy, although cruel, apparently worked, as the border was peaceful for decades. Severus may have intended to complete the conquest of the island of Britain, but while on this campaign he died at Eboricum (now the city of York, England) in 211.

Severus' son and successor, Caracalla, again dramatically increased the soldiers' pay from 2,000 to 3,000 sesterces a year, although this was offset by the introduction of a new coin called the *antoninianus*. The pay raises of the first two Severan emperors must have put an enormous strain on the imperial treasury: the Roman Empire's budget for military pay had increased 250 percent in only a decade! In 212, Caracalla issued a law called the Antonine Constitution granting Roman citizenship to virtually all the free inhabitants of the empire, thus eliminating the legal difference between legionaries and auxiliaries. Although he had a bad reputation among the senatorial historians who are our main sources for his reign, Caracalla was a competent commander-in-chief.

56. In a scene on the sarcophagus of Hostilian, who ruled Rome for one month in July 251 CE, the emperor is shown leading soldiers to victory over barbarians. In fact, Hostilian never fought in battle. Photo: Scala/Art Resource, NY.

Beginning in 213, Caracalla launched a series of successful campaigns, first defeating the German Cenni in a battle in which the Second Traiana distinguished itself, and then beating the Alamanni. The next year, he overcame the Dacians. In 215, he sailed to Alexandria and ordered the drafting of that city's citizens into the army. He may have done this to emphasize that his grant of universal citizenship entailed the responsibility of military service. The Alexandrians did not take kindly to this, however. The antidraft riot in the city was so serious that at least one legion had to be deployed and there was a massacre of the local populace. The next year, Caracalla launched an invasion of Parthia. Although the war was succeeding, and the city of Arbela (now Irbil in northeastern Iraq) had been taken, Caracalla was nonetheless assassinated by his Praetorian Prefect, Marcus Opellius Macrinus, who usurped the throne. The Parthians promptly defeated Macrinus at the Battle of Nisibis.

Anxious to end the war and secure his shaky throne, Macrinus paid an indemnity of 20 million sesterces to the Parthians. The new emperor was forced to cancel the army's recent pay raise to obtain sufficient money. This move gave Caracalla's aunt, Julia Maesa, an opportunity to convince the eastern legions to support the cause of her grandson, known to history as Elagabalus. At the Battle of Antioch in 218, Macrinus was defeated. The soldiers got their raise, though this must have caused a serious fiscal crisis. Elagabalus' government was dominated by three of his female relatives: his grandmother, Julia Maesa, his mother, Julia Soaemias, and his aunt, Julia Mamaea. These women were not only the political leaders in Rome, but also were involved in military decision making. Julia Mamaea even accompanied the army on campaign. The role of imperial women as actual (although not official) Roman rulers and commanders-in-chief has not been sufficiently appreciated by historians. Elagabalus was very unpopular, both with the army and the Senate, so Julia Mamaea arranged to have her thirteen-year-old son, Alexander Severus, made co-emperor in 221. The next year, the Praetorian Guard murdered Elagabalus and his mother, Julia Soaemias. Alexander Severus became the sole emperor, though Julia Mamaea ran the show.

Meanwhile, the Parthians were overthrown in Persia by a more aggressive and dangerous enemy, the Sassanid dynasty. In 224, Ardashir defeated the last Parthian king and was crowned the first Sassanid shah, or king, in 226. He reformed the Persian army, introducing very heavy cavalry called *clibinarii*. These horsemen wore iron mail and a metal face mask. (Both the medieval Western knight and the Japanese samurai are descended from this Persian heavy cavalryman.) The Sassanids' central Asian allies such as the Kushans, who lived in what is today Afghanistan, provided units of horse archers. The Sassanids also used war elephants. Infantry was less important: conscripted peasants provided low-quality spearmen, though Sassanid archers were better trained. The Sassanids also developed an effective siege train, unlike the Parthians. In 228, Ardashir tried, and failed, to take Hatra, whose king had now turned to the Romans for help. The next year the Persians succeeded in taking back Mesopotamia. It is noteworthy that some of the Roman garrisons there deserted to the invaders. Lack of discipline was a problem elsewhere as well. In 228, the Praetorian Guard murdered their commander, Ulpian, who was famous as a legal scholar rather than as a military man, indicating the changing nature of the Prefect's job.

In 231, Alexander Severus launched a counteroffensive against the Sassanids. He succeeded in reconquering Mesopotamia and won victories in Armenia and Media. Ardashir, however, defeated a Roman force that had penetrated to Ctesiphon, and an invasion by the German Alamanni forced Alexander to withdraw his forces to meet that danger. Alexander led an army to the threatened region, but then decided it was cheaper to buy off the enemy. At Rome, political and military decisions were now being driven by a lack of money in the imperial treasury. The troops were furious, and, led by an officer named Maximinus Thrax, they murdered Alexander Severus and his mother, Julia Mamaea, who was accompanying the army (235).

This military revolt ended the Severan dynasty, and ushered in a fifty-year period of instability referred to by historians as the Crisis of the Third Century. During this time there were endemic civil wars and increased incursions by the Germans from the north, by the Sassanid Persians in the East, and by desert tribes in North Africa. Remarkably, though, there were also campaigns of conquest, in which the soldier-emperors of the period tried to extend Rome's borders.

The new emperor, Maximinus Thrax (the Thracian), had been born a peasant and recruited as a common soldier. He was the first, though not the last, man to rise from poverty to the highest office in the Empire. The army was virtually the only institution in Rome that allowed such social mobility. A man of great size and strength, but also very intelligent, Maximinus became first a centurion, then was promoted to the equestrian order. Now emperor, he paid a large donative to the army and led it on a victorious campaign against the Alamanni. Maximinus not only led the army but also fought in the ranks. He subsequently made successful attacks on the Sarmatians and the Carpi.

In Africa, however, the governor, Marcus Antonius Gordianus, proclaimed himself emperor as Gordion I along with his son, Gordian II. The elder Gordian was in his seventies, was an experienced administrator,

57. Two legionaries shown in fighting poses from a relief found in the legionary fortress at Mogontiacum (Mainz). The lead soldier crouches with his *gladius* at the ready, while behind him a comrade shields him from above. Photo: Erich Lessing/Art Resource, NY.

and had military experience, having commanded the Fourth Scythica in Syria. The governor of the neighboring province, Numidia, remained loyal to Maximinus and invaded with the Third Augusta. The inexperienced Gordian II met him, leading a force of local militia, and was defeated at the Battle of Carthage in 238. At this point, the Senate elected two co-emperors, Marcus Clodius Pupienus and Decius Caelius Balbinus, on the model of the two consuls who had ruled during the republic. The thirteen-year-old grandson of Gordian I, who is called Gordian III, was made Caesar. Pupienus was put in charge of the army. It was said that he began his career as a *primus pilus*, which historians have doubted, but he certainly had held military command as a military tribune and legionary commander.

Maximinus marched south with his army to retake Rome. The Senate had ordered the land he had to traverse abandoned and stripped of supplies, and two Senators, Rutilius Crispinus and Tullius Menophilus, accompanied a small body of regular troops into Aquilea. The Senators led the soldiers and civilians of Aquilea in a spirited defense. Maximinus' advance bogged down in a siege of the city. He had not paid enough attention to his food supplies, but stubbornly refused to give up the siege. Finally, his hungry soldiers murdered him.

Pupienus had marched north with an army, but now prudently paid Maximinus' troops a large donative to return to duty. He returned to Rome triumphantly, guarded by an escort of German bodyguards. The co-emperors and the Senate, however, were unable to keep control over the Praetorian Guard, and when Pupienus, forgetting the example of Julius Caesar, dismissed his bodyguards, a group of Praetorians broke into the palace and murdered both Pupienus and Balbinus. Gordian III became the emperor, but it was the Praetorian Prefect, Gaius Furius Timesitheus, who wielded power. The arrangement worked out well, as the young emperor was popular and the Prefect was competent. This was fortunate, as serious fighting immediately broke out with Persia. Between 238 and 241, three important Roman border towns, Nisibis, Carrhae, and Hatra, fell to the Sassanids. Sufficient Roman forces did not arrive on the frontier until 242, due to the threat of German attacks on the Danube.

Timesitheus led the Roman army east and defeated the Persians at the Battle of Rhesaina (243). When Timesitheus died, Julius Philippus, an Arab-Roman officer from Palestine, became Praetorian Prefect. The next year (244), Philippus accompanied Gordian III, now eighteen, on a campaign that pushed the Persians all the way to Ctesiphon. Near the Persian capital either the emperor was killed in battle or was assassinated. In any case, Julius Philippus seized the throne.

Philip the Arab, as he is known to history, was an able commander and a strategic thinker. He negotiated a peace with the Persians, which allowed him to turn to the empire's northern border, where he defeated the Germans in 245, and another tribe, the Carpi, who had invaded Dacia, in 247. Unfortunately, Philip had demonstrated the ease in which a military man could become emperor. When he sent one of his generals, Gaius Messius Decius, to Pannonia to put down a revolt, the legions there proclaimed Decius emperor. The usurper invaded Italy and defeated and killed Philip at the Battle of Verona (249). Although historians generally dislike Decius – he is best known for his persecution of Christians – he did beat back a Gothic invasion of Thrace at Philippopolis. The Goths returned, however, defeating and killing Decius and his son at the Battle of Abrittus (in modern Bulgaria) in 251. The army raised a popular and capable general, Trebonian Gallus, to be emperor. Trebonian paid off the Goths, but unfortunately for him this did not leave enough money to pay what the new Persian king, Shapur I, had demanded for peace in the East. To make matters worse, a rival commander, Aemilius Aemilianus, marched against Trebonian, whose own troops defected. Aemilianus' own reign lasted only four months. He was defeated and replaced by Valerian, commander of the Upper Rhine army, who made his son, Gallienus, his co-emperor.

In 253, the Sassanid shah, Shapur I, invaded Roman territory. He first destroyed a Roman army at the Battle of Barbalissos and then captured and sacked Antioch. A few years later, the fortress of Dura Europus fell. The Persians besieged Edessa in 259. Valerian marched to relieve the city, but when he entered the Persian camp to negotiate a peace agreement, the Sassanids treacherously seized him. A Roman emperor had never before been captured alive. Near Shiraz in Iran there remains a large stone relief of Valerian kneeling before the Persian shah. According to one source, Shapur publicly displayed the captured emperor in a cage and then killed him, displaying his straw-stuffed body in one of his palaces. The Persians then attacked and defeated the now leaderless Romans, killing or capturing tens of thousands. Shapur went on to take both Edessa and Antioch.

From 253 to 260, while Valerian had been fighting in the East, his son Gallienus had defeated the Goths, and other German tribes, along the Rhine and Danube frontiers. On Valerian's death, Gallienus became sole emperor. Although he is far from famous, it was Gallienus who saved the Roman Empire. The year 260 was one of unprecedented revolt and invasion. In addition to the Persian onslaught, the Rhine defenses collapsed and the Franks, a German tribe, poured over the border, devastating southern Gaul. Facing this invasion without support from the central government, a general named Marcus Cassianus Postumus declared himself emperor. Postumus was a Batavian who had apparently worked his way up from the ranks to become a governor and general. The provinces of Britain, Gaul, Spain, and Germany recognized him, and Postumus defeated forces loyal to the central government. He was, however, unable to prevent the marauding Franks from moving into Spain, sacking Tarraco (now Tarragona), and crossing over into North Africa.

In the East, two generals named Macrianus and Callista gathered the remnants of Valerian's defeated eastern army and seized control of Mesopotamia. After subduing a Persian force that was plundering the area, they proclaimed Macrianus' two sons, one also named Macrianus and the other Quietus, to be Roman emperors. Simultaneously, there was a serious revolt in Pannonia, led by a general named Ingenuus, and an invasion of northern Italy by the Alamanni.

Faced with so many revolts and invasions, Gallienus acted decisively. He first defeated the Alamanni near Milan, then moved north into Pannonia and beat Ingenuus at the First Battle of Mursa (in what is now Croatia). In 261, Gallienus allied himself with Odenathus, the client king of Palmyra in Syria. He recognized the king's control over the eastern provinces in exchange for help in crushing Macrianus and Quietus. Gallienus' general Aureolus defeated Macrianus in Thrace, and Odenathus defeated Quietus in Syria. Odenathus was given the title "Corrector of All the East" and attacked the Persians in 264–265, recapturing Mesopotamia and besieging Ctesiphon. In the West, the rival emperor Postumus had set up a duplicate Roman administration with its own Senate and consuls. He ruled over Gaul, Britain, Spain, and Raetia (northern Switzerland).

Although he was busy defending the Roman frontier from German attacks, Gallienus was also committed to trying to reunite a divided Roman Empire. In 265, Gallienus invaded Postumus' Western Empire. He beat Postumus twice in battle but was himself seriously wounded by an arrow and forced to withdraw. In 267, two German tribes, the Goths and the Herulians, who lived in southern Russia, sailed across the Black Sea and attacked Asia Minor. Odenathus led an expedition against them but was assassinated during this campaign. His wife, Zenobia, took control, ruling on behalf of their young son, Vaballathus. She would continue to rule, and fight, in the East for years. Gallienus defeated the Goths and Herulians in 268, but his reign, and his life, would soon end through treachery.

For centuries, students of history have been asking why the Roman Empire fell in 476. Perhaps a better question would be why it did not collapse in the 260s. There had been simultaneous revolts in Gaul, Pannonia, Mesopotamia, and Syria. The Persians had broken through the eastern frontier and the Germans had poured over the Rhine and the Black Sea. What held Rome together?

One answer is certainly the army. Rome's soldiers remained loyal; they did not join the invading barbarians in looting and plundering, but fought them in hard and dangerous battles. Although local commanders raised themselves to the imperial throne, they took it upon themselves to defeat Rome's enemies in the regions they controlled rather than setting up power-sharing relationships with the barbarians, as they might have done. The personality and capability of the emperor himself was another important factor in Rome's survival of this period. While the Empire continued to teeter on the edge of collapse, it was Gallienus who held it together. He displayed extraordinary skill as a general and a political leader, suppressing revolts where he could and allying himself with those Roman rebels he could not crush. On the other hand, he was unremitting in his wars against foreign invaders.

Gallienus was also responsible for a number of important military reforms – for example, removing Senators from military command and replacing them with equestrians, which resulted in more effectiveness if not loyalty. He also significantly increased the number of cavalry in the Roman army, allowing the army to respond quickly to crises. In addition, Gallienus created a mobile reserve, called the *comitatus*, that he stationed around Mediolanum (now Milan) in northern Italy. The commander of the new *comitatus* force was Acilius Manius Aureolus, who had defeated Macrianus. Although he had loyally served Gallienus up to this point, Aureolus revolted in 268. At first he seems to have done so in support of the western emperor, Postumus, but later he claimed the throne himself. Gallienus led an army to Milan, but during the siege, his generals successfully conspired to murder him; he was replaced by one of them, named Claudius.

Until the reign of Claudius II (268–270), all the emperors of this period had been aristocrats, with the exception of Maximinus Thrax. For the rest of the third century, most of the emperors would be commoners who had risen to power within the military. These soldier-emperors would rebuild the empire; but they would also transform it. Claudius II reigned for only two years, but he did succeed in winning a decisive victory over an invading Gothic army at Naissus (modern Nish in Serbia). For this reason he is known to history as Gothicus – conqueror of the Goths. The next year, Claudius II defeated an invading force of Alamanni at the Battle of Lake Benacus (now Lake Garda in northern Italy). In 269, Western Emperor Postumus was murdered and succeeded by a series of short-lived soldier-emperors. Claudius II turned his attention westward, and in a series of campaigns Spain and southern Gaul were regained by the central government. While he was preparing an expedition against the Vandals, who had invaded Pannonia, Claudius II died in January 270, probably of smallpox or measles.

The middle of the third century also saw a severe economic crisis. The basic coinage was continuously debased with copper alloy, so it contained less and less silver. Partially as a result, there was a wild inflation that devastated the economy. With the money valueless, the emperors turned to taxing localities "in kind," requiring them to give food and clothing directly to the army. This system became known as the *annona*. However, the emperors did not shrink or debase the gold coins that were used to pay soldiers and bribe barbarians.

In addition to Gallienus' reforms, other changes were made within the military during this period. The senior centurion, the *primus pilus*, was removed from his combat command position in the late third century and made a supply officer. This may reflect the increasing difficulty in organizing logistics, given the confused circumstances of the time. In addition, the legionary cavalry was removed from their units and gathered together to form elite units called *promoti*. Due to the increased use of *vexillationes*, legions completely ceased to fight together as units. The last known legion to do so was the Second Parthica in the 240s. Another change was the addition of a new type of soldier called the *lanciarius*. There were actually two types of *lancea* (the word from which the English "lance" derives): one was a thrusting spear and the other a javelin. We find both infantry and cavalry *lanciarii*, both in the auxiliaries and in the legions.

After Claudius' death, a general of the Danubian army, Domitius Aurelianus, whom we call Aurelian, seized power. Aurelian was another key figure in the Empire's survival. The son of a poor tenant farmer, he had joined the army and risen through the ranks, serving with distinction on the Danube frontier. By the time he had reached his fifties he was commanding a cavalry unit in northern Italy. Now, as emperor, Aurelian was faced with a series of German invasions. In the years following 270, he defeated three invading barbarian armies – first the Juthingi (also known as Jutes), then the Vandals, and finally the Goths. Despite these victories, Aurelian decided to abandon Dacia. Although

58. A view of the walls of Rome built by the emperor Aurelian between 271 and 275 CE, which still surround much of the city. They were made of brick, ultimately 16 meters (52 feet) high, with towers every hundred Roman feet apart. Photo: Werner Forman/Art Resource, NY.

this made strategic sense, significantly lessening the length of Rome's northern border, it was a difficult decision for any Roman leader to deliberately reduce the empire's size. Aurelian had other concerns. He faced an invasion of the Sarmatian Iazyges from the steppes, which he defeated; but then he lost against a battle with a combined force of German tribes. When the Germans divided up their forces to plunder, however, Aurelian drove them over the border. Returning to Rome, Aurelian brutally put down an urban riot with his soldiers, earning him his nickname "The Iron Fist" (*manu ad ferrum*). He also began construction of the enormous baked brick walls around Rome. Originally rising to the height of 8 m (26.2 ft), they extended for 18.8 km (11.5 miles) and had 381 towers. Doubled in height in the fifth century, they can still be seen surrounding the city.

In the eastern provinces, Odenathus' widow, the Palmyrene queen Zenobia, had at first claimed to rule on behalf of Rome. By 270 she

Zenobia (ca. 240–ca. 285)

Zenobia Bat-Zabai was the daughter of an Arab sheik, Zabai, who had the Roman name Julius Aurelius Zenobius. It is possible that her mother was an Egyptian Greek, as she claimed to be descended from Cleopatra. We know nothing of her life until sometime around 260 she married Septimius Odenathus, the king of Palmyra, whose family had received Roman citizenship from one of the Severan emperors. On Odenathus' death in 267, Zenobia seized direct control of his realm, ruling on behalf of her son, Vaballathus. She led the Palmyrene armies personally, and in 269 captured Bostra (modern Bursa in Jordan) and Antioch. She then invaded Egypt and defeated its governor. The next year, she led another expediton, bringing Asia Minor under Palmyrene control.

In 272, Aurelian led an expedition to reconquer the East. Zenobia tried to stop the Romans at Antioch and again at Emesa, but was defeated both times. Returning to Palmyra, she took the title of Augusta, or Empress, probably in a desperate attempt to rally support. Aurelian took Palmyra, however, and although Zenobia escaped on camelback, she was soon captured. One tradition says that she died on the way to Rome; another claims that Aurelian displayed her in a triumph but her life was spared, and that she subsequently married a Roman Senator.

abandoned this pretense and seized control of Egypt and Asia Minor. In 272, she declared her son Vaballathus to be emperor. Almost immediately, Aurelian defeated the Palmyrene army in two battles at Antioch and at Emesa, then took Palmyra itself after a short siege. After his victory, Aurelian marched to the Danube and defeated an invasion by the Carpi. While there, he heard that Palmyra had revolted again, and in 273 he returned and obliterated the city. An uprising in Egypt, led by a wealthy merchant named Firmus in support of Palmyra, was also suppressed. Aurelian then marched to northern Italy where he defeated

59. A bronze medallion of the emperor Tacitus (275–276 CE), with the legend *adventus Aug(usti):* "Arrival of the Emperor (in Rome)." Tacitus is preceded by the goddess Victory and followed by two soldiers representing the army. Photo: Bildarchiv Preussischer Kulturbesitz/Art Resource, NY.

yet another barbarian incursion, and in the next year, he invaded the still independent Western Empire. He defeated the westerners at a battle near what is now Châlons-sur-Marne in France (274), bringing Gaul, Spain, and Britain back under central control.

After some fifteen years, the divided empire was again united under one rule. Aurelian made some monetary reforms, but neither he nor later emperors were able to solve a fundamental problem: it was increasingly difficult to raise the money that the empire's large standing army required. In 275 Aurelian went east to deal with the Sassanid Persians, but he was murdered en route in a conspiracy organized by one of his secretaries. There being no obvious successor, the army asked the

Senate to choose one. A senior Senator named Marcus Claudius Tacitus became the new emperor.

Although Tacitus was now seventy-five years old, he marched against the Goths, who had again invaded Asia Minor, and defeated them. He died in April 276, either from natural causes or assassination (the sources disagree on this point). The next emperor, Florian, reigned for only a few months before being murdered by his troops. The army then raised Marcus Aurelius Probus, another Danubian general of peasant origin, to the throne. Almost immediately, the Rhine frontier collapsed under the weight of German incursions. In 277 Probus defeated the Franks and the Alamanni in Gaul and the next year won victories over the Vandals and the Goths in Rhaetia. He also campaigned in Asia Minor and Egypt, suppressing bandit gangs that had grown into small armies. The army was clearly still able to fight effectively, but the soldiers were becoming increasingly difficult to control. When in 282 Probus tried to order some troops to perform manual labor on a building project, they murdered him. The Praetorian Prefect, Marcus Aurelius Carus, who may well have had something do with Probus' death, became the next emperor. Carus also did much campaigning in his short reign. In 282 he defeated the German Quadi and the Sarmatians along the Danube. The next year he led a successful expedition against Persia, capturing Ctesiphon. There he died – according to the official story, struck by lightning, but quite possibly assassinated. His son Carinus had only a short reign before he too died, probably murdered. A general named Diocles then defeated another son of Carus at the Battle of the River Margus. Diocles became emperor with the Latinized name Diocletian. With his accession, the dizzying succession of soldier-emperors was halted and the Empire put on a firm footing.

Links: Historia Augusta, *Septimius Severus* 8.6–11.9 (civil war); *the Two Maximini* 1.4–8.2 (Maximinus Thrax's rise from peasant to emperor); Fronto, *Letters to Lucius Verus* 2 (on the eastern campaign).

CHAPTER 14

ROME FIGHTS BACK

(285–378 CE)

Diocletian was the last, and greatest, of the third-century soldier-emperors. He created what we call the Late Roman Empire, which survived for another two hundred years in the West and in one form or another for twelve hundred years in the East. Diocletian was born in what is today Croatia. The Balkans had become an important recruiting ground for the Roman army and would remain so for hundreds of years. Diocletian joined the army and rose to command the cavalry of the Praetorian Guard, which put him in a position to seize power. After being proclaimed emperor by the Praetorians, Diocletian moved against Carinus, defeating him at the Battle of Margus (May 285). After this victory he named a fellow-soldier and friend, Marcus Aurelius Valerius Maximianus, known as Maximian, as vice-emperor. The next year, Diocletian again promoted him, to the rank of co-emperor, and assigned him the western part of the empire. Mediolanum (Milan), a major military base, was made the seat of the western emperor rather than the politically dangerous Rome, and in the East, Diocletian made the strategically located Nicomedia his capital.

The two men operated as a strategic team: Maximian suppressed a revolt of Gallic peasants who called themselves the Bacaudae, and Diocletian moved against barbarian invaders. The latter used a carrot-and-stick approach: in 288 he gave a Frankish chief the title "King of the Franks," but, on the other hand, he fought and defeated the Alamanni (288/9), Sarmatians (289, 292), and Arabs (290).

In 293 Diocletian established the political system known as the Tetrarchy: he continued as emperor in the East and assigned another risen-from-the-ranks general, Galerius, to be vice-emperor. Maximian remained emperor in the West, with Constantius Chlorus as western vice-emperor. The idea was to set up a regular succession of experienced soldier-emperors, without the need for civil war or accident of birth to provide quality leaders. Diocletian's idea of succession was based on the notion that the emperor should choose a capable – theoretically the most capable – military and political figure to succeed him. Although the system was not perfect, it had a lot to recommend it; but it had to compete with the powerful and entrenched idea of inheritance, whereby power and wealth were passed on to sons, regardless of their competence. The system also meant that those leading military figures who were shut out of the succession were very unhappy about it. For example, Carausius, commander of the Channel fleet, did not accept the Tetrachy and revolted, setting up an independent empire in Britain. Maximian could not dislodge him, but Constantius Chlorus took charge and defeated Carausius, a victory that led to the eventual return of Britain to Roman control.

In 297, Diocletian, with the help of a nomadic tribe called the Nobatae, crushed a revolt of the Blemmyes, a people who lived in Upper Egypt. Diocletian and his Caesar, or vice emperor, Galerius fought a series of very successful wars against the Persian shah Narses in 296–298. This resulted in the capture, for the first time, of territory on the eastern bank of the Tigris. Clearly a half-century of civil war had not quenched the Roman Empire's desire for expansion, only its ability to expand. Diocletian himself put down a revolt in Egypt led by Domitius Domitianus.

Diocletian also instituted a series of military reforms. Out of necessity, the third-century emperors had abandoned the linear, frontier defense of the early empire for a more mobile strategy. Diocletian recognized that, since the emperor now moved around the empire rather than staying in Rome, the lack of a mobile army was a great drawback. He was determined to develop such a force. Cavalry elements of the Praetorian Guard, called *equites promoti*, were combined to compose a force that could accompany the emperor wherever he went. Another new unit, the *protectores*, made up an elite force and served to groom candidates for high rank. *Vexillationes* of about a thousand men drawn from two elite legions, called the Herculiani and Ioviani, as well as other picked legionary and auxiliary forces, also marched with Diocletian. This new force, much more of an army than an imperial guard, was called the *comitatus* or *comitatenses*, meaning "those who accompany the emperor."

60. A scene from the Arch of Constantine, completed in 315 CE, probably represents the siege of Verona. Constantine's soldiers, with round shields and spears, attack Maxentius' – a rare example of Romans depicted killing other Romans. Photo © Archive Timothy McCarthy/Art Resources, NY.

61. Reenactors wear reconstructed equipment of fourth-century CE Roman infantry. The round or oval shields and scale armor are characteristic of the late Empire, as are the lances. Photo: The Batavi Late Roman Reenactment Group www.thebatavi.co.uk

The army as a whole, of course, still needed to guard thousands of miles of imperial borders, called in Latin the *limes*. There had been thirty-nine legions at the beginning of Diocletian's reign; by its end the number had almost doubled. This came about partly by combining and promoting auxiliary units. The number of auxiliaries was not increased, and the result was that any remaining distinction between legions and auxiliary units was lost. Diocletian assigned these frontier troops, called *limitanei*, to the task of linear defense. The *limitanei* were once thought to be a sort of peasant militia who were given land in exchange for military service. It is now known, however, that they were regular soldiers, although as frontier troops they were not as well paid as the mobile forces (*comitatenses*). *Limitanei* were generally kept in their posts and were recruited more and more from the children of soldiers, "barbarian" volunteers, and prisoners of war.

As a general rule, high officers in the mobile army bore the title of "count" (*comes*, pl. *comites*), but frontier armies were commanded by a "duke" (*dux*, pl. *duces*). These terms, however, were sometimes used loosely to mean "general" in any context. Diocletian further reduced the military functions of the Praetorian Prefects, which were gradually taken over by a new type of general, the *magister*. There were two types: *magister peditum* and *magister equitum*, literally "Master of Infantry" and "Master of Cavalry," collectively known as *magistri militum*, "Masters of Soldiers." These high-ranking officers not only took over the military administrative functions formerly carried out by the Praetorian Prefects, but also served as field commanders. One of Diocletian's most important reforms was regularizing the *annona*, or in-kind supply, that had sprung up as an ad hoc system in the chaotic years of the third century. He regularized the giving of "donatives," the gifts (or bribes) that soldiers had come to expect, which now became an element of the soldiers' pay.

In 305, Diocletian retired and forced a reluctant Maximian to do the same. Galerius now became the eastern emperor and appointed his nephew, Maximinus Daia, who had served as a cavalryman before entering the Imperial Guard, as vice-emperor. Galerius also arranged for another soldier from Illyria, Severus, to be vice-emperor to Constantius

Chlorus, now the western emperor. The Tetrarchy began to unravel when Constantius Chlorus died at Eboricum (York, England) in 306. Chlorus had been fighting a series of campaigns in Britain, accompanied by his son Constantine. The vice-emperor Severus duly became the new western emperor at Mediolanum, but the army in Britain proclaimed Constantine emperor. When Severus tried to register the plebeian population at Rome, apparently thinking of reintroducing conscription to fight Constantine, a revolt broke out. Maximian's son Maxentius led the uprising, and both Italy and Africa supported him.

When Severus marched on Rome with an army from Mediolanum in late 306, Maxentius made his father, Maximian, still popular with the troops, his co-emperor. When Severus arrived at the walls of Rome, there were massive desertions of his force to Maxentius and Maximian. Severus retreated to Ravenna, and when followed by Maximian, surrendered and abdicated. Maximian then went to arrange an alliance with Constantine, recognizing him as emperor and offering him his daughter Fausta (Maxentius' sister) in marriage. At this point, with a singular lack of paternal feeling, Maximian attempted to overthrow his son, but the army supported Maxentius and Maximian fled. In 308, Eastern Emperor Galerius, along with Diocletian and Maximian, held a conference. They decided to make Licinianus Licinius (also of peasant origin) the western emperor. Maxentius was declared a usurper. By now the Tetrarchy's elaborate system of succession had completely collapsed. By 311, when Galerius died, there were two emperors in the East, Licinius and Maximinus Daia, and two in the West, Constantine, who controlled Britain and Gaul, and Maxentius, who ruled Italy, Spain, and Africa.

In 312, although Maxentius' army outnumbered his by more than two to one, Constantine boldly invaded Italy. Moving rapidly, he won victories at Turin and Verona. Maxentius met Constantine with most of his forces, including the Praetorian Guard, at the Milvian Bridge, one of the major crossings over the Tiber. Constantine won a decisive victory over Maxentius and took Rome. Meanwhile, in the East, Licinius and Maximinus Daia had fallen out. Licinius allied himself with Constantine, and Daia with Maxentius. Hearing of the latter's defeat, Daia invaded

---

The Battle of Milvian Bridge (312 CE)

The Milvian Bridge crossed the Tiber just north of Rome. Two claimants for the Roman throne met there on October 28, 312 to determine control over the western half of the empire. Constantine commanded some fifty thousand men and his opponent, Maxentius, defended the capital with seventy-five thousand. The bishop Eusebius later claimed that Constantine told him that before the battle he had dreamed the Christian God told him to put *chi* and *rho*, the first two Greek letters in Christ's name, on the shields of his soldiers. Constantine is also said to have had a heavenly vision during the battle, in which a cross appeared in the sky bearing the words *In Hoc Signo Vinces*, "By this sign you will conquer." These stories are probably inventions, but they are more detailed than those of the battle's course, about which we know little.

The Battle of Milvian Bridge seems to have been decided primarily in cavalry fights on the flanks. Constantine's horse drove back his enemy. Maxentius' infantry force centered on the Praetorian Guard, which broke, leading to a general rout. Many soldiers, including Maxentius himself, retreated over a pontoon bridge; but when it collapsed, the emperor, and many of his troops, drowned in the river. After the battle, Maxentius' followers hastily, but carefully, buried the imperial regalia on the Palatine Hill to prevent them falling into Constantine's hands. They have recently been found, virtually intact, by archaeologists.

---

the Balkans with seventy thousand men, but was defeated at the Battle of Campus Serenus or Tzirallum in April 313.

There were now only two emperors, but Constantine considered that to be one too many. In 324, he defeated Licinius, first at Adrianople (now Edirne in the Balkans), then at Chrysopolis (now part of Istanbul). For the first time in decades, there was a single Roman emperor. Due to their opposition to him at the Milvian Bridge, Constantine disbanded the Praetorian Guard and demolished their camp. This ended three hundred years of Praetorian domination in the city of Rome. He replaced them with new Imperial Guard regiments called the *scholae*, five in the West and seven in the East. In addition, there was a personal bodyguard called *protectores* and *domestici*. Under Diocletian's reign the mobile army had been relatively small. Constantine expanded it considerably: he eventually set the *comitatenses* up in several strategic areas around the empire, such as at Milan and Trier. They served both as a reserve force and as a hedge against revolt. To administer the eastern half of the empire, Constantine built a second capital at the site of Byzantium, which he named New Rome. It was soon known as Constantinople and is today the city of Istanbul, Turkey.

Constantine left the static defense forces, now known both as river-bank troops (*riparii*) and frontier troops (*limitanei*) in place. Diocletian had tried to restore the field fortification system, and this trend was continued by Constantine, who also finished the job of dividing military and civilian authority. Praetorian Prefect was now a purely civilian post. Command of the military was now completely in the hands of the Master of Soldiers (*magister militum*). This change meant that the military and civilian bureaucracies were permanently separated. Although bureaucrats were technically soldiers and enrolled in one enormous "legion," this division resulted both in better military administration and in the ability to call up troops without affecting local government, even in rural areas. Thus divided, both civilian and military leaders could concentrate on their own spheres. This was more efficient than the previous administrative practice and also served as a check on rebellion. At some point in his reign, Constantine became a Christian and set the Roman Empire on the course of becoming a Christian one. Although Christian soldiers were no doubt favored, he made no effort to Christianize the military, and pagan (and Jewish) troops were allowed to worship as they pleased. He did use the army, though, to intervene in church affairs.

Despite his attention to military reform, Constantine did relatively little fighting after the civil war. The one major exception was in 332, when he repulsed a Gothic invasion on the Danube. Constantine completely rejected Diocletian's system of succession, dividing the empire among his three sons. Constantine II was assigned Britain, Gaul, and Spain; Constans, Italy, Africa, and Illyricum; and Constantius II, the eastern provinces. When Constantine was dying in 337, he expected that his three sons would rule together in fraternal harmony. Only three years after his death, however, Constantine II invaded northern Italy and was defeated and killed by his brother Constans at Aquilea (340). For the next ten years, the two brothers Constans and Constantius II ruled as the emperors of the East and West respectively. When, after a long period of peace with Persia, the Sassanids launched an invasion under Shapur II, Constantius II led the resistance. Shapur withdrew his forces after an unsuccessful siege of Singara (344), southeast of Nisibis, now in south-eastern Turkey.

In 350, there was a revolt against the Christian emperors led by a pagan Senator, Magnus Magnentius. He raised an army at Augustodunum (now Autun, in eastern France) and killed Constans. Constantius II then defeated Magnentius at the Second Battle of Mursa (351). Magnentius continued to resist until 353, when he finally committed suicide to avoid capture. Over the course of the fourth century, Christianity played an increasingly important role in the army. The replacement of pagan religion in the army by a militarized Christianity is evident in the stories of the saints. At first, Christians refused to bear arms, leading to stories of the soldier-martyrs (such as Saint Sebastian). Despite the injunctions against killing (or even thinking about killing) in the New Testament, by the fourth century the idea of a Christian soldier had become acceptable to virtually all Christians. The stories of martyrs like Saint George reflect this change. George was born into a Christian military family in Cappadocia in the 280s and rose to high rank, becoming a *comes*, or count, in the army of Diocletian. When, in the Great Persecution, Diocletian ordered all soldiers to sacrifice to the pagan gods, George refused, and was tortured and beheaded. (While Saint George was a real person, the story of his slaying a dragon is borrowed from an ancient Near Eastern myth.) Although Christian soldiers who killed enemies in battle were required to do penance, this does not

62. This gold *solidus*, minted in Antioch for the emperor Valens, mixes pagan and Christian images. In his left hand the emperor holds a statue of the goddess Victory and in the right a military standard, with a Christian cross prominently displayed. Photo: Bildarchiv Preussischer Kulturbesitz/Art Resource, NY.

seem to have seriously hampered their military careers. By the middle of the fifth century (if not before), Christians made up the vast majority of the regular army.

Constantius II now ruled as sole emperor. In 355, he appointed his nephew Julian as Caesar in the West. Julian faced some serious challenges in Gaul, but despite his lack of military experience, he rose to the occasion. He defeated the Alamanni in 355, and again at the Battle of Strasbourg in 357. He also campaigned successfully against the Franks in 356–359 and restored the Rhine frontier. Julian was more of a philosopher by inclination than a military man, but he lived the life of a simple soldier, which made him popular with his troops. He was also an innovator, and he settled defeated Franks in sparsely populated territory along the Rhine. In exchange for farmland, they would agree to fight for Rome – the first known use of *foederati*, or federate soldiers.

Meanwhile, in the East, the Sassanid ruler Shapur II had again attacked Roman Mesopotamia, capturing the fortress of Amida (now Diyarbakir in Turkey) in 359. Constantius II planned a counterattack, and demanded some of Julian's troops to assist him. The soldiers, not wishing to march east, made Julian emperor – by force, he claimed, although he may not have been as reluctant as he pretended. In any case, he revolted in 361. Consantius II marched against him, but died before reaching the West.

Julian (361–3) had been born and raised a Christian, but subsequently had become a secret pagan through his study of philosophy. Now, upon assuming the throne, he practiced the ancient religion openly. By this time, many, if not most, of Rome's soldiers were Christians. Although Julian did not persecute Christians, he did encourage pagans and Jews in official positions and in the army. After some time spent instituting administrative reforms, Julian moved to Antioch to prepare for an invasion of Persia. We know more about this campaign than any other Roman one in Mesopotamia because of the writings of Ammianus Marcellinus, the last great Latin historian of classical antiquity to survive. In early March 363 Julian marched eastward with eighty to ninety thousand men. His plan was complicated – perhaps overly so. It involved two separate columns as well as a large fleet on the Euphrates. This sort of two-pronged movement, although commonly used by the Roman army throughout its history, was difficult to carry out.

Julian sent thirty thousand men down the Tigris, while he led the rest of the army along the traditional route along the Euphrates. The two Roman armies were supposed to rendezvous at Ctesiphon, but Julian reached the capital first and defeated a Persian force under Shapur II. He decided, for some reason, to burn his fleet. The other Roman detachment had been defeated, and Julian was forced to retreat up the Tigris, being unable to return by the Euphrates route. The Persians employed a scorched-earth policy and constantly harassed the retreating Romans.

Ammianus Marcellinus (330–395 CE)

Ammianus Marcellinus was not only a historian but also a capable military officer. It is ironic that the last great Roman military historian to write in Latin was a native Greek speaker, born in the province of Syria in 330. He probably came from a wealthy and politically well-connected family, as evidenced not only by his fluent Latin but also by the fact that he was recruited into the elite Imperial Guard, the *protectores*, in his early twenties.

The emperor Constantius II assigned him to the staff of Ursicinus, who was the Master of the Soldiers in the East, stationed at Nisibis. When Ursicinus was assigned a campaign in northern Italy and Gaul against a rebel named Sylvanus, Ammianus accompanied him. He went back to the East with Ursicinus and participated in the siege of Amida in 359. When Ursicinus fell out of favor with Constantius II, Ammianus apparently went into retirement, but he returned when Julian took power, participating in Julian's successful war with the Alamanni, as well as in his disastrous Persian invasion of 363. It was at this point that Ammianus apparently left military service. He was living in Antioch in 371, and in the late 370s or early 380s traveled to Greece, the Black Sea region, and Egypt. In the mid-380s, he settled in Rome, where he wrote his history. We do not know the exact date of Ammianus' death.

Julian's forces suffered severely from lack of supplies. In late June 363, Julian went out to meet a Persian attack without his breastplate and received a fatal wound. He died of blood loss late that night, leaving his army in a very difficult position. Subsequently, it was claimed that a Roman Christian soldier had assassinated him, but his attacker has been identified as an Arab serving in the Persian army.

After Julian's death, the question of succession fell to a council of generals. They were divided into two factions. The older officers, who had been appointed by Constantius II, were mainly Christians, the newer ones, who had gained office under Julian, were pagans. The generals agreed on a compromise candidate, Jovian, a mid-level officer in the Imperial Guards. Although an orthodox Christian, he was young and popular with the soldiers. Anxious to secure his throne in Rome, the new emperor agreed to a very unfavorable treaty with the Persians, yielding territory that had been Roman since the reign of Septimius Severus. After a short and undistinguished reign of only eight months, Jovian died near Ancyra (now Ankara, Turkey) in late February 364.

Over the course of the fourth century the quality of the frontier troops (*limitanei*) gradually declined, until many became only paper units. Better forces were transferred to the mobile force and called *pseudo-comitatenses*, literally false mobile units, as, unlike the "real" ones, they continued to receive lower pay. The system of pay and support of the Late Roman army developed out of previous practice, but changed in important ways. Constantine introduced a gold coin called the *solidus*, which was used to pay the army (our word soldier derives from *solidus*). While regular pay (*stipendium*) continued, it became a smaller and smaller part of the soldiers' actual remuneration. Increasingly, rations of food and clothing became more significant benefits. The higher the rank, the larger the rations, and since they were too much to have been consumed by the soldier or even his family, the rations must have been bartered or sold for cash. The regular issue of a "donative" (*donativum*) to the soldiers supplemented their pay and rations. Originally a gold or silver gift issued in the name of the emperor to celebrate some event, it eventually became a standard method of pay for the troops.

After Jovian's death, Valentinian I, a tribune in the Imperial Guards, was elevated to the throne. His father had been a peasant who had risen to the rank of count (*comes*) in the army. After making his brother Valens emperor in the East, Valentinian spent most of his reign in the West defending the northern frontier against barbarians. From 363 to 375, Valentinian lived at Augusta Treverorum (now Trier, Germany), using it as a headquarters to fight the Alamanni. In 367, he defeated the Germans at the Battle of Solicinium (site unknown), though Roman casualties were heavy. Valentinian devastated the territory of

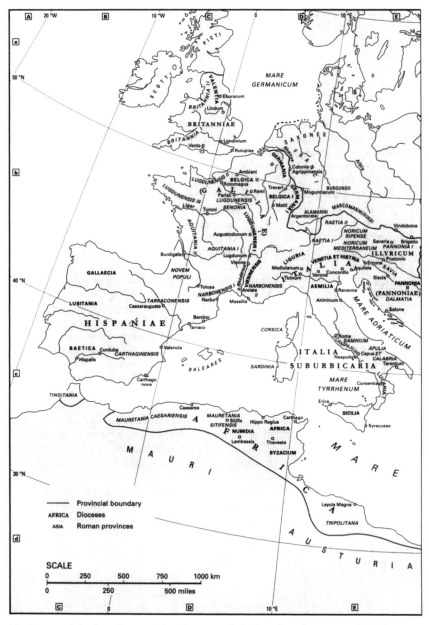

63. A map of the late Roman Empire around the late fourth century CE. Photo:
Copyright Cambridge University Press.

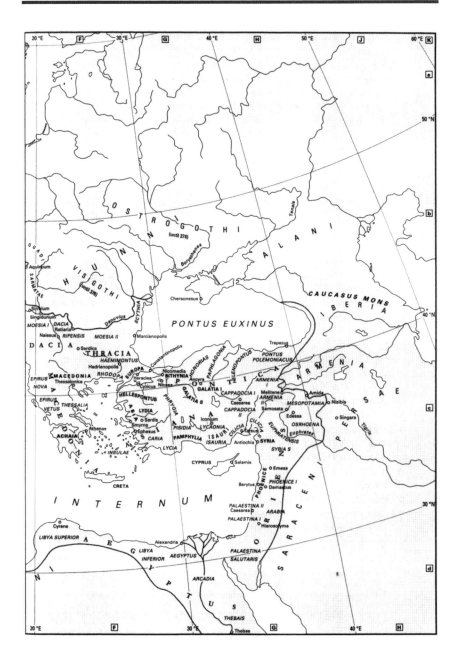

the Alamanni and restored the fortifications along the Rhine and Danube. The same year an expedition under one of Valentinian's most capable generals, Theodosius, defeated the Picts in the north of Britain. Valentinian now made his son Gratian, only eight years old, his co-emperor in the West.

In the East, Procopius, a relative of Julian, revolted in an attempt to reestablish the Constantinian dynasty. He managed to take Constantinople, but was betrayed by his German generals, defeated, and killed. In 367–368 Valens successfully campaigned against the Goths north of the Danube, imposing terms on them. Moving to Antioch in 370, he directed campaigns into Armenia and negotiated with Shapur II, the Sassanid shah. In 375 Valentinian II, the four-year-old son of Valentinian I, was raised to the purple by troops in Thrace. This was done without the consent of Valens or Gratian, but to prevent civil war, they agreed, giving him Italy, Africa, and Illyricum to rule. After Valentinian I died in 375, there were three emperors: Gratian and the young Valentian II in the West and Valens, the senior emperor in the East.

Meanwhile, the Huns, a nomadic steppe people who were sweeping westward from central Asia, had defeated the Goths along the Don River and pushed them, along with the Sarmatian Alans, out of their lands toward the Roman Empire. In 376, the Gothic leader Fritigern requested, and received, permission to settle in Roman territory on the southern bank of the Danube. They would become federates, as the Franks had in Gaul, but here the system collapsed due to the lack of sufficient farmland and poor treatment by local Roman officials. Starvation and humiliation led the Goths to revolt.

In 377, western Roman forces under a Frankish general, Ricimer, linked up with an Eastern Roman army and fought the Goths at a place called *Ad Salices* (By the Willows) in what is today Bulgaria. The fight was very bloody but indecisive. The next year, the Romans tried to put down the rebellion in a battle at Adrianople (378). The Goths under Fritigern were allied with a force of Alans. The emperor Valens himself led the Roman army. In a bloody fight, the Visigoths overwhelmed the

Roman army, destroying it and killing the emperor. Adrianople was certainly a disaster for the Romans. In fact, in the past, it has been seen as the "end of Rome," but it is clear that the army survived and continued to fight Rome's wars. Indeed, in the same year, the western emperor Gratian met and defeated an army of forty thousand Alamanni at the Battle of Argentaria, near modern Colmar in eastern France.

Links: Eusebius, *Life of Constantine* 27–29 (Battle of Milvian Bridge); Ammianus Marcellinus 23.4.1–14 (description of artillery), 24.1.1–2.15 (invasion of Assyria), 24.3.1–23 (death of Julian).

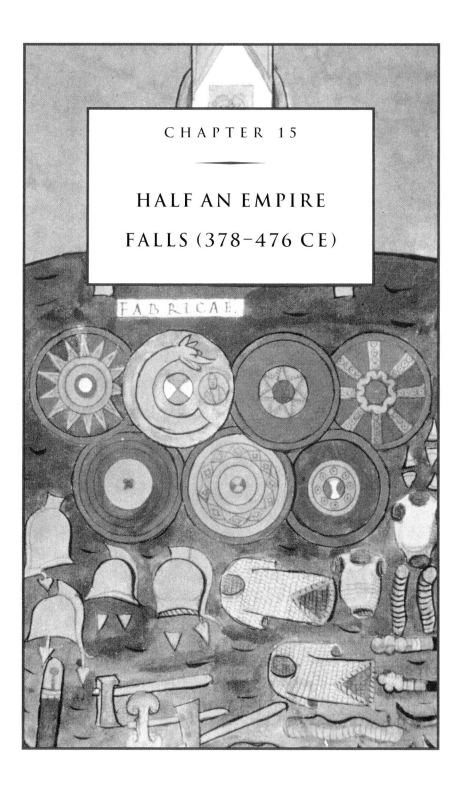

CHAPTER 15

HALF AN EMPIRE

FALLS (378–476 CE)

FABRICAE.

After the battle of Adrianople in which Valens was killed, an experienced Spanish general named Theodosius became emperor in the East while Gratian and his junior partner Valentinian II remained emperors in the West. In 380, Theodosius I made another agreement with the Goths, assigning them lands and rations to make them federates. This time they were treated fairly, and it was mainly with their help that the Romans stabilized the situation in the Balkans. Here is an example, which we shall see again and again, of "barbarians" fighting loyally for the empire and its survival. After Adrianople, the Imperial government relied more and more on federate forces.

Federates were used not, as has been claimed, because the Roman army had ceased to exist as an effective force. Rather, it was a cheaper way of providing military forces and helped to repopulate sparsely inhabited areas of the frontier. Successive epidemics of smallpox and other diseases had lowered the population and resulted in both civilian and military manpower shortages. The Germans provided an increasing proportion of the Roman field army. In the East, Arab tribes also began to be used as federates, particularly along the border with Persia. In general, federates and their commanders fought loyally and well for the empire.

Federates fought under their own kings and chiefs, but many Germans and others enlisted in the "regular" Roman army. Historians, following the views of many Roman aristocrats, tended to look at the "barbarian" forces disapprovingly. There was also popular dislike of such troops. Bad feelings in Thessalonica against a garrison made up mainly of German soldiers and officers led to rioting, during which several Gothic officers were killed and their bodies mutilated. This may have been the result of ethnic hostility, but the conflict was also religious in nature. While by this time the majority of soldiers and officers were Christians, the Goths were Arian Christians, a sect considered heretical by Orthodox Catholics, the faith of most Romans.

64. A scene from a mosaic of the third or fourth century CE shows two Roman soldiers taking part in a wild animal hunt. The symbol on the tunic of the pointing figure is a *crux gammata*, a Mithraic symbol that passed into Christian usage. Photo: Erich Lessing/Art Resource, NY.

The most significant change in this period, however, was that the army itself was divided between East and West. Now there were two Masters of the Soldiers (*magistri militum*), one for each half of the empire. What had once been merely an administrative division increasingly evolved into two different armies and, by default, two different empires. The mobile forces were now called praesental armies, as they served – in theory – in the presence of the emperor. As the quality of the frontier forces deteriorated, the praesental armies were left as the Romans' only regular military. While made up of quality soldiers, these armies had insufficient troops for major operations. Unable to draw on the frontier forces any longer, the army relied more and more on federates and on *laeti*, tribal forces that had been assigned Roman officers. While the federates and *laeti* generally fought well and loyally, as time went on and the political struggles between East and West intensified, federates and their kings began to act more and more independently. In addition, as had been the case with the Praetorian Prefects of the early Empire, the Masters of the Soldiers began to take political control, especially when there was a weak or unwarlike emperor.

In 383 a serious uprising took place in Spain led by a general named Magnus Maximus. He was a Spaniard and an orthodox Christian who had risen in the ranks to command of troops in Britain. He fought the Picts successfully, then crossed the channel to Gaul, defeating, capturing, and executing the western emperor Gratian at Lugdunum (now Lyons, France). In 387 Maximus drove Valentinian II out of Italy. The next year, 388, Theodosius I, leading both regular army units and Gothic federates, invaded and met Magnus at the Battle of the Save, now the Sava River in Croatia. Theodosius' forces won and he took control of Italy. Maximus was killed. Valentinian II was again placed on the throne, and the post of *magister militum* of the West given to one of Theodosius' generals, a Frankish-Roman named Flavius Arbogastes or Arbogast.

By the end of the fourth century there were five praesental armies, three in the East and two in the West, each led by a Master of the Soldiers. Under this commander were two officers: a Master of Infantry and a Master of Cavalry. These must have been primarily administrative commands, as field armies had both foot soldiers and mounted troops. It had become less and less normal for Roman aristocrats to serve as field officers. To help prevent revolts, senators were barred from doing so, and there were now many other routes to advancement. Many high imperial officials now trained as lawyers and served in the civil administration. The church was now also attracting young nobles. There were still some exceptions to this rule – for example, the famous general Flavius Aetius. Ethnic Germans increasingly took over positions of high military command, although it should be remembered that these all held Roman citizenship, and many were Senators or even consuls. Arbogast, Stilicho, and Odoacer are examples of Germans who rose to the highest levels of the Roman military.

Martinus (Saint Martin) (316–397 CE)

Saint Martin was born in Savaria (now Szombathely in Hungary), the capital of Pannonia Prima. His father had enlisted as a common soldier and had worked his way up to the rank of military tribune. Martin grew up in Ticinum in Cisalpine Gaul (now Pavia, Italy), where his father was stationed. According to his biographer, Sulpicius Severus, his parents were pagans, but Martin converted to Christianity when he was only ten. At the time, sons of soldiers were required to do military service, but it is noteworthy that Constantine enrolled Martin in the Imperial Guard. He was stationed in Samobriva, Gaul (now Amiens, France), possibly with the *equites catafractarii Ambianenses*, a unit of heavily armored cavalry known to have been garrisoned there. It is here that a famous incident supposedly occurred: seeing a poor man in rags, Martin divided his *pallium* or military cloak in two with his sword and gave the man half.

Martin continued his military service under the pagan emperor Julian. According to Sulpicius, when Julian was distributing a donative to the soldiers just before a battle, Martin refused to accept it, saying he was a "soldier of Christ." He was imprisoned, but released when the enemy decided to negotiate rather than fight. Martin subsequently left the army, ultimately becoming the bishop of Tours.

In 392, Valentinian II died, and Arbogast, the *magister militum*, arranged to have a puppet emperor, Eugenius, put on the western throne. Eugenius was a Christian, but he was tolerant of paganism and placed pagan Senators in important positions. Theodosius I marched west with an army that included twenty thousand Gothic federates under the command of Alaric, and defeated Eugenius and Arbogast at the Battle of the Frigidus River (394). Although both sides in this war were Christian, Theodosius I portrayed his victory as one of God over paganism. The difference between the two sides was that one was willing to tolerate paganism and Judaism, whereas the other was not. The victory of Theodosius was one of official intolerance. Increasingly pagans and other non-Christians were removed from positions of authority, including those in the military.

Theodosius I was the last undisputed sole emperor. When he died in 395 he left his sons as co-emperors: Honorius in the West and Arcadius in the East. Both sons were incompetent leaders and, to make matters worse, hated each other. Real power lay in the hands of various military and civilian officials, who fought relentlessly, ostensibly on behalf of the powerless emperors. The government of Arcadius was initially in the hands of two ministers, Rufinus and Eutropius. In the West, the younger son, Honorius, was dominated by Stilicho, whose father was a Vandal and mother a Roman. Stilicho is often called a German and considered a "barbarian," but he served loyally in the Roman army, rising to become Master of Soldiers in the West. In this capacity, he was made regent over Theodosius' son Honorius.

Alaric, who commanded the Gothic federates, had expected to be rewarded for his loyal service, including his assistance at the Battle of Frigidus River, where the Goths had taken heavy casualties. Disappointed, he led a revolt in 396, and the Visigoths elected him their king. The Visigoths headed to Constantinople but, faced with its fortifications, marched on to Greece. The invaders were aided by hostility between the East and West. Stilicho led a western force into the Balkans, but Arcadius, or rather his Praetorian Prefect, Rufinus, ordered the westerners out. The Visigoths sacked Corinth, Argos, and Sparta, selling the inhabitants into slavery. In 397, Stilicho returned with a force that forced Alaric out of Greece, but the plundering only ended when Alaric was made a Master of Soldiers.

Although he was technically a Roman general, in 401 Alaric decided to invade Italy along with another German leader named Radagaisus. Alarmed, Honorius ordered the coastal city of Ravenna fortified, and the walls of Rome doubled in height. The next year, Stilicho met and defeated Alaric and Radagaisus at the Battle of Pollentia (near modern Asti, Italy). Romans attacked the Visigoths while they were celebrating

65. This ivory diptych, a kind of ceremonial plaque, dates to around 395 CE and represents Flavius Stilicho, the half-Vandal, half-Roman officer, who rose to command the Roman armies of the Western Empire. Photo: Alinari/Art Resource, NY.

Easter, a fact that demonstrates that most of the so-called barbarians were devout Christians, albeit Arians, not Catholics. In 405, Radagaisus put together a large confederation of German tribes from outside the empire and led a massive invasion of Gaul. Stilicho, adding Alan and Hunnic troops to his small army, defeated Radagaisus at the Battle of Faesulae (406). The same year, the Vandals, along with a group of Alans and Suebians who had been living in Pannonia, migrated west. When they came to the Rhine, the Frankish federates fought hard to stop them, but the Vandals eventually forced the crossing, settling in Gaul.

After the death of Arcadius in 408, his son Theodosius II was crowned emperor of the East. He also reigned rather than ruled. During the early portion of his reign the effective ruler was a civilian named Anthemius, the Praetorian Prefect of the East, now the equivalent of an imperial prime minister. Theodosius II was also strongly influenced by his sister Pulcheria and wife Eudoxia. In the same year in the West, Stilicho's political enemies took advantage of a mutiny of soldiers at Ticinum (now Pavia, Italy) to have the *magister militum* ordered to Ravenna, where Stilicho was executed. This was a victory of palace intrigue over military necessity, and a bad omen for the future.

The year 408 also saw Alaric leading his Visigoths in another invasion of Italy. The next year, 409, the Vandals, under their king, Gunderic, and accompanied by the Alans and Suebians, invaded Spain. Britain was under attack from the Picts and requested aid, but in 410 the western emperor Honorius told the Roman authorities in Britain that they would receive no more military help from the government and would have to fend for themselves. Between 409 and 410 Rome was besieged three times by Alaric; but Honorius, and the imperial forces there, did not stir from the fortified city of Ravenna. The citizens of Rome parlayed with Alaric, and even planned to join with him against Honorius. Eventually, however, the Visigothic king lost patience with the protracted negotiations, and on August 23, 410, he moved in and sacked Rome.

Although it was no longer the seat of government, the Sack of Rome was a tremendous shock to the ancient world. The political danger soon passed, however, as Alaric died shortly afterwards. Honorius recognized Alaric's illegitimate son, Theodoric I, as king and gave the Visigoths land in Aquitania (southwestern France) in exchange for federate service. Theodoric, however, operated his kingdom as an independent state. In 411, the king of the Burgundians, Gundahar, and King Goar of the Alans supported the claims of a Senator named Jovinus, who managed to rule in Gaul for two years. In exchange, the Burgundians were given land on the left bank of the Rhine, ostensibly as a federate state, though it also was a de facto independent kingdom.

Given the rising power of the German kings, it is not surprising that many Roman leaders in the late fourth and early fifth centuries felt that the quality of the army had deteriorated fatally. Whatever the truth of this, there were suggestions for reforms. This was the main purpose behind the work of a high official named Flavius Vegetius Renatus. His book, called *On Military Affairs* (*De re militari* or *Epitome rei militaris*), is sometimes confusing to modern readers, as he claims to be writing about the army of a previous age. It is clear, though, that the organization of the legion, and the weapons and tactics he describes, are a mix from many different periods, and in some cases may be inventions.

It is important to understand, however, that the ancients always felt very nervous about reform (the Latin *res novae*, "new things," meant revolution). So reformers like Vegetius were careful to pretend that they were not proposing innovations, but rather returning to past practice. In some cases this even was so: Vegetius felt that the Romans should recruit soldiers from the body of citizens and not rely so much upon federate troops raised from barbarian tribes. He emphasized the importance of training and discipline. The "old style" legion he describes, however, never existed; for example, unlike any historical legion, it supposedly had a large component of cavalry. Although imaginary and never put into practice, Vegetius' legion was a well-thought-out system of reform. Vegetius' book may have been driven, however, more by an intense dislike of the Germans than out of real military need. In any case, given the political and economic situation of the fifth century, for all of its military promise Vegetius' reform had virtually no chance of being put to the test.

The anonymous author of a book called the *De rebus bellicis* (*On Warfare*) was also trying to enhance the military strength of the Empire, in his case by inventing new types of weapons. The late Empire is often viewed as a period of stagnation, yet there were many technological developments. Some of the author's suggested innovations were quite good. For example, he posits a paddlewheel ship powered by oxen turning a wheel: similar ships were developed in Sung China centuries later and were very effective. There is no evidence, however, that any of the inventions in the *De rebus bellicis* were adopted; nonetheless, they show a creative mind.

The real problems in the Empire were not strictly military, but economic, political, and social. One major difficulty was the tax system. It relied on the cooperation of the wealthiest Romans, who were increasingly able to resist paying. Many nobles had moved to fortified villas on enormous estates in the countryside. They raised private armies, called *bucellarii*, in part to protect against bandits, but also against tax collectors. Increasingly, there were insufficient funds to pay regular troops, which resulted in the emperors increasingly turning to federates, who were less expensive. Both the East and the West were functioning more and more like independent states, and their courts were riven by rivalries. As the Western Empire increasingly became separated from the rest, it became more difficult to fund its army, as the wealthier eastern provinces had previously subsidized the poorer western ones.

As the Western Empire fell apart, the state factories (*fabricae*) that produced arms also ceased production. There is evidence, though, of the continued issuing of standard equipment well into the fifth century. A broad belt with a ring buckle was worn by virtually all soldiers, as was a cloak. Infantry continued to wear tunics, as they had for a thousand years. Cavalrymen, however, increasingly wore trousers. Vegetius states that in the fourth century infantry rarely wore helmets or armor, but pictorial and archaeological evidence has led historians to question this. Certainly infantry helmets were still made, and still had the ridge of third- and fourth-century examples, but we also see the use of "coifs" or head coverings made of chain mail or scale armor. Armor was made

66. This page from the *Notitia dignitatum*, dating to the 420s C.E., refers to the Master of Offices (*magister officiorum*) of the West. It shows the shield patterns of units under this official's command, as well as equipment made by arms factories (*fabricae*) that he managed. Photo: The Bodleian Library, Oxford University.

67. Late Roman heavy cavalry, or *clibinarii*, are shown marching past the Arch of Constantine in a painting by Christa Hook. Photo: From *Rome at War AD 293–696*, by Michael Whitby (Oxford: Osprey Publishing Ltd, 2002).

either of bronze or iron chain or scales, mounted on linen or leather. Infantry generally fought with a spear, but we also see lances, and long and short swords. Throwing axes (*franciscae*) were used by German federates, especially Franks.

Many cavalry helmets sported a ridge, but we begin to see the conical helmet typical of the early Middle Ages. Specialized horse-archer units continued to be used, though most cavalry apparently used a long sword or spear in battle. Very heavily armored cavalry, called cataphracts or *clibinarii*, who carried a long spear, a sword, and a bow, were the predecessors of the medieval knights. Both infantry and cavalry continued to carry a large oval shield all though the fifth century. The shields of all soldiers were painted with distinctive designs, indicating their units. We have examples of these on the *Notitia dignitatum*, an organization chart or order of battle of the late Roman army. The dating (ca. 400) and interpretation of this document is complex, but it gives us a great deal of information.

Late-fifth-century forts tended to be quite small. Unlike the earlier legionary camps, they were located up on heights. Square shapes with projecting towers were common, but the walls of forts often took advantage of natural features. The army was now relying on defensive positions to make up for a lack of combat capability. The fifth century also saw a great deal of wall building around cities. The walls of Rome are a good example, though of course on a much larger scale than in any other place. The eastern capital, Constantinople, was also heavily fortified. The custom of daily marching camps had been almost entirely abandoned.

The late Roman army was still capable of launching offensives against foreign powers. Responding to the persecution of Christians by the Sassanid Persians, Theodosius II declared war and sent his general Ardabur, an Alan, into Armenia, where he defeated a Persian army and laid siege to Nisibis in northern Mesopotamia. An attack into Dacia by King Rua of the Huns, however, led to a Roman-Persian peace in 422.

In 423, the western emperor Honorius died, childless, and a high official in Rome, Joannes, took control. Theodosius II immediately launched an expedition against the West, and Joannes sent one of his followers, Flavius Aetius, a Roman general from Moesia, to the king of the Huns to ask for aid. Although the Huns responded with a large army, it arrived too late; Joannes had already been betrayed by one of his generals at Ravenna (425). The eastern emperor paid off the Huns, gave Aetius the rank of *magister militum*, and installed Valentinian III as emperor at Rome. While in Italy, Theodosius II enacted a decree mandating that pagans, Jews, and nonorthodox Christians be expelled from the military. All soldiers now had to be Orthodox Christians, as defined by the emperor.

In the West, Valentinian III reigned for thirty years, but like Theodosius II, he was a figurehead; the real power was wielded by the *magister militum* Aetius. The government in Rome, however, was increasingly unable to control the western provinces. In 425, Aetius managed to defeat Theodoric I and his Visigoths at the Battle of Arles, forcing them back into Aquitania. A few years later, in 429, under their king Gaiseric, eighty thousand Vandals moved from Spain into North Africa. They had been invited there by the military commander of Africa, Boniface, who hoped to use them in a power struggle with Aetius. Though he ended up not needing them, he could not get rid of them. The Vandals took the city of Hippo Regius in 430 (Saint Augustine died in this siege), and in 439 they captured the provincial capital, Carthage. Boniface took an army to Italy and in 432 met Aetius in the Battle of Rimini. Although he won the battle, Boniface was mortally wounded, leaving Aetius as the strongman of the West.

Aetius fought hard to maintain control against the rising power of the German kingdoms. In 436, he defeated the Visigoths at the Battle of Narbonne; and the next year, employing an army of Huns, he destroyed the Burgundian kingdom. The Romans resettled the Burgundians as federates in 443, but they promptly began creating another independent kingdom. The Alans, under their king, Goar, created another kingdom in Gaul. The Visigoths had been settled in Spain in 418, and by the middle of the century had created an independent kingdom there. In Britain, an invasion of Angles, Saxons, and Jutes led to a desperate appeal

---

The Battle of the Catalaunian Plains (451 CE)

Attila the Hun is a figure who still resounds in history. There is no question that his invasion of the Roman Empire almost resulted in its being replaced by a Hunnic one. In 451, Attila was in the midst of a campaign to conquer Gaul when he was challenged by the Roman general Flavius Aetius. Aetius had put together a coalition of Germans, who by this time were functioning as independent kingdoms. Although hostile to the government in Rome, both the Visigoths and the Alans were convinced by Aetius that the Huns were a common threat. The allies met the Huns on the Catalaunian Plains, near the modern French city of Châlons. We do not know the numbers of forces on each side and estimates vary considerably.

The broad outlines of the battle can be reconstructed, however, from an account by the historian Jordanes. The Visigoths were on the right, under their king, Theodorid. Sangiban and the Alans were in the center, with the Roman army under Aetius on the left. Attila and his Huns were in the center, with his allies, the Ostrogoths and the Gepids, on his flanks. Theodorid was killed, but instead of demoralizing the Visigoths, this inspired them, and they drove the Ostrogoths off the field. At that point, Attila retreated into his fortified camp. Rather than attacking the camp, Aetius allowed Attila to retreat. We do not know why he made this decision. Perhaps he was afraid of a trap or a reversal of fortune. Contemporaries, however, blamed Aetius for Attila's escape and accused him of corruption, and even treason.

---

for troops in 446, to no avail. The island province was divided up into small German kingdoms.

A rising threat, that of Attila the Hun, made any chance of giving aid to Britain impossible. Attila had been born around 400 and, after the death of his father, had ruled jointly with his brother Bleda. Attila and Bleda led the Huns on an invasion of Illyria (in the modern Balkans) in

441. They sacked a number of major cities, and even the recall of troops from North Africa by Theodosius failed to stop them. In 442 the Huns took the important city of Naissus (Nish in modern Bulgaria) using sophisticated siege machines, battering rams, and towers. They moved on Constantinople, destroying a Roman army sent to stop them. At this point, Theodosius made a substantial, and ongoing, payment in gold to Attila. The Huns withdrew. In 445, Bleda died, perhaps murdered by Attila, who became sole king. Two years later, Attila renewed his assault on the Eastern Empire. He defeated a Roman army under the Master of Soldiers Arnegisclus at the Battle of the Utus River (in what is now Bulgaria). The Huns plundered their way through the Balkans as far as the borders of Greece.

As dangerous as the Huns themselves were the increasing tension and hostility between the western and eastern courts. When, in 450, Attila decided to move westward and attack the Visigoths, Emperor Valentinian III encouraged him to do so, despite the obvious danger to the Western Empire. By 451, Attila had reached Gaul. Aetius gathered an army and formed an alliance with the kings of the Alans and Burgundians. They met and defeated Attila at the Battle of the Catalaunian Plains (Châlons, France). The next year Attila invaded Italy, and although he ravaged the Po Valley he turned away from Rome. In 453, Attila was planning an invasion of the East, but he suddenly died of an internal hemorrhage. Attila's sons fought each other for power, and the Gepids, one of their most important German vassals, revolted.

In 453 Aetius had been killed by the hand of Valentinian III himself in the course of an internal power struggle. The German federates had by this time taken control of virtually the entire Western Empire. In 454, the Ostrogoths and the Gepids defeated the Huns at the Battle of Nedao or Nedava, in Pannonia, in 454. The Romans were not involved in the fighting. In 455, Maximus became emperor in the West, and the same year the Vandals under Gaiseric sacked Rome. Finally, in 476, Odoacer deposed the last emperor in the West, Romulus Augustulus, a young boy put into power by his father, Flavius Orestes, the *magister militum*. Odoacer took the title of King of Italy.

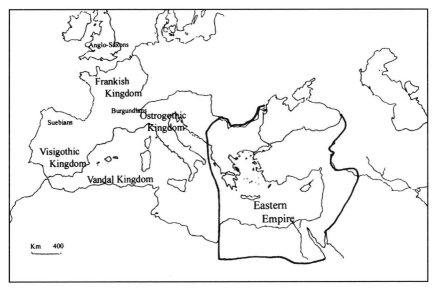

68. A map showing the political situation after the collapse of the Western Roman Empire. Photo: Copyright Antonio Santosuosso.

In many respects the date 476 for the Fall of the Roman Empire is an artificial one. Indeed, the Western Roman army outlasted the removal of Romulus Augustulus by Odoacer. As late as 489, the Italian praesental army fought hard against the invasion by Theodoric the Ostrogoth. By the year 500, however, the Roman army had completely disappeared in the West.

For the last fifteen hundred years, historians have been debating the reasons for the "Fall of Rome." Everything from sexual immorality to lead pipes to Christianity have taken the blame. Students often picture hordes of wild barbarians rolling over hapless Roman defenders. The truth is that Germans and other non-Romans often fought hard to maintain the empire. The causes of Rome's fall were complex, but certainly war and the army played an important role. As we have seen, the army and its soldiers were central to the Roman Empire's political, social, and economic system. Right up to the collapse of the Western Roman Empire in the fifth century, the army maintained its importance. It is very difficult for historians to judge what the active strength of the army was and to what extent its quality had deteriorated. Nevertheless, it is clear that the military forces of Rome were enormous, at least on paper. Paying for the army still played a key role in circulating currency, and generals were often the powers behind the throne, although few actually assumed imperial power themselves. Indeed, the reluctance of military figures to become emperors may have been a factor in Rome's decline.

Up until recently, military historians have relied almost entirely upon textual evidence. There is very little in the way of historical texts, and the religious writings (which are voluminous) tend to take a dim view of the army. In the past few decades, however, archaeologists have begun excavating more intensively in the many Late Roman fortresses spread around the Empire. What *is* clear is that, through the fifth century, these military garrisons were not only held but extended and improved. Although the details are still unclear, the Roman army seems to have been much more active, and reliable, in the late Empire than was previously thought.

It is not surprising that, as the Empire in the West disintegrated, war and strife became a common part of daily life. However, wars were not simply a matter of barbarians breaking through Roman defenses. Rather, one sees political and military struggles between various court factions, often divided by religious views. Each side was backed by both Roman and barbarian generals and troops, and increasingly by the independent German kings and their followers. The end of the Empire did not bring liberation. Rather, the security provided by the army disappeared, and those who had complained of too much government discovered the danger of too little.

Links: Theodosian Code 7.20.2 (rights of veterans); Vegetius, *Military Epitome* (prologue); Sulpicius Severus, *Life of Saint Martin*.

TIMELINE

BCE *(Before the Common Era)*

753   Traditional date of founding of Rome according to
M. Terentius Varro. Dates in other ancient sources
range from 758 to 728. The actual date is unknown and
controversial.

578–535   Traditional dates of King Servius Tullius, who is
supposed to have introduced hoplite warfare to Rome
(the Servian Reform) and built Rome's walls (the
Servian Walls).

535–510   Traditional dates of King Tarquinius Superbus (the
Proud). By his reign, Rome seems to have controlled all
of Latium.

510   Traditional date of the overthrow of the monarchy and
the establishment of the Roman Republic.

Ca. 490   Battle of Lake Regillus, perhaps a legendary victory
over the Latins, supposed date of the First Treaty of
Cassius (*foedus Cassianum*)

Ca. 450   Romans defeat and absorb the Sabines.

Ca. 430   Romans defeat the Volsci and Aequi.

Ca. 400–396   Siege of Veii (traditional dates are 406–396). Romans
defeat the Etruscans.

Ca. 390	Battle of Allia River. Gauls defeat the Romans and sack Rome.
376	Office of consul, and command of Rome's army, opened to plebeians.
Ca. 370	Rome's Servian Walls are rebuilt.
358	Romans defeat the Latins and Hernici and impose the Second Treaty of Cassius.
343–341	Traditional dates of the First Samnite War.
341–338	Great Latin War. Antium (Anzio) conquered.
326–304	Second Samnite War, after initial defeats, Rome defeats Samnium.
321	Battle of the Caudine Forks. Samnites trap a Roman army, forcing it to surrender.
312	Appian Way (Via Appia) is begun, eventually linking Rome with Brindisium.
298–290	Third Samnite War. Rome conquers Samnium.
295	Battle of Sentinum. Romans defeat Samnites.
280–275	Pyrrhic War. Pyrrhus wins costly victories, but fails to win war.
279	Battle of Asculum. Pyrrhus defeats Romans ("One more such victory and we shall be undone").
264–241	First Punic War. Romans defeat Carthage.
260	Battle of Mylae. Roman fleet defeats Carthaginians.
255	Battle of Tunis. Carthaginians repel the Roman invasion of Africa under M. Atilius Regulus.
249	Battle of Drepana. Carthaginian fleet defeats Romans.
241	Battle of Aegates Islands. Romans crush Carthaginian fleet to end First Punic War.
236	Gates of the Temple of Janus are closed.
229–228	First Illyrian War. Romans defeat Illyrians.
224	Battle of Telamon. Romans annihilate Gauls in Cisalpine Gaul.
222	Beginning of consular year moved to the Ides of March (March 15).

220–219	Second Illyrian War. Romans complete the conquest of Illyria.
218–202	Second Punic War. Romans decisively defeat Carthage.
216	Battle of Cannae. Carthaginians under Hannibal destroy the Roman army.
215–205	First Macedonian War. Rome, allied with the Aetolian League and Pergamum, defeats Philip V.
202	Battle of Zama. Romans under Scipio Africanus defeat Carthaginians under Hannibal.
200–196	Second Macedonian War. Rome, allied with Rhodes and Pergamum, defeats Philip V.
200–191	War with the Cenomani and Boii. Romans drive these tribes out of Cisalpine Gaul.
197	Battle of Cynoscephelae. Romans under Flamininus defeat Philip V.
195	Roman-Spartan War. Romans defeat Nabis, tyrant of Sparta.
191–188	Roman-Syrian War: Rome, along with Pergamum, Rhodes, and the Achaean League, defeats the Seleucid king Antiochus III and the Aetolian League.
190	Battle of Magnesia. Romans under L. Cornelius Scipio and Eumenes II of Pergamum defeat Seleucids under Antiochus III.
181–179	First Celtiberian War. Romans defeat tribes along the Ebro River in Spain.
171–168	Third Macedonian War. Rome defeats King Perseus.
168	Battle of Pydna. Lucius Aemilius Paullus' legions win over the Macedonian phalanx.
155–139	Lusitanian War. After many defeats, the Romans defeat the Lusitani under Viriathus.
154–151	Second Celtiberian (or First Numantine) War. Numantines repel Roman attempts at conquest.
153	Beginning of consular year moved to Calends of January (January 1).

150–146	Fourth Macedonian War. Romans defeat pretender Andriscus and conquer Macedonia.
149–146	Third Punic War. Romans under Scipio Aemilianus conquer and annex Carthage.
146–145	Achaean War. Achaean League is defeated and Corinth razed.
143–133	Third Celtiberian (or Second Numantine) War. After several further defeats, Scipio Aemilianus takes and destroys Numantia.
135–132	First Servile War. Unsuccessful slave uprising in Sicily.
125–121	Ligurian War. Rome conquers and annexes Liguria.
122–120	War with the Allobroges and Averni. Gallic tribes defeated by Domitius Ahenobarbus and Fabius Maximus.
113–101	Cimbrian War. German Cimbri and Teutones migrate into Roman territory.
105	Battle of Arausio (Orange). Roman army is destroyed by Cimbri and Teutones.
104–103	Second Servile War. Unsuccessful slave uprising in Sicily.
102	Battle of Aquae Sextae. Gaius Marius decisively defeats the Cimbri and Teutones.
100	Birth of Julius Caesar.
91–88	Social War. Revolt of Italian allies is suppressed, but Italians gain citizenship.
90–85	First Mithridatic War. After initial defeats, Rome and Bithynia defeat King Mithridates VI of Pontus.
88–87	First Marian-Sullan Civil War. Cornelius Sulla marches on Rome and seizes control of the government from the Marians.
83–81	Second Mithridatic War. Pontus defeats a Roman invasion.
83–72	War of Sertorius. Marian general holds Spain before being defeated by Caecilius Metellus and Pompey.

82–81	Second Marian-Sullan Civil War. Sulla defeats the Marians and retakes control of the Roman government.
75–65	Third Mithridatic War. First Licinius Lucullus and then Pompey defeat Pontus.
73–71	Third Servile War. Spartacus and a slave army defeat several Roman forces before being defeated by Marcus Licinius Crassus.
66	Battle of Nicopolis. Pompey decisively defeats Mithridates VI.
59–51	Gallic Wars. Julius Caesar conquers Gaul and suppresses revolts against Roman rule.
58	Battle of Bibracte. Caesar defeats the Helvetii.
55	Caesar's first invasion of Britain.
54	Caesar invades Britain a second time.
53	Licinius Crassus invades Parthia, is defeated and killed at the battle of Carrhae.
52	Siege of Alesia. Caesar defeats Gauls under Vercingetorix.
49	Battle of Ilerda. Caesar defeats a Pompeian army under Lucius Afranius and Marcus Petreius.
49–45	Caesarian-Pompeian Civil War.
48	Battle of Pharsalus. Caesar defeats Pompey, who flees to Egypt where he is murdered.
45	Battle of Munda. Decisive defeat of Pompeian forces in Africa.
44	Julius Caesar is assassinated. Antony's army is besieged at Mutina, which is taken by Octavian.
44–36	Caesarian-Republican Civil War. Struggle for control of Rome after Caesar's assassination.
43	Second Triumvirate established (Octavian, Antony, Lepidus). Octavian and Antony defeat Republicans Brutus and Cassius at the Battle of Philippi.
41–40	Perugine or Perusian War. Lucius Antonius (Antony's brother) is defeated by Octavian.

40–38	Parthian invasion. Pacorus leads an attack by Roman Syria, joined by Labienus and other Romans. Defeated by Publius Ventidius.
36	Octavian's fleet under Agrippa defeats Sextus Pompeius at the Battle of Naulochus. Antony invades Parthia, unsuccessfully besieges Phraaspa, then retreats.
32–30	Civil war between Octavian on one hand and Antony and Queen Cleopatra VII of Egypt on the other.
31	Battle of Actium. Octavian's fleet defeats that of Antony and Cleopatra.
29	Octavian closes the gates of the Temple of Janus.
29–19	Cantabrian Wars. Roman armies under Octavian, and later Agrippa, conquer northern Spain.
27	Octavian becomes Augustus.
25	Aelius Gallus leads an unsuccessful invasion of Arabia.
25–22	Indecisive war with Meroë (Ethiopia).
15	Drusus and Tiberius conquer Raetia.
12–9	Systematic "pacification" of Pannonia.
9	Drusus defeats German tribes, reaches the Elbe, and builds forts there.
4	Revolt in Judaea suppressed by Quinctilius Varus.
Ca. 1	Expeditions to Yemen and Armenia.

CE (In the Common Era)

4	War with Marcomanni under King Maroboduus.
6–9	Major revolt of the Pannonians in Illyria, led by two kings named Bato.
9	Battle of Teutoburger Forest. Germans under Arminius destroy three legions commanded by Quinctilius Varus.
14–16	Tiberius leads punitive expeditions into Germany.
17–24	War against Tacfarinas in Numidia.
21	Revolt of Julius Sacrovir and Julius Florus in Gaul.
39	Caligula leads a military "expedition" to Germany, but there is no fighting.

40–42	Aedemon's revolt in Mauretania.
43	Conquest of Britain by Aulus Plautius. Claudius arrives briefly to take credit for the victory.
54–64	War with Parthia. King Vologaeses I enjoys initial success but is forced by Domitius Corbulo to negotiate peace.
60/61	Suetonius Paulinus takes druid stronghold at Mona (Anglesey).
60/61–62	Revolt of Boudicca in Britain.
66–73	First Jewish War (or Great Revolt). Jewish rebellion suppressed by Vespasian and Titus.
69	Year of the Four Emperors. After Galba's murder, Otho takes control but is defeated by Vitellius in the First Battle of Bedriacum (April 15). Antonius Primus, a supporter of Vespasian, defeats Vitellius at the Second Battle of the Bedriacum (October 24). A Batavian named Julius Civilis leads a revolt, which is put down by Petillius Cerialis.
70	Romans under Titus take Jerusalem after a five-month siege.
Ca. 70–75	Occupation of the Agri Decumates (Black Forest region), straightens out Rome's northern frontier.
71–79	Brigantes, largest tribe in Britain, are defeated, first by Cerialis then by Agricola.
73	Masada, the last holdout of Jewish rebels, is taken after a siege of a few weeks.
74–84	Romans conquer Wales, the Lake Country, and southern Scotland.
84	Battle of Mons Graupius. Romans under Agricola defeat Britons under King Calgacus.
87–88	Roman-Dacian war. Romans are defeated at the First Battle of Tapae (87) but win the Second Battle of Tapae (88).
89	A revolt led by Antonius Saturninus, governor of Germany, is suppressed by loyal troops. Domitian unsuccessfully attacks Quadi and Marcomanni; an invasion by Sarmatian Iazyages is repelled, but an entire legion is lost.

101–103	First Dacian War. Trajan defeats King Decebalus and forces him into client status.
105–106	Second Dacian War. After Decebalus revolts, Trajan invades again, defeats Decebalus, and annexes the region.
115–117	Trajan invades Parthia and captures Ctesiphon. A Jewish revolt (War of Quietus or Kitos) in Cyrenaica, Egypt, and Judaea is suppressed by Lusius Quietus but it forces Trajan to withdraw from Parthia.
117	Siege of Hatra. Trajan fails to take the city.
120	Construction on Hadrian's wall begins in Britain.
132–135	Second Jewish War. Jews revolt under Simon Bar Kosiba (or Bar Kokhba). Revolt is suppressed by Julius Severus.
144–152	Incursions by the nomadic Gaetulians in North Africa.
Ca. 145	Antonine Wall is built. It is abandoned about twenty years later.
Ca. 154	Revolt of Brigantes in Britain is suppressed.
161–166	War with Parthia. After initial Roman defeat by Vologaesus IV, Parthians are defeated by Avidius Cassius and Ctesiphon is burned.
162–166	Calpurnius Agricola suppresses revolts in northern Britain.
168–173	First Marcomannic War. Marcus Aurelius campaigns against Marcommani and other German tribes.
170–175	War with Sarmatian Iazyges is ended by negotiation.
175	Revolt of Avidius Cassius.
177–180	Second Marcomannic War. After some success, Marcus Aurelius dies and Commodus negotiates a peace.
191–197	Murder of Commodus starts a civil war between Clodius Albinus, Pescennius Niger, and Septimius Severus, the ultimate victor.
194	Battle of Issus. Septimius Severus defeats Pescennius Niger.
197	Battle of Lugdunum: Septimius Severus defeats Clodius Albinus.
197	Septimius Severus invades Parthia, captures and burns Ctesiphon.

199	Romans unsuccessfully besiege Hatra.
204–205	Septimius Severus campaigns in North Africa.
208–211	Septimius Severus fights the Caledonians in Britain.
213–214	Caracalla's wars along the Rhine.
215	Caracalla brutally suppresses an antidraft riot in Alexandria.
216–218	Caracalla unsuccessfully invades Parthia.
218	Battle of Antioch. Forces loyal to Elagabalus defeat Macrinus.
231–233	Alexander Severus campaigns against Sassanid Persians.
233	Alamanni invade Upper Germany and Raetia.
235–236	Maximinus Thrax campaigns north of the Rhine and Danube.
238	Battle of Carthage. Forces loyal to Maximinus Thrax defeat Gordian II. Siege of Aquilea by Maximinus Thrax fails.
238–244	Sassanid Persians invade and capture Nisibus and Carrhae. They are driven out, but Roman invasion of Mesopotamia fails.
245–247	Invasion of Carpi and Goths defeated by Philip the Arab.
249	First Battle of Verona. Decius defeats and kills Philip the Arab.
249–251	Gothic invasion of Thrace. Goths defeat Romans at the Battle of Abrittus (251).
253–259	War with Sassanid Persians. Shapur I invades and decisively defeats Romans, ultimately capturing the emperor Valerian.
253–260	Incursions by Marcommani, Goths, Franks, and other Germans.
260	Franks move into Gaul, Spain, and North Africa, Alamanni invade Italy. Revolts by Postumus (in Gaul), Macrianus and Callista (in Mesopotamia), Ingenuus (in Pannonia).
264–265	King Odenathus of Palmyra defeats Sassanids on Rome's behalf and captures Ctesiphon.

267–268	Goths and Herulians invade Asia Minor.
268	Claudius II defeats Goths at the Battle of Naissus (Nish).
270–273	Aurelian Walls are built around Rome.
272	Aurelian defeats Palmyrenes at Antioch and Emesa.
274	Battle of Châlons-sur-Marne. Aurelian reunites Empire.
276	Massive invasion across the Rhine and Danube by Franks, Alamanni, Vandals, and Goths. Defeated by Probus in 277.
282	Carus defeats Quadi and Sarmatians, captures Ctesiphon.
284–286	Revolt of Bacaudae in Gaul.
285	Battle of Margus. Diocletian defeats Carinus.
296–298	War with Sassanid Persians. Romans defeat King Narses. Revolt of Domitius Domitianus in Egypt.
306	Revolt of Maxentius, who seizes control of Rome.
312	Battle of the Milvian Bridge. Constantine defeats Maxentius and takes Rome.
313	Licinius defeats Maximinus Daia at the Battle of Campus Serenus or Tzirallum.
324	Constantine defeats Licinius at the Battle of Chrysopolis.
332	Constantine defeats the Goths.
350–351	Revolt of Magnus Magnentius, who takes control of the West.
351	Second Battle of Mursa. Constantius II defeats Magnus Magnentius.
355–359	Julian campaigns against the Alamanni and Franks.
357	Battle of Strasbourg. Julian defeats the Alamanni under Chnodomar.
359	Siege of Singara. Romans hold out against Persians under Shapur II.
363	Julian unsuccessfully invades Persia. Wins Battle of Ctesiphon, but fails to take the capital and is killed in a skirmish.
363–375	War with the Alamanni.

367	Battle of Solicinium. Romans under Valentinian I defeat Alamanni.
367–369	War with Goths. Valens defeats them and imposes term.
376	Theodosius I defeats Picts.
376–378	Gothic federates revolt under the leadership of Fritigern.
376–382	Gothic War.
377	Indecisive Battle of Ad Salices (By the Willows) between Goths and Romans.
378	Battle of Adrianople. Goths and Alans under Fritigern wipe out a Roman army and kill the emperor Valens.
383–388	Revolt of Magnus Maximus.
388	Battle of the Save River. Forces of Theodosius I defeat Magnus Maximus.
394	Battle of the Frigidus River. The western emperor Eugenius, and Arbogast, lose to the forces of Theodosius I.
402	Battle of Pollentia. Romans under Stilicho defeat Visigoths under Alaric.
406	Battle of Faesulae. Stilicho, leading a force of Romans, Huns, and Alans, defeats a coalition of Germans and Alans under Radagaisus.
406–409	Vandals, Alans, and Suebi under Vandal king Gunderic invade Gaul and Spain.
408–410	Visigoths invade Italy.
410	Siege of Rome. Alaric takes and sacks the capital.
421–422	War with Persia. The Romans invade Mesopotamia and besiege Nisibis.
425	Battle of Arles. Aetius defeats the Visigoths under Theodoric I.
429	Vandals invade North Africa.
430	Siege of Hippo Regius. Vandals take the city.
432	Battle of Rimini. The forces of Boniface defeat those of Aetius, but Boniface is mortally wounded.
436	Battle of Narbonne. Aetius defeats Visigoths under Theodoric I.

439	Siege of Carthage. Vandals, under Gaiseric, take the African capital.
447	Battle of the Utus (Vit) River. Huns led by Attila defeat an Eastern Roman army.
451	Battle of the Cataulonian Plains (Châlons). Aetius defeats Huns under Attila.
455	Siege of Rome. Geiseric and Vandals take and sack the city.
476	The last Western Roman emperor, Romulus Augustulus, is deposed by the German general Odoacer, who takes the title of King of Italy. The Roman Empire continues in the East, with its capital at Constantinople. It is traditionally called the Byzantine Empire from this date.

GLOSSARY

accensus (pl. *accensi*): Originally a member of the fifth class in the Republican legion, armed as a slinger. Later the term was used for a military servant or orderly.

acies (pl. *acies*): The front line of battle, used generally for a line or for the battlefield.

acies triplex (pl. *acies triplices*): A three-line formation used by the Romans.

aerarium militare: Military treasury established by Augustus to pay pensions.

ala (pl. *alae*): In the early Republic, the "wing" of allied infantry who fought on the flank of the Romans. In the late Republic and Empire, it referred to an independent cavalry unit of auxiliaries.

ambulatura (pl. *ambulaturae*); or *ambulatio* (pl. *ambulationes*): A military practice march.

annona (pl. *annonae*): In-kind taxes used to support the army.

antesignanus (pl. *antesignani*): Soldier stationed in front of the standards, in the front line of battle.

arma (pl. *armae*): Weapons and military equipment.

assiduus (pl. *assidui*): A Roman citizen with sufficient property to serve in the Republican army.

auxilia: The noncitizen forces under the Empire. Called the auxiliaries or auxiliary forces in English.

ballista (pl. *ballistae*): A torsion artillery piece used to throw stones. Often called a catapult in English.

bucellarius (pl. *bucellarii*): In late Rome, an armed retainer or private soldier of a general or wealthy landowner.

calo (pl. *calones*): A military slave.

Campus Martius: Place in Rome where the army mustered.

cassis (pl. *cassides*): A helmet.

castrum (pl. *castra*): A military camp.

cataphractus (pl. *cataphracti*): An armored cavalryman.

catapulta (pl. *catapultae*): A torsion artillery piece used to shoot bolts. Often called a ballista in English.

centuria (pl. *centuriae*): A subunit of the legion. Originally a hundred men (thus the name), under the Republic it had varying sizes, and in the imperial period it contained eighty legionaries. Called a century in English.

centurio (pl. *centuriones*): The commander of a century. Senior centurions also commanded cohorts. Called in English a centurion. See *primus pilus*.

classis (pl. *classes*): A fleet.

cliens (pl. *clientes*): A "client" was a free Roman who attached himself to a "patron" in exchange for legal protection and financial benefits. In return, clients were expected to support their patrons with votes, and in at least one case, military service.

clipeus or *clipeum* (pl. *clipei*): A hoplite-style shield used by the early Roman army. See *scutum*.

cognomen (pl. *cognomina*): The third or surname of a Roman (such as Caesar). Also, the name of a legion (such as Valeria Victrix).

cohors (pl. *cohortes*): One of ten subunits of a legion or an independent unit of auxiliaries.

comes (pl. *comites*): A later Roman military office.

comitatus (pl. *comitatus*): Originally the friends and advisers of a general, who formed a kind of staff. Later it referred to the mobile army created by Gallienus. Soldiers in it were called the *comitatenses*.

consul (pl. *consules*): One of two military and political rulers of Rome, elected to one-year terms. The highest officer in Rome, he held *imperium* and frequently led Rome in war. The office lost its power under the emperors, but consuls were appointed until the sixth century CE.

contubernales: Tent mates.

contubernium (pl. *contubernia*): The smallest subunit of a legion, made up of soldiers who shared a tent (or later a barracks room). Under the Empire it contained eight men.

cornu (pl. *cornua*): A G-shaped instrument used to give tactical signals in battle.

corvus (pl. *corvi*): A bridgelike device with a hook at the end, designed to grab enemy ships and allow them to be boarded. Literally, a raven.

cuniculus (pl. *cunicula*): A mine dug under a besieged city's walls. The word literally means a rabbit hole.

custos armorum (pl. *custodes armorum*): An armorer.

dictator (pl. *dictatores*): An absolute, but temporary, military and political ruler under the Republican constitution. Also called the *magister populi*, or army commander. The office was revived and extended in the Late Republic.

diploma (pl. *diplomata*): A discharge document.

donativum (pl. *donativa*): A cash bonus given to troops, in the Late Empire it became the standard method of pay.

dux (pl. *duces*): A Late Roman military office.

ensis (pl. *enses*): A long sword (as opposed to the short sword or *gladius*).

eques (pl. *equites*): A horseman. Term used both literally for cavalry and also for the second highest class of Romans, after the Senators, called equestrians or knights in English. The *equites singulares* were cavalry attached to the Praetorian Guard.

evocatus (pl. *evocati*): A discharged veteran who returns to military service.

exercitus (pl. *exercitus*): An army.

Fetialis (pl. *Fetiales*): War priest. Members of the college of *Fetiales* performed the rituals to ensure that Rome's wars were just in the eyes of the gods.

foederati: In the Late Empire, tribal forces that fought for the Romans under their own leaders. In English, federates.

frumentarius (pl. *frumentarii*): Originally a soldier involved in collecting supplies, later used as a sort of secret service.

furca (pl. *furcae*): A forked stick that served as a sort of backpack for Roman soldiers. Introduced in the time of Marius and used well into the Imperial period.

garum (pl. *gara*): A fish sauce, an important part of the military diet.

gens (pl. *gentes*): A clan. Under the monarchy and early Republic, the army was organized around these clans. Clan leaders provided Rome's military commanders for centuries.

gladius (pl. *gladii*): A short sword.

glans (pl. *glandes*): A slingshot bullet, literally an "acorn."

hasta (pl. *hastae*): A spear. The main armament of the early Roman legions, it reappeared in Imperial times.

hastatus (pl. *hastati*): Soldiers of the second class, who stood in the front line of battle.

hibernacula: Winter quarters.

honesta missio (pl. *honestae missiones*): Honorable discharge.

immunis (pl. *immunes*): A legionary who was exempt from fatigue duty due to his rank or duties.

imperium: Command. This word expressed the right of a commander not only to lead the army but to execute soldiers, and civilians, within his jurisdiction. See *provincia*.

laeti: In the late Empire, a tribal force that fought under Roman officers.

lanciarius (pl. *lanciarii*): A Late Roman soldier armed with a lance or javelin.

legatus legionis (pl. *legati legionis*): Under the Empire, the commander of a legion. Called a legionary legate in English.

legio (pl. *legiones*): A military unit made up of Roman citizens. Of varying size, units bore this name from the early Republic to the Late Empire. Called a legion in English.

limitanei: Late Roman border troops. Also called *riparii*.

lorica (pl. *loricae*): A breastplate. The *lorica squamata* was made of scale armor and the *lorica segmentata* of strips of iron sewn together with leather.

magister (pl. *magistri*): Late Roman military office, as in the *magister militum* (Master of Soldiers), *magister equitum* (Master of Cavalry), and *magister peditum* (Master of Infantry).

manipulus (pl. *manipuli*): A subunit of the legion made up of two centuries.

mensor (pl. *mensores*): An expert in measurement who laid out a camp or other installation.

miles (pl. *milites*): A soldier.

numerus (pl. *numeri*): A military unit raised from tribal forces who fought under their own chief.

Optimas (pl. *Optimates*): A member of a political "party" or faction associated with the wealthy and the aristocratic rulers of Republican Rome.

optio (pl. *optiones*): A century's second-in-command.

parma (pl. *parmae*): A small, round shield used by light infantry and cavalry.

patera (pl. *paterae*): A flat dish used as a mess kit.

patricius (pl. *patricii*): A member of Rome's hereditary, aristocratic elite during the Republic. Called a patrician in English.

pilum (pl. *pila*): A light throwing javelin.

plebs: The common people. Called plebeians in English.

Popularis (pl. *Populares*): A member of a political "party" or faction in Rome associated with the poor and disenfranchised. Called a populist in English.

populus (pl. *populi*): The people. In early Rome, it meant the army or the armed population. Later, the population as a whole.

posca (pl. *poscae*): A drink made of sour wine (or vinegar) and water, commonly drunk by soldiers.

praefectus (pl. *praefecti*): The Roman commander of an allied or auxiliary force, also used for other military offices. Called a prefect in English.

praefectus castrorum (pl. *praefecti castrorum*): The third-ranking officer in a legion. Literally "camp commandant," he was generally a very senior centurion.

praefectus praetorio (pl. *praefecti praetorio*): The commander of the Praetorian Guard. Called a Praetorian Prefect in English. In the Late Empire, a civilian administrator.

praesentales: In the Late Empire, soldiers who fought in the emperor's presence. Later the term for all *comitatenses*.

praetor (pl. *praetores*): Second-highest military and political office in the Roman Republic. Praetors had *imperium* and often commanded armies.

praetorianus (pl. *praetoriani*): A member of the Praetorian Guard, the imperial guards established by Augustus Caesar in 27 BCE and disbanded by Constantine in 312 CE.

praetorium (pl. *praetoria*): A military headquarters.

primus pilus or *primuspilus* (pl. *primipilares*): The first or senior centurion of the legion.

principia: The parade-ground of an imperial camp or fort, placed where the Via Decumana and Via Principalis met.

principis (pl. *principes*): A soldier of the first class during the Republic.

probatio (pl. *probationes*): The medical examination for soldiers.

proletarius (pl. *proletarii*): A citizen without enough property to serve in the army, before the Marian reform. Called a proletarian in English.

promoti: Late Roman cavalry units.

prorogatio (pl. *prorogationes*): The practice according to which the Senate kept in or returned to command an officer with *imperium*. A consul became a proconsul and a praetor a propraetor. Called prorogation in English.

provincia (pl. *provinciae*): The area of operations assigned to a military commander under the Republic. Later, a political division ruled by a governor.

pseudo-comitatenses: Late Roman units transferred from the *limitanei* to the *comitatenses*.

pteryges: Leather strips used to protect a soldier's groin.

pugio (pl. *pugiones*): A dagger.

quaestorium (pl. *quaestoria*): A building used for storing and administering supplies.

quincunx (pl. *quincunces*): Arrangement of units on the field to resemble the "five" on a die.

rex (pl. *reges*): A king. In early Rome, probably a war chief.

rostrum (pl. *rostra*): The beak or ram of a ship.

sacramentum (pl. *sacramenti*): A military oath.

sagum (pl. *sagî*): A military cloak.

schola (pl. *scholae*): A unit of the Late Roman imperial guard.

scorpio (pl. *scorpiones*): A type of light ballista, handled by a single soldier.

scutum (pl. *scuta*): A convex shield used by the Romans through most of their history; the term came to refer to any shield.

sestertius (pl. *sestertii*): A silver coin.

signifer (pl. *signifera*): A standard bearer. Types included the *aquilifer*, who carried an eagle; an *imaginifer*, who carried the emperor's portrait; a *vexillarius*, who carried a flag; and in the Late Empire a *draconarius*, who carried a dragon standard in the cavalry.

signum (pl. *signa*): A military standard used for identification and signaling.

socius (pl. *socii*): An ally or allied soldier.

spatha (pl. *spathae*): A long sword.

spolia opima: The highest distinction a Roman could win: obtainable only by a Roman commander who killed an enemy commander in hand-to-hand combat.

stipendium (pl. *stipendii*): Military pay.

tiro (pl. *tirones*): A recruit.

triarius (pl. *triarii*): The oldest legionaries, who fought in the third line in the Republican legion.

tribunus militum (pl. *tribuni militum*): A tribune of the soldiers, a military rank. In early Rome, the commander of a tribal levy; later, one of the officers in a legion. In Imperial times there was one of senatorial rank, the *tribunus laticlavius*, and five of equestrian rank, the *tribuni angusticlavii*.

tuba (pl. *tubae*): A military trumpet. A straight instument, it is not to be confused with the modern tuba. It was used to sound charges and retreats.

valetudinarium (pl. *valetudinarii*): A military hospital.

veles (pl. *velites*): A lightly armed soldier used for skirmishing. Originally called a *rorarius* (pl. *rorarii*).

veteranus (pl. *veterani*): A military veteran.

vexillatio (pl. *vexillationes*): Part of a legion detached as a task force for a specific mission.

vexillum (pl. *vexilla*): A flag used as a standard for a cavalry unit or *vexillatio*.

via (pl. *viae*): A road. The Roman camp was bisected by the Via Decumana and Via Principalis.

viaticum: Military travel pay.

vir militaris (pl. *viri militares*): In the Imperial period, an aristocrat who chose the military profession.

virtus (pl. *virtutes*): Physical courage, especially in battle.

vis (pl. *vires*): Physical and military strength.

GLOSSARY OF PEOPLE

Aetius (Flavius Aetius): ca. 396–454 CE. *Magister militum* of the West. Victor of the Battle of Châlons (451).

Agricola (Gnaeus Julius Agricola): 40–93 CE. Governor of Britain and conqueror of northern Wales, the Lake Country, and southern Scotland. Father-in-law of Tacitus.

Agrippa (Marcus Vipsanius Agrippa): ca. 63–12 BCE. Lifelong supporter of Octavian. Victor at Actium. See biography in Chapter 8.

Alaric: ca. 370–410 CE. King of the Visigoths. Sacked Rome in 410.

Ammianus Marcellinus: ca. 330–395 CE. Military officer and historian. His history of the emperor Julian's campaigns is the last significant surviving Roman military history in Latin.

Appian: ca. 95–165 CE. Politician, lawyer, and historian. Born in Alexandria, his book on Roman history, in Greek, survives only in fragments but is a major source for the period of the late Republican civil wars.

Arbogast (Flavius Arbogastes): (d. 394 CE). A Frankish-Roman general, he seized control in the West in 392 and was defeated at the Battle of the Frigidus River.

Arrian (Lucius Flavius Arrianus): ca. 86–160 CE. Roman general and writer. His most famous work is on Alexander's campaign, but he also authored a Greek description of his campaign against the Alans in 135 CE.

Avidius Cassius (Gaius Avidius Cassius): 130–175 CE. Roman general and governor. Victor in wars against the Parthians.

Brutus (Marcus Junius Brutus): 85–42 BCE. Roman politician and general. One of Julius Caesar's assassins, he committed suicide after losing the Battle of Pharsalus. Not to be confused with another of Caesar's assassins, Decimus Junius Brutus.

Caecilius Metellus (Quintus Caecilius Metellus Numidicus): ca. 150– ca. 91 BCE. Optimate commander in the Jugurthine War.

Caesar (Gaius Julius Caesar): 100–44 BCE. General, politician, and writer. His "Commentaries" are a major source for Republican warfare. One of the great military commanders in history, he became dictator for life and was famously assassinated on the Ides of March.

Camillus (Manius Furius Camillus): ca. 445–365 BCE. General and politician of the early Republic. See biography in Chapter 1.

Cicero (Marcus Tullius Cicero): 106–43 BCE. Politician. His younger brother, Quintus Tullius Caesar (102–43 BCE) served in Gaul under Julius Caesar.

Cleopatra (Cleopatra VII Thea Philopater): 69–30 BCE. Queen of Egypt, she commanded Egyptian forces allied with Antony.

Constantine (Flavius Valerius Aurelius Constantinus): ca. 280–337 CE. Roman emperor 306–337. Victor at the Battle of the Milvian Bridge (312).

Corbulo (Gnaeus Domitius Corbulo): ca. 3 BCE–66 CE. One of Imperial Rome's greatest generals. See biography, Chapter 10.

Crassus (Marcus Licinius Crassus): ca. 115–53 BCE. Roman general and politician. A member of the First Triumvirate, he was killed at the Battle of Carrhae.

Decebalus: ca. 40–105 CE. Dacian king. He was defeated by Trajan.

Dentatus (Manius Curius Dentatus): ca. 335–ca. 270 BCE. Roman general in the Third Samnite and Pyrrhic Wars.

Dio Cassius: ca. 155–ca. 230 CE. Roman Senator, governor, and historian. His eighty-book Roman history in Greek is our main source for the wars of the second century.

Diocletian (born Diocles; also Gaius Aurelius Valerius Diocletianus): ca. 245–ca. 312 CE. Roman general and emperor 284–305.

Drusus (Nero Claudius Drusus): 38–9 BCE. Augustus' stepson. A general, he campaigned in Germany and Pannonia.

Fabius (Quintus Fabius Maximus Verrucosus, also called Cunctator or Delayer): ca. 275–203 BCE. Roman general. Dictator in 216 BCE. Developed "Fabian" tactics of delay and avoiding battle in order to wear down Hannibal.

Frontinus (Sextus Julius Frontinus): ca. 40–103 CE. Governor of Britain, he initiated the conquest of Wales. He also authored a famous book on stratagems.

Gallienus (Publius Licinius Egnatius Gallienus): 218–268 CE. Roman emperor 253–268. He reformed the late Roman military, increasing the number of cavalry.

Gellius Egnatius: ca. 340–295 BCE. Samnite general, defeated and killed at Sentinum (295).

Germanicus (born Nero Claudius Drusus; after 4 CE, Germanicus Julius Caesar): 16/15 BCE–19 CE. Son of Drusus, adopted by Tiberius. General and governor, he fought successfully in Germany and Pannonia.

Hamilcar Barca: ca. 270–228 BCE. Carthaginian general. Father of Hannibal and two other Carthaginian generals, Hasdrubal and Mago.

Hannibal Barca: 247–183 BCE. Carthaginian general, victor at Cannae and many other battles, defeated at Zama (202).

Hiero II: 306–215 BCE. King of Syracuse and Roman ally in the First Punic War.

Josephus (Flavius Josephus): 37/8–ca. 100 CE. Jewish aristocrat, general, and historian. His history, in Greek, of the Jewish War of 66–73 CE (in which he fought) is among the best accounts of an Imperial military campaign.

Jugurtha: ca. 160–104 BCE. Numidian king. Led a long, but ultimately unsuccessful, resistance to the Romans.

Julian (Flavius Claudius Julianus): 331–363 CE. Roman emperor 361–363. Won victories against the Alamanni, died fighting the Persians.

Julius Caesar (Gaius Julius Caesar): 100–44 BCE. Roman general and politician. See biography in chapter 7.

Lepidus (Marcus Aemilius Lepidus): ca. 90–13 BCE. Roman general and politician. A member of the Second Triumvirate with Antony and Octavian.

Livy (Titus Livius): 59 BCE–17 CE. Historian whose history of Rome is our main Latin source for early Roman history.

Lucullus (Lucius Licinius Lucullus): ca. 118–56 BCE. General and politician. Consul in 74/73. He defeated Mithridates, but was thwarted by lack of support from Rome.

Marius (Gaius Marius): 157–86 BCE. Populist general and politician. Consul seven times. The Marian Reforms, principally the recruiting of proletarians, is attributed to him.

Mark Antony, also Marc Antony (Marcus Antonius): 83–30 BCE. A key lieutenant of Julius Caesar, he fought first the Republican forces and then Octavian. Defeated at Actium (31 BCE).

Mithridates: 132–63 BCE. King of Pontus. He fought four wars against the Romans, but was ultimately killed by his own son.

Octavian (born Gaius Octavius; from 44 BCE, Gaius Julius Caesar Octavianus, and from 27 BCE, Imperator Caesar Augustus): 63 BCE–14 CE. General and politician. First Roman emperor.

Odoacer (Odovacer): 435–493 CE. General of Italian federates who deposed the last Roman emperor and took the title King of Italy in 476 CE.

Philip V: 238–179 BCE. King of Macedonia, he was defeated by the Romans in two wars.

Plutarch (Lucius Mestrius Plutarchus): ca. 50–120 CE: Greek priest and writer. His "Parallel Lives," comparing great Greek and Romans, contains much information about military figures.

Polybius: ca. 200–118 BCE: Greek politician and historian. Exiled to Rome, his account of the Republican army and its campaigns is the best we have.

Pompey the Great (Gnaeus Pompeius Magnus): 106–48 BCE. General and politician. He helped suppress the Italians in the Social War, fought for Sulla, campaigned against Sertorius in Spain, crushed pirates throughout the Mediterranean, conquered most of the East, and was a member of the First Triumvirate. Defeated by Caesar, he was murdered in Egypt.

Pyrrhus: 319–272 BCE. King of Epirus. A second cousin of Alexander the Great, he won several battles over the Romans, but heavy losses caused his retreat from Italy.

Rullianus (Quintus Fabius Maximus Rullianus): ca. 364–ca. 290 BCE. General and politician, one of the commanders at the Battle of Sentinum. See biography in Chapter 2.

Sallust (Gaius Sallustius Crispus): 86–35 BCE. Historian who wrote a history of the war with Jugurtha.

Scipio Aemilianus (Publius Cornelius Scipio Aemilianus Africanus Minor): 189–125 BCE. Roman general. Victor in the Third Punic War and Third Celtiberian War.

Scipio Africanus (Publius Cornelius Scipio Africanus Major): 236–183 BCE. Roman general. Victor in the Second Punic War.

Septimius Severus (Lucius Septimius Severus): 146–211 CE. General and emperor, he defeated two rivals for the throne and campaigned successfully in Persia and Britain.

Sertorius (Quintus Sertorius): ca. 130–72 BCE. General who held Spain for years against several Sullan generals, including Pompey.

Servius Tullius: Sixth-century BCE king of Rome. He is said to have introduced the hoplite system and to have built Rome's first stone walls.

Spartacus: ca. 120–70 BCE. Thracian ex-soldier who led a revolt of slave-gladiators.

Spurius Ligustinus: ca. 217–ca. 178 BCE. Veteran centurion of the Republic, lauded by Livy.

Stilicho (Flavius Stilicho): ca. 359–408 CE. *Magister militum* in the late empire, he defeated both Alaric and Radagaisus, but was executed by order of the emperor.

Suetonius Paulinus (Gaius Suetonius Paulinus): ca. 1 CE–70 CE. Suppressed revolts in Mauretania and Britain.

Sulla (Lucius Cornelius Sulla): 138–78 BCE. General and politician, he helped defeat Jugurtha. He seized control of Rome by force and made himself dictator, a key turning point that led to the end of the Republic.

Tacitus (Publius [or Gaius] Cornelius Tacitus): ca. 55–ca. 120 CE. Senator and historian. His *Annals* and *Histories* are good sources for first-century warfare, as is his biography of his father-in-law, Agricola.

Theodosius (Flavius Theodosius): 347–395 CE. Roman general and emperor 379–395, he defeated Arbogast at the Frigidus River and speeded up the process of Christianizing the army and the empire.

Tiberius (Tiberius Claudius Nero; after 14 CE, Tiberius Caesar Augustus): 42 BCE–37 CE. Augustus' stepson. One of Rome's greatest generals, he campaigned in Germany and served as emperor 14–37 CE.

Tiberius Gracchus (Tiberius Sempronius Gracchus): 163–132 BCE. Tribune of the plebs who tried to restore Rome's army through a series of reforms.

Tiberius Julius Alexander: ca. 15–ca. 85 CE. A Jewish-Roman general, he commanded a legion in Egypt and later helped suppress the Jewish Revolt. He may have become Praetorian Prefect.

Trajan (Marcus Ulpius Traianus): 53–117 CE. Roman general and emperor, he rose from military tribune to emperor, conquered Dacia, and fought the Parthians.

Varus (Publius Quinctilius Varus): 46 BCE–9 CE. Roman general and governor (of Syria and Germany). Suppressed the Jewish Revolt of 4 BCE. He was defeated and killed at Teutoburger Forest.

Vegetius (Flavius Vegetius Renatus): Late fourth–early fifth centuries CE. Author of an important late Roman work, in Latin, on the Roman army's organization and training.

Vespasian (Titus Flavius Vespasianus): 9–79 CE. Given the mission of suppressing the Jewish Revolt of 66, he revolted and seized power in Rome, establishing the Flavian dynasty.

Viriathus: ca. 180–139 BCE. Lusitanian leader.

Zenobia (Zenobia Bat-Zabai, also Julia Aurelia Zenobia): ca. 240–ca. 285. Queen of Palmyra, she led an army against Valerian.

Zosimus: ca. 460–ca. 530. Late Roman writer, in Greek. The last pagan historian of the Roman Empire, he gives an account of the fall of the Western Empire from a non-Christian perspective.

BIBLIOGRAPHY

Adcock, F. E. *The Roman Art of War under the Republic*. Cambridge, MA: Harvard University Press, 1940.

Alston, Richard. *Soldier and Society in Roman Egypt: A Social History*. New York: Routledge, 1995.

Anglim, Simon, Phyllis Jestice, Rob Rice, Scott Rusch, and John Serrati. *Fighting Techniques of the Ancient World*. New York: Thomas Dunne Books/St. Martin's Press, 2002.

Austin, N. J. E., and N. B. Rankov. *Exploratio: Roman Political and Military Intelligence from the Second Punic War to the Battle of Adrianople*. New York: Routledge, 1995.

Bagnall, Nigel. *The Punic Wars*. New York: Thomas Dunne Books, 1990.

Bishop, M. C., and J. C. N. Coulston. *Roman Military Equipment*. Oxford: British Archaeological Reports, 1993.

Bowman, Alan K. *Life and Letters on the Roman Frontier*. London: British Museum Press, 1994.

Burns, Thomas. *Barbarians within the Gates of Rome: A Study of Roman Military Policy and the Barbarians, ca. 375–425 A.D.* Bloomington: Indiana University Press, 1994.

Campbell, Duncan. *Greek and Roman Siege Machinery 399 B.C.–A.D. 363*. Oxford: Osprey Publishing, 2003.

Campbell, J. Brian. *The Emperor and the Roman Army, 31 BC–AD 235.* New York: Oxford University Press, 1984.

———. *The Roman Army: A Sourcebook.* New York: Routledge, 1994.

———. *War and Society in Imperial Rome.* New York: Routledge, 2002.

Cheesman, G. L. *Auxilia of the Roman Army.* Oxford: Clarendon Press, 1914.

Connolly, Peter. *Greece and Rome at War.* Englewood Cliffs, NJ: Prentice-Hall, 1981.

Cowan, Ross. *Imperial Roman Legionary, A.D. 161–284.* Oxford: Osprey Publishing, 2003.

Crump, G. *Ammianus Marcellinus as Military Historian.* Wiesbaden: Steiner, 1975.

Davies, Gwyn. *Roman Siege Works.* Stroud, Gloucestershire: Tempus, 2006.

Davies, Roy W. *Service in the Roman Army.* New York: Columbia University Press, 1989.

Davison, D. P. *The Barracks of the Roman Army from the First to the Third Centuries A.D.* Oxford: British Archaeological Reports, 1987.

Dillon, Sheila, and Katherine Welch, eds. *Representations of War in Ancient Rome.* New York: Cambridge University Press, 2006.

Dixon, Karen, and Pat Southern. *The Roman Cavalry from the First to the Third Century A.D.* London: Batsford, 1992.

Dodgeon, M. H., and Samuel N. C. Lieu. *The Roman Eastern Frontier and the Persian Wars, AD 226–363: A Documentary History.* New York: Routledge, 1991.

Dyson, Stephen L. *The Creation of the Roman Frontier.* Princeton, NJ: Princeton University Press, 1985.

Elton, Hugh. *Warfare in Roman Europe, A.D. 350–425.* Oxford: Clarendon Press, 1995.

———. *Frontiers of the Roman Empire.* Bloomington: Indiana University Press, 1996.

Erdkamp, Paul. *A Companion to the Roman Army.* Malden, MA: Wiley-Blackwell, 2007.

————. *Hunger and the Sword: Warfare and Food Supply in Roman Republican Wars, 264–30 B.C.* Amsterdam: Gieben, 1999.

Evans, John K. *War, Women and Children in Ancient Rome.* New York: Routledge, 1991.

Ferrill, Arther. *The Fall of Rome: The Military Explanation.* New York: Thames & Hudson, 1986.

————. *Roman Imperial Grand Strategy.* Lanham, MD: University Press of America, 1991.

Fink, R. O. *Roman Military Records on Papyrus.* Cleveland, OH: Press of the Case Western University, 1971.

Frere, S., and Lepper, F. A. *Trajan's Column: A New Edition of the Cichorius Plates.* Gloucester, UK: Alan Sutton, 1988.

Gabba, Emilio. *Republican Rome: The Army and the Allies.* Trans. P. J. Cuff. Berkeley: University of California Press, 1976.

Gabriel, Richard A., and Karen S. Metz. *A History of Military Medicine.* Vol. 1. New York: Greenwood Press, 1992.

Garlan, Yvon. *War in the Ancient World.* Trans. Janet Lloyd. New York: Norton, 1975.

Garnsey, P., and C. R. Whittaker, eds. *Imperialism in the Ancient World.* New York: Cambridge University Press, 1978.

Gilliver, Catherine. *The Roman Art of War.* Stroud, Gloucestershire: Tempus, 1999.

————. *Caesar's Gallic Wars: 58–50 B.C.* Oxford: Osprey Publishing, 2002.

Goldsworthy, Adrian. *The Roman Army at War, 100 B.C.–A.D. 200.* Oxford: Clarendon Press, 1996.

————. *The Punic Wars.* London: Cassell, 2000.

————. *Roman Warfare.* London: Cassell, 2000.

————. *Caesar's Civil War, 49–44 B.C.* Oxford: Osprey Publishing, 2002.

————. *The Complete Roman Army.* London: Thames & Hudson, 2003.

Goldsworthy, Adrian, and I. Haynes, eds. *The Roman Army as Community.* Portsmouth, RI: Journal of Roman Archaeology, Supplementary series No. 34, 1999.

Grant, Michael. *The Army of the Caesars*. New York: Charles Scribner & Sons, 1974.

Greatrex, Geoffrey, and Samuel N. C. Lieu. *The Roman Eastern Frontier and the Persian Wars. Pt. 2, AD 363–630: A Narrative Sourcebook.* London: Routledge, 2002.

Harris, William V. *War and Imperialism in Republican Rome, 327–70 B.C.* Oxford: Oxford University Press, 1979.

Heather, P. J. *Goths and Romans, 332–489.* New York: Oxford University, 1991.

Holder, P. A. *Studies in the Auxilia of the Roman Army from Augustus to Trajan.* Oxford: British Archeological Reports, 1980.

Hyland, Ann. *Training the Roman Cavalry: From Arrian's Ars Tactica.* Dover, NH: Alan Sutton, 1993.

Isaac, Benjamin. *The Limits of Empire: The Roman Army in the East.* Rev. ed. New York: Oxford University Press, 1992.

Kennedy, D. L., and David Braund. *The Roman Army in the East.* Ann Arbor, MI: Journal of Roman Archaeology, 1996.

Keppie, Lawrence. *The Making of the Roman Army.* New York: Barnes & Noble, 1984.

Lazenby, J. F. *Hannibal's War.* Norman, OK: University of Oklahoma Press, 1978.

Le Bohec, Yann. *The Imperial Roman Army.* New York: Hippocene Books, 1994.

Lendon, J. E. *Soldiers and Ghosts: A History of Battle in Classical Antiquity.* New Haven, CT: Yale University Press, 2005.

Lepper, F. A. *Trajan's Parthian War.* Oxford: Oxford University Press, 1948.

Lloyd, Alan B., ed. *Battle in Antiquity.* London: Duckworth, 1996.

Luttwak, Edward. *The Grand Strategy of the Roman Empire.* Baltimore, MD: Johns Hopkins University Press, 1976.

MacDowall, Simon. *Late Roman Infantryman, A.D. 236–565.* Oxford: Osprey Publishing, 1994.

MacMullen, Ramsey. *Soldier and Civilian in the Later Roman Empire.* Cambridge, MA: Harvard University Press, 1963.

Mann, J. *Legionary Recruitment and Veteran Settlement during the Principate*. London: University of London, 1983.

Marsden, Eric W. *Greek and Roman Artillery: Historical Development*. Oxford: Clarendon Press, 1969.

Mattern, Susan P. *Rome and the Enemy: Imperial Strategy in the Principate*. Berkeley: University of California Press, 1999.

Maxfield, Valerie. *The Military Decorations of the Roman Army*. Berkeley: University of California Press, 1981.

McCall, Jeremiah B. *The Cavalry of the Roman Republic*. London: Routledge, 2002.

McDonnell, Myles. *Roman Manliness:* Virtus *and the Roman Republic*. Cambridge: Cambridge University Press, 2006.

Milner, N. P. *Vegetius: Epitome of Military Science*. Liverpool: Liverpool University Press, 1993.

Morrison, J. S., and J. F. Coates. *Greek and Roman Oared Warships*. Oxford: Oxbow Books, 1996.

Nicasie, Martinus. *Twilight of Empire: The Roman Army from the Reign of Diocletian until the Battle of Adrianople*. Leiden: J. C. Gieben, 1998.

Parker, H. M. D. *The Roman Legions*. Oxford: Oxford University Press, 1928.

Peddie, John. *The Roman War Machine*. Conshocken, PA: Combined Publishers, 1994.

Phang, Sara. *The Marriage of Roman Soldiers (13 BC–AD 235): Law and Family in Imperial Society*. Leiden: E. J. Brill, 2001.

Raaflaub, Kurt, and Nathan Rosenstein. *War and Society in the Ancient and Medieval Worlds: Asia, the Mediterranean, Europe and Mesoamerica*. Cambridge, MA: Harvard University Press, 1999.

Rich, John, and Graham Shipley, eds. *War and Society in the Roman World*. New York: Routledge, 1993.

Richmond, Ian. *Trajan's Army on Trajan's Column*. London: British School at Rome, 1982.

Robinson, H. Russell. *The Armour of Imperial Rome*. London: Arms and Armour Press, 1975.

Rodgers, William. *Greek and Roman Naval Warfare: A Study of Strategy, Tactics and Ship Design from Salamis (480 B.C.) to Actium (31 B.C.).* Annapolis, MD: United States Naval Academy Institute, 1964.

Rosenstein, Nathan. *Imperatores Victi: Military Defeat and Aristocratic Competition in the Middle and Late Republic.* Berkeley: University of California Press, 1990.

Rossi, Lino. *Trajan's Column and the Dacian Wars.* Ithaca, NY: Cornell University Press, 1971.

Roth, Jonathan P. *The Logistics of the Roman Army at War,* 264 B.C.–A. D. 235. Leiden: E. J. Brill, 1999.

Roxan, Margaret M. *Roman Military Diplomas, 1954–1977.* London: Institute of Archaeology, 1978.

———. *Roman Military Diplomas, 1978–1984.* London: Institute of Archaeology, 1985.

———. *Roman Military Diplomas, 1985–1993.* London: Institute of Archaeology, 1994.

Saddington, D. B. *The Development of the Roman Auxiliary Forces from Caesar to Vespasian.* Harare: University of Zimbabwe Press, 1982.

Santosuosso, Antonio. *Storming the Heavens: Soldiers and Civilians in the Roman Empire.* Boulder, CO: Westview Press, 2001.

Sekunda, Nick. *Republican Roman Army: 200–104 B.C.* Oxford: Osprey Publishing, 1996.

Simkins, Michael. *The Roman Army from Hadrian to Constantine.* Oxford: Osprey Publishing, 1979.

———. *The Roman Army from Caesar to Trajan.* Oxford: Osprey Publishing, 1984.

Smith, Richard E. *Service in the Post-Marian Roman Army.* Manchester: Manchester University Press, 1958.

Southern, Pat. *The Late Roman Army.* New Haven, CT: Yale University Press, 1996.

———. *The Roman Army: A Social and Institutional History.* Santa Barbara, CA: ABC-Clio, 2006.

Speidel, Michael. *Riding for Caesar: The Roman Emperor's Horse Guards.* Cambridge, MA: Harvard University Press, 1994.

Starr, Chester. *The Roman Imperial Navy 31 B.C.–A.D. 324.* New York: Barnes & Noble, 1960.

Stephenson, I. P. *Roman Infantry Equipment: The Later Empire.* Stroud, Gloucestershire: Tempus, 1999.

Treadgold, W. *Byzantium and Its Army, 281–1081.* Stanford, CA: Stanford University Press, 1995.

Watson, George. *The Roman Soldier.* Ithaca, NY: Cornell University Press, 1969.

Webster, Graham. *The Roman Imperial Army.* Norman: University of Oklahoma Press, 1985.

Whitby, Michael. *Rome at War, 293–696.* Oxford: Osprey Publishing, 2002.

Whittaker, C. R. *Frontiers of the Roman Army: A Social and Economic Study.* Baltimore, MD: Johns Hopkins University Press, 1994.

For Younger Readers

Blacklock, Dyan. *The Roman Army: The Legendary Soldiers Who Created an Empire.* New York: Walker & Co., 2004.

Butterfield, Moira. *Going to War in Roman Times.* New York: Franklin Watts/Grolier, 2001.

Connolly, Peter. *Tiberius Claudius Maximus: The Cavalryman.* Oxford: Oxford University Press, 1988.

———. *Tiberius Claudius Maximus: The Legionary.* Oxford: Oxford University Press, 1989.

MacDonald, Fiona. *How To Be a Roman Soldier.* Washington, DC: National Geographic, 2005.

Mulvihill, Margaret. *Roman Forts.* New York: Gloucester Press, 1990.

Nardo, Don. *The Roman Army: An Instrument of Power.* San Diego, CA: Lucent Books, 2004.

Ross, Stewart. *A Roman Centurion.* Vero Beach, FL: Rourke Enterprises, 1987.

Shuter, Jane. *Life in a Roman Fort.* Chicago: Heinemann Library, 2005.

Simkins, Michael. *Warriors of Rome: An Illustrated Military History of the Roman Legions.* London: Blandford Press, 1990.

Stewart, David. *Avoid Being a Roman Soldier!* Brighton, UK: Book House, 2006.

Wilkes, John. *The Roman Army*. Minneapolis: Lerner Publications, 1973.

Windrow, Martin. *The Roman Legionary*. New York: F. Watts, 1984.

Websites

www.perseus.org (texts, archaeology, and many links).

www.romanarmy.net (Roman Military Research Society).

www.roman-empire.net/army/army.html (general description).

www.vindolanda.com (on the camp and ongoing excavations).

www.wikipedia.org (many articles on the Roman army and warfare).

INDEX